Tourism in the Age of
Alliances, Mergers and Acquisitions

OMT·WTO·BTO

TOURISM IN THE AGE OF ALLIANCES, MERGERS AND ACQUISITIONS

Original: French

ISBN: 92-844-0514-9

Published by the World Tourism Organization

Supervised by the Market Intelligence and Promotion Section of the World Tourism Organization

Printed by the World Tourism Organization
Madrid, Spain

CHARTS

NOTE TO READERS

This report has been produced by the Chair in Tourism, School of Business Management, Université du Québec à Montréal, under the direction of Michel Archambault, PhD, Professor and Holder of the Chair in Tourism.

The World Tourism Organization whishes to express its gratitude to the Production Team, directed by Michel Archambault, PhD: Chantal Neault, consultant, Project Leader and Co-ordinator; Chantal Neault, Chantal Caron, Jean-François Charest, Michèle Laliberté and Claude Péloquin (Chair in Tourism), Design, Research and Development; Yves Tinard, economist and professor, Groupe ESCP-EAP (Paris), Contributor; and Edith Skewes-Cox, Translation.

The research for this study was completed in mid-August 2001. However, given the upheaval following the September 11 attacks we thought it advisable to add an initial assessment of the repercussions on the tourism industry. This section, entitled "Introductory Remarks Relating to the Events of September 11, 2001," has been placed at the beginning to put the report's subject matter in perspective and reflect the situation as it stood in early October 2001.

FOREWORD

This document draws a portrait of the current situation in three key sectors of tourism: the airline industry, the distribution network and the hotel industry. However, to take into account the upheaval affecting the global travel industry following the tragic events of September 11, 2001, and to put this overview in perspective, we have added an introductory section that summarizes various repercussions on travel destinations and the three sectors examined.

Since the ties that bind the airline industry, the distribution network and the hotel industry are increasingly structured, many business decisions are now made because they are mutually beneficial. This brings us to the essence of our theme, "Tourism and the Trend Towards Consolidation."

In today's business environment, creating alliances with complementary partners is an attractive option for many firms and destinations, regardless of size. The concept of "tourist experience" involves establishing agreements, often between different sectors, so as to provide tourists with the desired products and services. And these types of partnerships appear at all levels: local, regional, national and international. This study differentiates among the various types of alliances, highlighting the specific issues affecting the airline industry since this is of special interest if we are to better understand the impact of these alliances and recognize business opportunities.

While the airline industry has been influenced primarily by the creation of alliances instigated by the carriers themselves, the distribution network and hotel industry have been affected by the phenomenon of mergers and acquisitions. This study therefore looks at the openings created by this new dynamic for businesses that continue to operate independently in any of these sectors. It would seem that associations of businesses are also inevitable. And so the question arises, if the future of the industry lies in large integrated travel conglomerates supported by new financial players, is there still a place for independent companies? What niches remain for hotel industry firms to exploit? These are just some of the topics of discussion we invite the reader to consider. With these questions in mind, the document also examines how technology plays an innovative and facilitating role. For example, technology influences the decision behaviour of consumers purchasing tourism products, in the case of e-consumers. It also enables companies to more efficiently manage their operations and adapt their strategies to create true value-added products and services.

Part 1 of the document provides an overview of the consolidation phenomenon in the travel industry, situating it on a global scale. It discusses the specific realities characterizing each of the three sectors, and then describes some of the more important players in detail. This section also identifies the keys to success for businesses interested in pursuing an alliance-based strategy. However, the accuracy of this portrait may be somewhat limited, given the rapidity with which changes are occurring within travel groups around the world. It is inevitable that shifts will take place between the time we go to press and the time the document is distributed. That said, we do hope that the information collected reflects reality as accurately as possible.

Part 2 highlights the effects of consolidation on each sector as well as its impact on destinations. In Part 3, we attempt to identify the new opportunities created by economic globalization by looking at current practices in the travel industry. This section also attempts to define the strategies that can optimize a destination's tourism potential and enhance the competitiveness of its businesses, while still meeting the requirements of an increasingly sophisticated clientele. Finally, Part 4 provides additional information in the form of statistics and data that complement the report as a whole.

Tourism-based businesses and players cannot ignore the phenomenon of market restructuring that is profoundly altering the industry as a whole. Furthermore, responses to this trend that can help us better define and understand the issues and challenges facing us all are often found outside one's country or immediate sector. The ultimate aim of this document is to contribute to the discussion that must be held if players are to make appropriate choices that will successfully distinguish them from the competition.

The Authors

INTRODUCTORY REMARKS RELATING TO THE EVENTS OF SEPTEMBER 11, 2001

The tragic events of September 11, 2001 disrupted the established order of things and had serious repercussions on the airline and travel industries. To an already bleak economic outlook was added a crisis the magnitude of which remains to be seen. Overnight, millions of passengers became fearful of travelling by plane and many companies placed restrictions on, or even prohibited, air travel for their employees. Although it is still too early to fully evaluate the impact of these events, we have attempted to assess their immediate consequences and examine the possible long-term effects on destinations and the tourism industry as a whole.

STOCK PRICES PLUMMET

The value of airline stocks in the U.S. fell dramatically. When Wall Street reopened, United Airlines stocks had declined in value by 43 per cent and American Airlines by 40 per cent. Hotel sector stocks were also affected, dropping in value between 20 per cent and 70 per cent: Starwood H & R, owner of the Westin and Sheraton brands, was down by almost 30 per cent at closing. European hotel companies with American hotels also experienced declining share prices but many of them have already rebounded to pre-September 11 levels. Nevertheless, results for the rest of 2001 will be lower than forecast since investments are being approached more cautiously and markets are still reacting.

The impact of the September 11 tragedy is also being felt in the on-line travel sector. The table below shows the decline in share value for the major American players as at September 28, 2001.

Decline in share value for on-line travel sites	
Agencies	Change (%) in share value between September 10 and 28, 2001
Travelocity	-39.6
Expedia	-33.0
Sabre	-32.2
Priceline.com	-24.0
Hotel Reservations Network (HRN)	-38.9

Source: Chair in Tourism, Université du Québec à Montréal (2001)

However, once the initial wave of panic had passed, the Dow Jones index rose 7.4 per cent during the week of September 21 and shares for the 20 largest hotel companies increased in value by 12.8 per cent. However, as long as U.S. military and diplomatic activity leaves room for uncertainty, the effectiveness of security measures remains unproven and the economy remains in a slump, market instability will persist.

TURBULENCE IN THE AIRLINE INDUSTRY

Every air carrier felt the impact of the disaster, but those in the United States—where national and international flights were cancelled for several days—were particularly hard-hit. Moreover, since connecting flights to North America were cancelled until September 13, the attacks' repercussions were also felt by European and Asian carriers. The temporary closing of air space and the significant decrease in air traffic led to the loss of more than 120,000 jobs, including more than 50,000 in aircraft construction (see Table A). Unless the airline industry recovers significantly, this trend may well continue. Bombardier reportedly has further layoffs planned that could amount to 6,500 people cut, or 17 per cent of its workforce. By way of comparison, Boeing announced that it has laid off 15 per cent of its employees.

Table A
Repercussions in the airline industry

Carriers	Employees laid off	Decrease in flights (%)
• *United States*		
United Airlines	20,000	20
American Airlines	20,000	14
Delta Air Lines	13,000	15
Continental Airlines	12,000	21
US Airways	11,000	23
Northwest Air	10,000	10
American West Airlines	2,000	14
American Trans Air	1,500	19
Other (regional)	3,040	20
• *Europe, Asia*		
Alitalia	4,000	17
British Airways	7,000	12
Iberia	2,516	n/a
Sabena	12,000	n/a
Swissair/Crossair	3,000*	12
Ansett Australia	16,000	100**
Korean Air	n/a	4 to 5
• *Canada*		
Air Canada	9,000	20
Transat A.T.	1,300	23

* Only with respect to its airline activity

** The crisis aggravated Ansett's financial problems, leading to its closure. A financial bailout is currently under discussion.

Sources: La Presse, September 27, 2001, page A1, and the Chair in Tourism, Université du Québec à Montréal (2001).

Moreover, according to Pierre Jeanniot, Director General and CEO of the International Air Transport Association (IATA), the September 11 attacks, coupled with the economic slowdown already estimated to have cost the international airline industry more than US$2.5 billion, will cost the industry US$7.5 billion in 2001. Add in the estimated deficits of U.S. domestic carriers, and the global airline industry will probably lose a total of over $10 billion. Low-cost carriers appear to be the least affected by the crisis, since many of them enjoyed better financial health prior to the September 11 attacks. Some of them have already taken over the routes that the larger carriers, due to their recent difficulties, have been forced to abandon.

To compensate the U.S. airlines for their losses, the American government has passed an aid package of US$5 billion with almost no strings attached. This amount is only a first instalment, since Congress and the White House have agreed to grant a total of US$15 billion in the form of secured loans. The European Commission believes it is similarly justified in adopting various assistance measures for carriers: state aid schemes, legislation on airport slots, insurance problems, assumption of the additional costs of security and even compensation for the direct losses suffered in the days following the attacks. Agreements and specific amounts have not yet been disclosed. The adoption of these measures—both in the U.S. and Europe—is not being greeted by carriers with universal approval. Many companies in financial difficulty fear that these sums will only help their more powerful rivals buy them out. It is reasonable to suppose that the airline industry will undergo a new round of consolidation.

For example, SAir Group's strategy with the Qualiflyer alliance has turned out to be a financial abyss for Swissair, which is fighting for survival even as Sabena declares bankruptcy. America's Midway Airlines suspended all flights as of September 12. The future of US Airways appears problematic unless a major player buys it out and Continental's stock prices have plummeted. According to then-United Airlines CEO James Goodwin (who has since resigned), even this industry giant—which expected to lose $1 billion this year due to the economic slowdown—may well disappear off the map next year if the economic fallout from September 11 does not rapidly clear. As for American Airlines, which was particularly hard-hit by September's tragic events and the crash—again in New York—of one of its planes two months later, it was fortunate enough to have healthy cash reserves of $1 billion. Although the continued lack of travellers makes the financial picture bleaker than ever, American Airlines can and will survive the current crisis, although recovery will be slow. Canada's second-largest carrier—Canada 3000—was forced to close down.

The outright disappearance of certain players or their inability to fulfil their roles in various alliances could change the landscape and lead to the creation of new, hitherto unimaginable partnerships. It is rumoured that U.S. antitrust authorities will be more flexible regarding upcoming mergers and acquisitions in order to facilitate the airline industry's recovery. We may also see a return to public investment in this sector as governments could, in exchange for the loans granted, demand shares in airline companies, thus obtaining more influence and control over the carriers' operations.

The airline industry—indeed, the entire tourism industry—is currently faced with the considerable challenge of winning back consumer confidence. An essential step towards attaining that goal is the strengthening of existing security measures and the introduction of new ones. However, this will inevitably entail additional costs that companies will pass on to consumers through higher ticket prices. Lufthansa, KLM, Iberia, Air Canada and Thai Airways have already announced that they will be raising airfares due to the increased costs of tighter security and insurance. Other carriers are looking at similar measures. Air France, for example, is projecting a substantial fare increase. In addition to paying more for tickets, passengers will be obliged to endure lengthy boarding and deplaning procedures, which will only add to the delays and inconvenience already associated with air travel. Also, if they need to be at the airport two or three hours before their flight leaves to go through all the security checks, business travellers may well turn to other means of transportation, or avoid trips altogether through the use of new technologies such as video-conferencing.

The new government-legislated security measures are likewise a cause of concern for airports, since their costs will also go up considerably. Some smaller airports are even wondering if they will be forced to close down. Member countries of the International Civil Aviation Organization (ICAO) have agreed in principle to financially assist poorer countries in their efforts to increase airport security. Furthermore, many of the expansion projects planned by larger airports have been put off indefinitely to enable them to adjust to the new security logistics and because air travel is expected to decline. Some of the airports that have announced they are suspending or rethinking their expansion activities are the Los Angeles, Minneapolis-St-Paul, Charlotte-Douglas (North Carolina), San Francisco and Boston international airports.

THE HOTEL SECTOR IN DISARRAY ON SEVERAL CONTINENTS[1]

Already suffering from the declining economy, the American hotel industry has been slow to recover from the events of September 11. In the days following the attacks, occupation rates for New York and Boston hotels that previously stood at 80 per cent to 90 per cent were down to 30 per cent and 40 per cent. The impact was felt as far away as Florida (a 30% to 50% occupation rate), California (a 30% rate for San Francisco) and Las Vegas. For the week of September 9 to 15, Smith Travel Research has estimated average daily losses of US$45 million for the American hotel industry. The devastating effects were felt around the world: in the days following the attacks, the Georges V in Paris, the Savoy and Claridge's in London, and the Imperial and the Okura in Tokyo all noticed an absence of American clientele and a drop in occupation rates.

U.S. forecasts for the rest of 2001 paint a gloomy picture: record lows in the revenue per available room (RevPAR) for the final quarter, less-than-anticipated improvement for 2002 and profits reduced to 1998 levels[2]. According to PricewaterhouseCoopers, a 3.5 per cent to 5 per cent drop in the RevPAR for 2001 would be the worst performance in the 33 years for which they have records. This drop can be explained by a decrease in long-distance pleasure travel, disrupted flights, the decline in business travel caused by the slowing economy, heightened security concerns, market volatility and the costs and inconvenience associated with the new security measures.

The cancellation or deferral of numerous conferences has also significantly affected hotel performance. Autumn is usually the high season for conferences, yet the attacks set off a wave of cancellations, particularly in the United States. For example, in the eight days immediately following September 11, nearly 200 conferences and business meetings that were to be held in Las Vegas over the upcoming three months were cancelled, representing a loss of 45,000 visitors and US$55 million.

These unfortunate consequences have resulted in massive layoffs and reduced work hours. Many hotel expansion projects are also in jeopardy, despite favourable interest rates. Marriott Hotels is re-evaluating plans to develop 60,000 rooms. With its share values declining, Accor scaled back its fourth quarter operations, and is doing the same with future investments. According to estimates made by PricewaterhouseCoopers, 6 per cent of the projects planned for 2002 and 2003 will either be cancelled or postponed.

The European hotel industry will certainly feel the after-effects of the attacks, but it is still too soon to know to what extent. Arthur De Haast, Director, European division, for Jones Lang LaSalle Hotels, has predicted that the European markets most affected will be those that rely heavily on American demand. This means London, not only because of the influx of American travellers but also because of its role as entry point into Europe and its unconditional support of U.S. military action. It also means 5-star hotels in Paris, Rome, London and Amsterdam. It means cities that are host to numerous conferences, such as Paris, Berlin, Madrid and Frankfurt. On the other hand, because of the size of their domestic market and the extensive use of alternate transportation methods (such as high-speed trains and highways), European

---

[1] All hotels, but more specifically those rated 4- or 5-star.

[2] PricewaterhouseCoopers, "PricewaterhouseCoopers Forecasts Further Contraction in Lodging Industry," September 18, 2001.

hotels will probably escape the prolonged downturn resulting from the general insecurity regarding air travel.

Although the figures for 2001 will probably be the worst since the Gulf War, the hotel industry is nevertheless in better shape than it was at that time. With nine years of continuous growth behind it and lower financing costs, the industry has more room to manoeuvre and is in a better position to handle the situation. Analysts remain optimistic and predict that, in the absence of another major attack, the impact on the tourism industry will be short-lived.

THE TRAVEL AGENCY SECTOR DEALS WITH NUMEROUS CANCELLATIONS

The impact of the disastrous events has been felt, not just by the American travel industry, but worldwide. As in other sectors, there have been many layoffs: as many as 6,000 to 10,000 workers in Canada alone lost their jobs. In Germany, Thomas Cook (with 26,000 employees) has cut its workforce by 10 per cent. Disney (in Orlando) has asked that staff accept a 20 per cent reduction in work hours and pay.

In the days immediately following the attacks, travel agency business plummeted. For cancellations involving American destinations, many agencies waived the usual penalty. People only travelled if they absolutely had to, and reservations were low. Data for changes in the total number of reservations made through global distribution systems such as AMADEUS show a decline for Western Europe, with a drop of 28 per cent between September 11 and 14 (i.e., a decrease of 1.6 million reservations). One of Italy's largest operators, a specialist in the American market, announced the cancellation of hundreds of U.S. tours, while Japan Travel Bureau received 9,500 cancellations for U.S. packages, causing losses of US$13 million. The Australians have a similarly pessimistic outlook, projecting $2.5 billion in losses over the next 12 months. Cancelled bookings have resulted in 20 per cent fewer visitors to France (the most popular tourist destination in the world), a 13 per cent decrease in American domestic tourism and–compared to the same month last year–a 22 per cent drop in the number of Japanese travellers, who are famous for their lavish spending habits.

In the United States, according to the American Society of Travel Agents (ASTA), the industry is experiencing a 40 per cent to 50 per cent cancellation rate, which works out to a loss of more than US$51 million per day. In Canada, the Association of Canadian Travel Agents (ACTA) forecast a 30 per cent to 40 per cent decrease in sales in the fourth quarter and a 20 per cent to 30 per cent drop over a six-month period[3]. This kind of behaviour is normal among tourists and has been observed in similar situations in the past. The wave of panic now appears to be receding. Following the drop in reservations and, to a lesser degree, a drop in the number of cancellations, many European wholesalers are seeing sales for the coming weeks and reservations for winter start to pick up. However, recent American actions are creating a renewed climate of uncertainty.

Already feeling the impact of a weaker economy and slower financial markets, on-line agencies were greatly affected by the attacks. One of the first to fall was Biztravel.com, a specialist in business travel and a subsidiary of the Rosenbluth Interactive group. On September 27, 2001, it announced it was suspending all business activities. The impact on other players has been equally negative: in the week following the attacks, reservations at on-line travel agent Expedia's sites dropped between 60 per cent and 65 per cent, compared to figures for the week preceding the tragedy. Hotel Reservations Network (HRN) saw its reservations decrease between 20 per cent to 30 per cent. It is worth mentioning that one hotel room out of every 100 in New York is reserved through HRN. However, more than three weeks after the tragedy, a number of sites were recording traffic comparable to pre-September 11 levels.

Internationally, some tour operators and travel agents had already been in financial difficulty before September 11, and thereafter had to close down. According to ACTA, the decrease in sales activity, which registered 60 per cent as of October 11, has caused a number of

---

[3] Monique GIGUÈRE, "Le monde du voyage perd la moitié de son volume d'affaires," *Le Soleil*, September 27, 2001, p. A3.

companies to merge, sell or go out of business. In the U.K., 13 tour operators have had to close down since the attacks, compared to only two within the same period the previous year. Similarly, one of Brazil's biggest tour operators–Soletur–was forced to declare bankruptcy.

LEARNING FROM THE PAST

The 1991 Gulf War is one of very few bases for comparison from which to assess the outcome of current events. At that time, as today, large areas of the world suddenly became potentially unsafe for travellers. Without actually registering a decline in the total number of arrivals, tourism growth nevertheless suffered a setback. However, the following year there was a noticeable jump in international travel: 8.3 per cent that year compared to 1.2 per cent in 1991. The most significant drops were in the numbers of American tourists: 22 per cent in Europe, 21.6 per cent in Israel and 26 per cent in the U.K. Air traffic declined by 5 per cent, with resultant losses of US$4.8 billion. In 1991, it took seven months for the airline industry to get back on track, and four more for it to return to its long-term growth curve.

Similarly, during the war in Kosovo, international arrivals rose 3.8 per cent in 1999 (the first year of the conflict) and 7.4 per cent in 2000. In both cases, tourists stayed away from the actual war zones as well as the areas they believed were too close to the conflicts. In fact, demand shifted as tourists chose new destinations, particularly within a region or within their own country.

In 1997, at the time of the terrorist attacks in Luxor, the number of tourists travelling to Egypt dropped, although arrivals to the Middle East as a whole did not. Two years later, the number of international travellers to Egypt had grown by 40 per cent—the result of a tourism policy aimed at the most promising tourist-generating countries.

In 1997 and 1998, the financial and economic instability of several countries in Southeast Asia, coupled with the region's social problems, caused the number of tourists to that part of the world to drop sharply. However, over the next two years the number actually grew, by 10.8 per cent and 14.7 per cent respectively, a recovery that was much faster than most observers had thought possible.

UNCERTAINTY REIGNS IN THE TOURISM INDUSTRY

Because the airline industry exerts a domino effect on the other sectors in the tourism industry, the fear of flying will significantly affect all other players: tour operators, travel agents, hotels, attractions, destination management organizations at the local, regional and international levels, convention centres, etc. There is still too much uncertainty in the industry to predict the economic consequences of the catastrophe on the travel industry over the next several months. The rate of recovery for this particular market will depend on future military action, consumer confidence, the state of the economy, the effectiveness of security measures and how quickly the airline industry recovers.

Fear of reprisals may cause many travellers to avoid American hotel chains and airlines, thus checking their international expansion. Growth in international travel will slow down, and it is believed that North America and Islamic countries will be the most affected[4]. Middle Eastern and North African destinations that are popular with Europeans–Dubai, Egypt, Morocco and Tunisia–will probably experience a drop in the number of visitors, while European destinations may enjoy a corresponding increase in popularity. The prevailing uncertainty will likely increase domestic tourism as people will choose to stay close to home. The main challenge facing these destinations will be to convince travellers from Western Europe, Japan, Southeast Asia, Australasia and North America that their region has not suddenly turned into a war zone. Tourism boards should become proactive, and reassure travellers through large-scale marketing campaigns that emphasize the numerous security measures their countries have implemented. This was done successfully by Egypt in the aftermath of the terrorist

---

[4] The Syndicat national des agents de voyages (SNAV) in France has announced almost 11,000 cancellations, principally in the United States/Canada (5,000), Tunisia (1,800) and Egypt (1,200). One of Japan's biggest travel agencies had a 25 per cent cancellation rate for its package tours to Hawaii, Guam and the Americas; Australia's overseas reservations dropped by the same percentage amount.

attacks in Luxor and more recently by the British Tourist Authority in response to hoof-and-mouth disease. It is important to clarify the situation and explain all the steps that are being taken to ensure the safety of people visiting the country. Fear can be self-perpetuating, so an effective means of boosting the number of visitors in difficult times is to initiate first-rate public relations campaigns and fam tours aimed not only at public figures but also tour operators working in the primary tourist-generating countries. Rather than turning away from foreign tourists, it is crucial to try and regain their confidence.

There is no "miracle" capable of lessening the impact of current events. Rather, the crisis calls for a concerted approach at the regional level, involving all players, both public and private. No single company or government can provide solutions to all the problems posed by security and a lack of traveller confidence. As we have already seen, the damage is widespread: forecasts for tourist travel to the United States for the last quarter of 2001 have been lowered and the outlook for the first six months of 2002 is subdued. However, the United States has already launched a three-point recovery plan: research to assess travel plans and security perceptions; a huge tourism marketing campaign; and a partnership between the government and the tourism industry to reinforce security measures and ensure the industry's economic vigour. Destination management organizations in other countries such as India, the Middle East and Europe should also adopt a concerted regional marketing approach–develop new products and specifically promote activities focussed on "profitable" markets such as the Russian Federation–to counter the negative effects of the terrorist attacks.

It is still too soon to predict how long this unusual state of affairs will last and how consumers will react in the days and the years to come. However, the experience of recent armed conflicts has proven that the tourism industry can rally. After all, one of the strengths of this industry is that it should foster understanding among peoples of the world and pave the way for peace between countries.

PART 1: AN OVERVIEW OF THE CONSOLIDATION PHENOMENON AND ANALYSIS OF THE THREE SECTORS

I.1 TOURISM AND THE TREND TOWARDS CONSOLIDATION

I.1.1 THE EMERGENCE OF A GLOBAL MARKET

Major advances in information technology, economic development in Third World countries and policy changes in numerous countries around the world are just some of the factors accelerating the growth of a global market. With the right strategy, companies can now penetrate formerly inaccessible markets and take advantage of the new opportunities created by globalization. Trade agreements have proliferated steadily on every continent, opening up the global economy. The North American Free Trade Agreement (NAFTA) has promoted trade throughout the hemisphere. According to economist Ricardo Petrella, founder of the Lisbon Group, an organization set up to examine the social consequences of economic globalization, Canadian and American corporations have helped create approximately 30,000 companies in Mexico since NAFTA was signed. Over the years, the free trade zone has extended beyond the borders of North America all the way to Chile. Other co-operative trade and investment agreements have already been signed with Mercosur and the Central American Common Market, and the Andean Common Market is not far behind. The current goal is to create the Free Trade Area of the Americas (FTAA), which will unite 34 countries representing a market of over 800 million inhabitants and a gross domestic product (GDP) of $11 trillion[5]. The heads of state of the 34 democracies in the region have already agreed to complete the negotiations required to create this agreement by the year 2005.

Europe and its common market also subscribe to this open vision, forming another major economic player alongside the Americas. Through the Asia Pacific Economic Co-operation (APEC) organization, even Asia is working to establish a regional system of free and open trade and investment. APEC now includes all the major economies in the Asia Pacific region.

Despite all this economic liberalization, it is vital to remember, as Ricardo Petrella reminds us, that most global trade is conducted by 40,000 businesses who belong to international networks, and that a third of this trade takes place between subsidiaries and parent companies while another third is conducted by multinationals. Therefore, the new world economy operates in practically a closed market[6]. It is also true that the recent explosion in mergers and acquisitions (M&As) has produced gigantic multinationals. Some examples are AOL/Time Warner and VodaphoneAirTouch/Mannesmann, both worth upwards of US$100 billion, and Bell Atlantic/GTE, Philip Morris/Nabisco and Viacom/CBS.

I.1.2 MERGER MANIA

Mergers and acquisitions are becoming an increasingly popular method for companies to strengthen their position in the global marketplace. Although business partnerships are by no means a new phenomenon, today there are many different types, uniting a variety of sectors and activities. These new entities may be short-term or permanent, deal with advertising, marketing or shared expertise, and involve partners from various regions and sectors.

---

[5] One trillion equals 10^{12}.
[6] Louis-Bernard ROBITAILLE, "Refus global," magazine *En Route*, September 2000, p. 60.

A definition of international mergers and acquisitions

International mergers and acquisitions are unions involving companies from different countries of origin. M&As require that one company take control of all of another's business activities. In any M&A, only one entity remains once the transaction is complete. Generally speaking, M&As provide added value through synergy effects. A merger tends to succeed when strategies, personnel, products and production tools are integrated quickly. For this to happen, the newly created company must focus on sharing expertise, assisting and reassigning employees and harmonizing working conditions.

In the year 2000, mergers and acquisitions totalled an impressive US$3.5 trillion worldwide[7]. But with the expected slowdown in world economic growth and market volatility, the trend towards mergers and acquisitions was starting to lose steam by the end of the year. Even Europe–expected to dominate in that area since its market is more fragmented than that of the U.S., which has almost reached the saturation point–experienced a reduction in the number of transactions compared to 1999 and felt the results of the slowdown much earlier in the year. However, this European decline is expected to be of short duration. Although new "marriages" between major corporations are still possible, and the mergers and acquisitions trend will definitely continue in 2001, some experts believe that the global phenomenon is now slowing down. In fact, in the first quarter of 2001, the number of mergers and acquisitions dropped off sharply, following stock market declines and a general slowing of the economy. Not only are there fewer actual transactions but–and this is an important indicator of future activities–there is also less talk of upcoming agreements. In spite of the recent slowdown, there are still powerful forces behind the consolidation movement. It seems more appropriate to speak of a "hiatus" rather than a decline, a hiatus that will end when financial markets and the world economy (and the American economy in particular) regain their strength.

According to international equity expert Chris Jenkins of Rothschild Asset Management, "the global merger trend will likely continue for many years. [...] The initial phase is merging in your own country with allies or competition to achieve market dominance. Once you go outside your country, chances are you might get a merger, but it's probably going to start to get a bit hostile, because you're going to be taking over companies that don't want to be taken over, and they will fight to defend their position"[8]. However, M&As can have a downside for shareholders. According to a study by consulting firm KPMG, half of all mergers had reduced shareholder value and a third did not have the desired effect. Mergers often simply involve combining two operations under a single name.

Chart 1
International Alliances and M&As

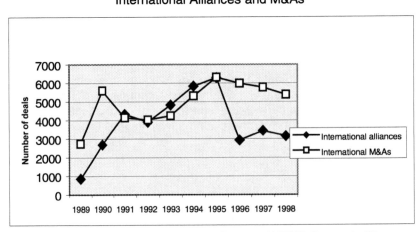

Sources: Thomson Financial Securities Data and KPMG Corporate Finance

---

[7] "The Great Merger Wave Breaks," *The Economist*, January 27, 2001, p. 59.

[8] André BILSKY, "Un seul monde : Stratagème global pour l'investisseur", magazine *En Route*, Summer 2000, p. 48-50.

I.1.3 STRATEGIC ALLIANCES

The number of international strategic alliances, in all sectors, has grown exponentially over the last decade, rising from just over 1,000 in 1989 to 7,000 in 1999. This is because they give businesses the flexibility needed to respond to globalization, the increased consolidation of economic power, the high cost of keeping up with constantly changing technologies and a highly competitive business environment. International strategic alliances represented 68 per cent of all alliances during this ten-year period, ample proof that they are indeed a response to globalization[9].

One of the primary goals of strategic alliances is to strengthen and expand a firm's market presence. However, businesses sometimes form alliances because of threats from the competition, or because alone they do not have the internal resources needed to meet new challenges. Each partner uses its strengths to compensate for the weaknesses of the other—in capital, expertise or personnel—or partners share the increased risk and costs related to certain activities, such as the development of a major project.

From 1990 to 1999, the most common co-operative alliances dealt with joint sales and marketing activities (29%), manufacturing and production (25%) and research and development (17%). However, these three major purposes of strategic alliances are not the only factors behind the recent growth in alliances because they now account for less than half of all alliances. This trend can be explained in part by the fact that strategic alliances in service sectors such as business services are proliferating faster than those in manufacturing.

Definition of a strategic alliance

Strategic alliances can take a variety of forms, ranging from an arm's-length contract to a joint venture. But the core of a strategic alliance is an inter-firm co-operative relationship that enhances the effectiveness of the competitive strategies of the participating firms by the trading of mutually beneficial resources such as technologies, skills, etc. Strategic alliances have the following three characteristics:

- The two or more firms that unite to pursue a set of agreed goals remain independent subsequent to the formation of the alliance.

- The partner firms share the benefits of the alliance and the control over the performance of assigned tasks.

- The partner firms contribute on a continuing basis in one or more key strategic areas (e.g., technology and products).

Source: OECD, *International Strategic Alliances: Their Role in Industrial Globalisation*, July 2000.

I.1.4 THE TRAVEL BOOM: A MAJOR CHALLENGE FOR THE INDUSTRY

Economic globalization, more accessible markets and the advent of new technologies have all combined to create a boom in travelling. This trend is likely to continue and the World Tourism Organization predicts that the number of international travellers will jump from 664 million per year to more than one billion by the year 2010 and that the figure will reach 1.6 billion by 2020. This steady growth will no doubt lead to an increase in air traffic encouraged by international trade, the desire to discover new destinations and travel experiences, and the need to better manage time, a resource of increasing importance in the traveller's decision-making process.

According to the International Air Transport Association (IATA), international air traffic is expected to rise 5.6 per cent annually in the next few years, which means over 150 million

---

[9] OECD, *International Strategic Alliances: Their Role in Industrial Globalisation*, July 2000.

passengers more in the next five years, for an annual total of 643 million by 2005. By the year 2010, the number of person-trips by plane could surpass 2.3 billion per year. The International Civil Aviation Organization (ICAO) notes that its 185 members transported a total of 1.6 billion passengers[10] in the year 2000. North American carriers dominate this market, conveying 36 per cent of the world's air traffic, including cargo and mail, compared to 28 per cent for European carriers and 27 per cent for those in the Asia-Pacific region.

To successfully serve all the new markets, tourism-based businesses have had to develop new strategies. The industry's response has been to create international strategic alliances and enter into mergers and acquisitions with partners already established in coveted markets. Sharing resources, risks and costs is a fast, efficient and, most importantly, less costly way of expanding one's influence. Whether it is for marketing or the purchase of goods and services, partners combine their strengths and multiply their economies of scale.

Tourism calls on the resources of many different companies to meet the client's needs. Working together is essential, for no one service provider (attractions, transportation companies, distribution networks, hotels, tourism associations, etc.) can single-handedly welcome clients and integrate the development of a tourism destination.

I.1.5 THE GROWTH OF TECHNOLOGY: THE INTERNET REVOLUTION

The Internet explosion of the last few years has been truly impressive. In the first quarter of 2001, there were over 429 million Internet users around the world. The United States and Canada account for the most users, with 41 per cent, while Europe, Africa and the Middle East come second with 27 per cent. This North American domination will not last. In Europe, the number of Internet users is expected to increase by an average 38 per cent each year, reaching 255 million by 2004.

The amazing popularity of the Internet can largely be explained by its affordability and user-friendliness. With a minimum of computer expertise, consumers can browse the Internet and access any number of commercial sites where it is possible to purchase products and services.

Table 1
Number of Internet users, by Region (in millions)

United States / Canada	175.9
Europe / Africa/ Middle East	115.8
Asia Pacific	85.8
Latin America	17.2

Source: Nielsen/Netratings (June 2001)

"Lack of information" bothers 80 per cent of Internet users

According to new research conducted by Axance, the primary reason that 80 per cent of Internet users do not complete on-line transactions is a lack of information, both about products and payment methods.

The biggest problem occurs when a potential consumer has trouble distinguishing among various products when making a purchase. Also, users complain that there is not enough information about the products and that the products described are not the same as those pictured. The Axance survey illustrates that there is also a lack of information about the order itself, the method of payment and delivery, and the conditions.

Source: Axance. *E-commerce* (June 2001)

E-commerce: The wave of the future

Electronic commerce is an inescapable reality for businesses. Data show that this sector is growing exponentially, despite consumer concerns about security and confidentiality. There are two types of e-commerce: business-to-business (B2B) and business-to-consumer (B2C).

The first type of e-commerce, or B2B, is by far the most common. Retail e-commerce has not developed as quickly simply because not as many homes as businesses have Internet access. A lack of confidence about the security of Internet transactions has also limited the growth of e-commerce. B2C commerce in particular has suffered due to consumers' concerns about the security of financial transactions and the transmission of personal data.

---

[10] Domestic and international passengers.

The third barrier to growth is of a legal nature. Since the Internet crosses political borders, it is somewhat difficult to define the legal liabilities involved. Although the Web improves a business's access to foreign markets, national laws regulating imports and exports apply to all electronic transactions.

As more and more businesses develop Web sites, those not on-line will be forced to adopt the technology as well. E-commerce has tremendous potential, both in the United States and elsewhere, as the Web gains millions of new users every year.

E-commerce enjoyed spectacular growth in 2000. Nearly 36 million Americans visited a retail site for the first time and approximately half of them made at least one on-line purchase. North American Internet retail sales totalled US$47.5 billion in 2000 and should reach just under US$200 billion by 2004, according to eMarketer. However, while North America currently accounts for 80 per cent of the world's Internet sales, this share should drop to 46.2 per cent by 2004.

Table 2 Retail e-Commerce Market (B2C) (in billions of US$)					
Region	2000	2001	2002	2003	2004
North America	47.5	74.4	110.6	135.2	197.9
Latin America	0.7	1.8	3.3	5.5	8.1
Europe	8.1	16.5	37.1	81.8	182.5
Africa / Middle East	0.2	0.3	0.6	1.1	1.6
Asia	3.2	8.3	15.6	26.4	38.0
Worldwide	59.7	101.1	167.2	250.0	428.1

Source: eMarketer (2001)

According to a report from Nielsen/NetRating, one out of six Europeans used the Internet to shop during the first six months of 2001. The European e-commerce market should double this year to reach US$16.5 billion and is expected to climb even higher by 2004. In Europe, potential Internet users are seeking affordability and quick access. Moreover, communications charges have dropped dramatically since the telecommunications sector was deregulated in 1998.

Mobile commerce (m-commerce)

The emergence of information technologies has had a major impact on consumer habits, enabling consumers to actively and thoroughly research their purchases before buying. With new tools, more personalized products and services can be developed to better fit consumer needs. One example is mobile telephony combined with wireless application protocol (WAP) technology, which seem particularly suited to the latest demands of e-consumers. The WAP protocol converts Web pages into a format that can be read from a mobile phone handset, enabling people to use their phones to access the Internet and enjoy its interactive features. The attraction of m-commerce is that consumers are no longer tied to a PC in a home or office; they can order products and services at any time, from anywhere.

Table 3 Percentage of Internet Users Who Engage in On-line Shopping, by Country	
Sweden	26
Switzerland	17
Denmark	16
Norway	14
Austria	12

Source: Nielsen / NetRating (2001)

Although the travel industry could be an ideal application for wireless Internet-ready phones, some experts question the actual market potential of WAP.

I.1.6 DEVELOPING ALLIANCES TO MEET THE DEMANDS OF TOURIST TRAFFIC

The phenomenon of consolidation observed in the tourism sector for the past several years continues to cause structural upheavals that affect not only the businesses involved but the various clienteles as well. As we examine whether the consumer will benefit from all these changes, the question arises: How is the trend towards consolidation playing out in each of the major sectors of the tourism industry?

Faced with the inevitable increase in air traffic, airlines must position themselves to take full advantage of the surge in travelling. Some crucial decisions must be made now if this demand is to be met. Firstly, carriers must think about upgrading their fleets to meet new market demands in terms of capacity, range, comfort and onboard services (e.g., the new Airbus A380 with a range of nearly 13,000 kilometres, designed to transport 550 to 650 passengers). Secondly, airport authorities must improve, enlarge, modernize, and even rethink their infrastructures to be able to receive the air traffic of tomorrow. At the moment, only twenty airports in the world are big enough to accommodate the new Airbus A380 aircraft. In the next 20 years, airlines are planning to spend US$1.2 trillion on more than 16,000 planes, bringing the total number of commercial aircraft to some 31,000 worldwide. To successfully support the growth in air traffic and adapt to new realities, airport authorities must commit to investing US$350 billion, a figure which does not include the investment required to enhance airport access (highways, rail links, etc.). Many airports are already taking steps to prepare for the demands of carriers and travellers, in particular: Reagan National Airport in Washington, DC, Dallas-Ft. Worth Airport, Changi Airport in Singapore, Kuala Lumpur International Airport and Roissy-Charles-de-Gaulle Airport, to name a few. In 2000, the 25 largest airports in the world[11] received more than one billion passengers, an increase of 6 per cent compared to the year before. This increase can be broken down as follows: 8 per cent more travellers in both the Asia-Pacific region and in Europe; 7 per cent more in the Middle East; 6 per cent more in Africa; 2 per cent more in Latin America/the Caribbean; and 4 per cent more in North America. However, the tragic events of September 11, 2001, are likely to change this situation, at least in the short term.

To satisfy travellers, airports must work to minimize the time passengers spend on the ground by reducing the waiting times of various terminal operations. When passengers are forced to spend time in the terminal, they must have access to a range of leisure, business and educational activities. Technology can become an indispensable tool for resolving this logistical challenge and helping create a positive travel experience from the moment a traveller arrives at the airport to the moment he leaves. These changes in airport services must be determined today if the requirements of tomorrow are to be met. And it is this philosophy that must guide carriers in alliances, tour operators and airport authorities as they strive to harmonize their alliance, merger and acquisition strategies and investment decisions with the growth in tourism traffic.

Market Share, by Continent, in 2000

According to the figures from 2000, the number of international tourists reached 699 million, a 7.4 per cent increase over 1999, and the highest increase in ten years. The East Asia-Pacific region was popular once more, receiving 14.7 per cent more travellers and setting a new record of over 111.9 million international arrivals. Other regions like the Middle East (12.9%) and South Asia (11.0%) also recorded major gains compared to 1999.

Continental Europe is still the most popular destination with some 403 million international tourists. In 2000, Europe registered a 6.1 per cent increase, the biggest since 1994. The Americas recorded less-than-average increases for the fourth year in a row. However, the growth recorded in 2000 (5.5%) was twice as high as that recorded in 1999 (2.3%). The Caribbean enjoyed the strongest growth (7.5%), particularly in the Turks and Caicos Islands (28.9%) and the U.S. Virgin Islands (16.5%).

Finally, Africa welcomed 27.6 million international tourists in 2000, the smallest increase (4.4%) over 1999, compared to the other regions of the globe.

---

[11] Sixteen of them are located in the United States, six are in Europe and three are in Asia.

Chart 2
International Tourist Arrivals, by Region, 2000

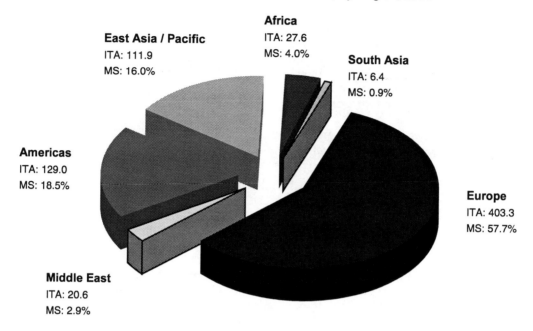

East Asia / Pacific
ITA: 111.9
MS: 16.0%

Africa
ITA: 27.6
MS: 4.0%

South Asia
ITA: 6.4
MS: 0.9%

Americas
ITA: 129.0
MS: 18.5%

Europe
ITA: 403.3
MS: 57.7%

Middle East
ITA: 20.6
MS: 2.9%

ITA: International Tourist Arrivals (in millions)   MS: Global Market Share

Source: World Tourism Organization (WTO)

I.2 THE AIRLINE INDUSTRY

I.2.1 BACKGROUND AND ISSUES

Since the airline industry was deregulated in North America and Europe, all international air transportation has been governed by bilateral open skies agreements. These agreements define in detail which cities can be served, the number of carriers that can offer flights, flight frequency or capacity on routes, and approved rates. In some cases, the agreements are highly restrictive and competition is tightly regulated. Others are more liberal, allowing more than one carrier in each country to fly on routes between countries (multiple designation) and creating greater flexibility in terms of cities served and rates.

Open skies agreements have fostered the development of international alliances that are nevertheless subject to the approval of the U.S. Department of Transport (DOT), the European Commission, the Canadian Transportation Agency, the African Civil Aviation Commission, etc., depending on the origin of the carriers involved.

Development of Hubs

In the decade since deregulation, one of the main accomplishments has been the creation of strategically situated hubs from which an impressive number of routes radiate. These airports are used by the larger carriers as transfer points for passengers travelling to and from the surrounding region as well as to foreign destinations. This system has a number of advantages for travellers living in the immediate area, who see a substantial increase in the number of flights and destinations available from their airport. It becomes hard to compete in the local market, however, and overpricing often results. Both the United States and Canada have developed hubs very successfully. However, Europe and Asia still have a long way to go before they have a true hub system interconnecting many cities.

Airlines have developed this system because it enables them to serve many more markets than they could with direct flights. The number of seats sold from and to small municipalities is also higher with the hub-and-spoke system, which in turn brings down operating costs and therefore ticket prices.

For example, a small community of 100,000 cannot by itself generate enough passengers to a single destination, but it can generate enough travellers to a variety of destinations to fill a plane. A carrier operating from a hub offering a large number of destinations is thus able to provide travellers connections to other of its own flights. Using the hub as the transfer point, it keeps a customer that it might otherwise have had to transfer to another carrier.

Geographic Location: A Key Consideration

Geographic location is the chief consideration in setting up a hub; next is the size of the local market. Airlines prefer to set up their base of operations in a place where there is already heavy traffic, either because local customers travel a great deal or because the destination is popular with other travellers.

Nonetheless, operating out of a hub airport requires a large ground staff, given the baggage handling and passenger assistance required for making connections.

Restrictions on share-holding

In Canada and the U.S., legislation limits foreign ownership of a domestic airline to 25 per cent of voting shares, while this figure is 49.9 per cent in Europe. This means that a North American airline can own almost half of a European airline, while the same European airline can only own 25 per cent of a North American airline.

In Asia, government restrictions on the foreign ownership of national carriers have been easing gradually, but differ from country to country. In Thailand, the percentage allowed has risen from 10 per cent to 30 per cent, while the government of the Republic of Korea raised the foreign ownership limit–formerly 7 per cent for individuals and 26 per cent for groups–to 50 per cent.

I.2.2 A TYPOLOGY OF INTERNATIONAL ALLIANCES

Various types of alliances

Alliances among airlines consist of one or more co-operative agreements between two or more carriers, and may be divided into two main categories according to the nature and degree of involvement of the partners in each others' affairs: non-equity alliances and equity alliances.

According to Tretheway and Oum,[12] there are basically two kinds of **non-equity alliances**: sharing of specific routes and commercial alliances. They consist in a series of inter-company co-operative agreements, such as joint marketing agreements, promotion of specific routes, combined frequent flyer plans, standardization of services, or co-ordination of flight timetables and baggage handling. They are thus the more flexible and less constrictive type of alliance, at least at first. As this type of alliance does not require a major initial commitment, it imposes no constraints. Interlining and code sharing, which are described below, fall into this category of strategic alliance.

Equity alliances necessarily imply a higher degree of involvement of members in each others' affairs. This type of strategic alliance is more highly integrated, although the extent varies enormously from one agreement to another. When a significant interest is held, it leads to the establishment of a number of joint activities, such as price setting, standardizing of equipment, services and supplies, development of common image and brand identity, revenue and profit sharing and, in the case of some international alliances, it guarantees immunity from prosecution under antitrust laws.

Interlining: The ancestor of modern alliances

Historically, unrelated air carriers entered into agreements to facilitate transfers of passengers at airports. Under these agreements, the carriers concerned would charge a lower price for a combined ticket than they normally would for two tickets purchased separately. The carriers were also supposed to simplify the ticketing and baggage handling for these connections. Although there are still some interlining agreements, they are rare nowadays.

Code sharing: An agreement on specific routes

Code sharing accounts for 70 per cent of the alliances between airlines. Originally national and regional carriers shared code, then the practice spread to international routes. In its simplest form, code sharing is defined as a business agreement between two carriers who maintain their full independence, wherein each of them purchases a block of seats on the other one's flight and then sells them as if they were its own. This allows allied carriers to extend their network of routes without making a major investment, which would be necessary if they had to purchase their own aircraft to fly the same routes.

It's Easy To Lose Track!

Swissair and Sabena (Qualiflyer Group) have code-share agreements with American Airlines (oneworld Alliance) on the Dallas–Zurich–Chicago and Washington–Boston–Brussels routes, while Air Canada (Star Alliance) and Delta (SkyTeam Alliance) have been offering cross-border code-share flights between Canadian gateway cities and Delta's American hubs, Atlanta, Cincinnati, Dallas and Salt Lake City since October 29, 2000. This arrangement replaces the ten-year business agreement on multiple-code flights that Air Canada and Canadian cancelled with American Airlines after Canadian was acquired by Air Canada.

---

[12] OUM, PARK and ZHANG, *Globalization and Strategic Alliances,* Pergamon, 2000, 252 p.

So a flight to Cancún may be operated by Mexicana Airlines but listed as both a Mexicana flight and a United flight, thus giving the *impression* that United offers a greater number of flights to a wider range of destinations. These code-share agreements involve specific routes, and their extent may vary tremendously from one alliance to the next: they may apply to a single route in a single market, or to a number of routes and several markets. A separate agreement must therefore be drawn up for each pair of cities that the carriers wish to serve.

A major issue in code sharing is a carrier's hub and the availability of time slots at that hub. An alliance will be attracted to a given carrier if it needs some access at the carrier's main hub. The way in which carriers' hubs and slots complement each other is key to the establishment of code-share alliances.

Code sharing: Healthy competition?
A number of code-share alliances involving a limited number of specific routes have failed because the partners had to compete to sell their share of the seats on each flight for which they shared code, instead of co-operating and harmonizing their activities. One-third of the 50 alliances involving specific routes approved by the U.S. Department of Transport in 1995 no longer exist, because they did not achieve the anticipated revenues or passenger traffic.

Also, competition between the partners continues to be just as fierce on other routes for which they have no code-share agreement. Some carriers that are members of a specific group do not hesitate to enter into code-share alliances with partners that are members of competing groups.

Antitrust immunity: A step towards integration
Code sharing can take several forms and be part of a more general marketing alliance in which two carriers make other changes to offer the same rates, share revenues, and co-ordinate timetables, fleets, gate access, service levels, baggage handling and frequent flyer plans. To do so, they must enjoy immunity from antitrust laws.

As a general rule, the authorities confer antitrust immunity when they deem that consumers will benefit. Immunity means that the alliance is not anti-competitive, and enables foreign carriers to operate as if they were a single company. This brings them to a new stage in their integration, while leaving them free in the most important areas. This type of business relationship is the most likely to generate significant profits for the partners since they work closely together instead of competing to sell seats. Nonetheless, some people see this as a loss of competition for the industry and consumers.

Antitrust Immunity in the North Atlantic

In May 2000, Swissair, Sabena and American Airlines obtained antitrust immunity in the North Atlantic from the U.S. Department of Transport, which enabled them to offer a greater number of code-share flights between Europe and the U.S., while at the same time co-ordinating their timetables and prices. Antitrust immunity went into effect on August 6, 2000.

Alliances based on resource sharing
This type of alliance allows a number of economies of scale. Carriers often share aircraft and resources when they penetrate a new market. Co-operation lasts until the market can support both carriers. Agreements are highly specific, however, and do not usually entail any exchange of business information.

I.2.3 PORTRAIT OF THE BIG FIVE INTERNATIONAL ALLIANCES

The primary objective of an alliance is to strengthen and expand an airline's market presence by offering passengers "seamless" flights — in which seats are assigned from beginning to end right from the point of origin — to a large number of destinations. An alliance allows each airline to offer a wider range of itineraries without actually serving all the destinations itself. The variety of destinations offered, especially when combined with frequent flyer programs, is what draws customers. The alliance also makes it possible to cut costs by sharing airport facilities such as business-class lounges and pooling equipment maintenance and catering services. Hence the bitter competition between the major groups for new members.

Generally speaking, an international alliance requires an agreement between a major European airline and a North American airline, as passenger air traffic between North America and Europe represents 54 per cent of the world's air traffic. It is on this basis that the five biggest international alliances were formed: oneworld Alliance, Star Alliance, SkyTeam Alliance (the new alliance between Delta and Air France), Qualiflyer and Wings, the KLM-Northwest alliance. Together, the five account for 60 per cent of all air traffic.

The situation described below is current as of August 2001, but a number of carriers are undergoing a complete restructuring of their network of allies. For more details, see the supplemental information in Part 4 of this document.

Table 4
The Big Five Alliances

Name (date founded)	Members	Destinations (in 2000)	Passengers/yr (in millions) (in 2000)	Cumulative sales, 1999 (in billions of US$)
Star Alliance (May 1997)	Air Canada, Air New Zealand, ANA, Ansett Australia, Austrian Airlines, British Midland, Lauda Air, Lufthansa, Mexicana, SAS, Singapore Airlines, Thai Airways, Tyrolean Airways, United Airlines, Varig	894	317.6	82.2
oneworld (February 1999)	Aer Lingus, American Airlines, British Airways, Cathay Pacific, Finnair, Iberia, Lanchile, Qantas	565	209.0	51.0
Wings (1993)	KLM, Northwest, Continental*	480	n/a	26.7
Qualiflyer (March 1998)	Air Europe, Air Lib**, Air Littoral, TAP Air Portugal[13], Crossair, LOT Polish Airlines, PGA Portugal Airlines[14], Sabena, Swissair[15], Turkish Airlines, Volare Airlines	332	over 53	17.5
SkyTeam (June 2000)	Air France, Aeromexico, Delta Airlines, Korean Air, CSA Czech Airlines, Alitalia***	472	177	30.4

*   Continental is not a real member, but is included in the alliance here because of Northwest Airlines' major holdings in Continental.
**   Merger of Air Liberté and AOM.
*** Agreement signed July 27, 2001. Expected to take effect in November 2001.

---

[13] January 2000.
[14] April 2000.
[15] Will be taken over by Crossair (former regional carrier) on October 28, 2001.

Wings

Although this group has very few members, it is the most highly integrated alliance of all. KLM and Northwest have already merged their business teams and their frequent flyer plans are interchangeable. In addition, as they enjoy antitrust immunity, the two carriers can easily harmonize their rates and co-ordinate their timetables.

Nonetheless, this very strong desire to create a single company has engendered a few conflicts, most significantly the withdrawal of Alitalia: the ties between the Italian carrier and KLM have been cut once and for all. The future of this alliance is a subject of debate since it does have very few members and covers a relatively limited geographic area.

Star Alliance

Star bills itself as a "consensual" alliance, meaning a sort of co-operative in which the identity of each operator is recognized and each maintains its freedom. Its management board, on which all group members sit, is an excellent means of communication. It is heading towards a single management in charge of implementing the measures decided by the chairmen of the member companies, including:

- Product development: common facilities at various airports, single agencies in big cities where all companies are represented, with each one able to work for the others
- Group purchases of parts, fuel and aircraft
- Business strategy; harmonization and reciprocity of frequent flyer plans; harmonization of domestic and international timetables and routes of all members; integrated reservation systems facilitating check-in and connections; pooling of resources and brands; sharing of information systems
- Marketing communications: integration of staff and brand identity

Right now, Star is also the most global alliance, with 894 destinations in 129 countries on every continent.

Qualiflyer

Until very recently, this alliance was based entirely on the financial ties between SAirGroup, Swissair's holding company, and all the partners: Swissair held a 34 per cent to 49.5 per cent interest in each of the carriers in the alliance, with the exception of Turkish Airlines which was completely independent of Swissair. This equity investment strategy ultimately proved unsuccessful: following a series of financial setbacks, Swissair filed for bankruptcy protection in late September 2001. As part of a bailout, the UBS and Crédit Suisse banks bought Swissair's 70 per cent interest in Crossair and gave both companies the cash needed to facilitate the transfer of activities. Swissair will be taken over by regional carrier Crossair, formerly its subsidiary, in late October 2001. The future of this alliance is uncertain as its members are in a shaky financial position following Swissair's withdrawal from its obligations. Swissair was supposed to purchase an 85 per cent interest in Sabena[16], a 34 per cent interest in TAP Air Portugal–a sale that was part of a plan to privatize the carrier–, and buy shares of Turkish Airlines. Swissair has also sold off its French arm consisting of Air Liberté, AOM and Air Littoral[17].

This group is expected to undergo more upheaval in the coming months. The developing European airline industry is bound to create fierce competition among the various member airlines of Qualiflyer, thereby causing serious internal tension despite the partners' high level of commitment and shared activities: single frequent flyer program, same reservation classes, agencies representing all members, etc.

oneworld

Oneworld is the "bluff" alliance of British Airways (BA) and American Airlines (AA), so called because these two carriers cannot offer code-share flights between the U.S. and Great Britain. There is, as yet, no open skies agreement between the two countries. However, in

---

[16] Sabena has obtained legal protection until November 30. This puts off an immediate liquidation and buys it some time to put together a restructuring plan.

[17] Suffering from financial difficulties, AOM and Air Liberté announced they would merge their activities in March 2001. Since September 22, 2001, the newly created company has been called Air Lib.

early August 2001, the two airlines announced that they had reopened negotiations with American, European and British regulatory authorities aimed at strengthening the alliance and ultimately forging an open skies agreement. Until such an agreement is signed, the oneworld alliance cannot be ratified. Furthermore, because they already control most of the traffic between England and the States, the two carriers had to divest themselves of 167 time slots at Heathrow to encourage competition. They now maintain that they hold fewer slots at this hub–38 per cent–than their competitors do in their respective hubs[18].

Furthermore, the presence of two relatively ambitious carriers such as British Airways and American Airlines in an alliance can spell problems for a long-lasting agreement. That is why we have seen the members of this alliance be mutually wary in their dealings with one another. However, oneworld has managed to develop an integrated international timetable, common baggage-handling and passenger-handling protocols, frequent flyer reciprocity and unified technology. It has also nearly doubled its membership in just over a year, making it the fastest-growing alliance. The future of the alliance, which cannot offer code-share flights between the U.S. and Great Britain, remains unclear. We will have to wait for the results of the negotiations begun in August 2001 on an open skies agreement between London and Washington.

SkyTeam

Launched officially on June 23, 2000, SkyTeam is the most recent strategic alliance, with an initial ten-year contract. Delta Airlines was looking for a bigger European hub to improve its position on the transatlantic market, which it obtained with Air France and the Roissy-Charles-de-Gaulle Airport. SkyTeam also has a foothold in Latin America thanks to Aeromexico and in Asia with Korean Airlines. Together, these four partners already cover 80 per cent of the world's air traffic routes and, through Canada, serve the partners' main hubs — providing access to over 450 destinations around the world. From the outset, SkyTeam was planning to recruit other European carriers and this plan was implemented when CSA Czech Airlines joined in April 2001 and Alitalia followed in August of the same year. Other airlines are poised to join the alliance, notably Royal Air Maroc and Aeroflot. The regional partners of each alliance member are involved as associates rather than full-fledged members of SkyTeam.

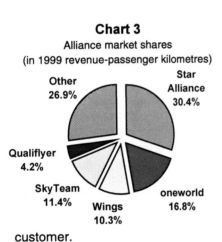

Chart 3

Alliance market shares
(in 1999 revenue-passenger kilometres)

Other 26.9%
Star Alliance 30.4%
Qualiflyer 4.2%
SkyTeam 11.4%
Wings 10.3%
oneworld 16.8%

With its current members, SkyTeam is not a large alliance. However, that is not its goal. Instead, it is committed to focussing on the customer.

And that is the state of the industry in August 2001, an industry in flux, attempting to consolidate itself around four or five major alliances, which could in most cases be termed marriages of convenience.

I.2.4 ALLIANCES, MERGERS AND ACQUISITIONS IN THE AIRLINE INDUSTRY

Following the deregulation of the airline industry, international carriers created strategic alliances at a frantic pace to respond to the increase in bilateral agreements, which were often very restrictive. More and more, governments are granting airlines antitrust immunity and are even allowing mergers between major carriers, leaving still fewer players in the industry.

---

[18] Northwest-KLM (Qualiflyer) hold 70 per cent of the slots in Amsterdam; United-Lufthansa-SAS (Star) control nearly 70 per cent of the slots in Frankfurt; and Delta-Air France-Alitalia (SkyTeam) have 55 per cent of the slots at the Paris de Gaulle airport.

The airline industry is now characterized by its super-alliances. By integrating their networks, the five major international alliances provide member carriers with better access to a greater number of destinations and countries. Competition no longer occurs among individual airlines; it is now a battle of the alliances. Consequently, most carriers feel they must join an alliance, not simply to compete, but to survive.

Despite these developments, the airline industry remains much less consolidated than many other tourism sectors, as well as most of the highly competitive modern industries such as information technology (IT), communications or automobile manufacturing.

I.2.5 FROM CODE SHARING TO EQUITY INVESTMENT

The North American market
In the United States, the airline industry is leaning more towards mergers and acquisitions than strategic alliances. There are a number of reasons for this. Firstly, there are few opportunities for growth, given the maturity of the market and the development of mega-airports. Secondly, shareholders are putting more and more pressure on airlines to maintain a high return on their investment. Mergers and acquisitions are therefore aimed at increasing shareholder value by accelerating the growth of carriers.

In May 2000, United Airlines, the largest U.S. carrier, announced a buyout of US Airways, the sixth largest carrier, thus strengthening its position as the largest airline in the world. The deal would also give United control over 25 per cent of the American market. However, the U.S. Department of Justice (DOJ) blocked the proposed merger on July 28, 2001, saying that such a merger would reduce airline competition in the United States to the detriment of the public[19].

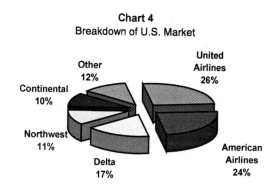

Chart 4
Breakdown of U.S. Market

In January 2001, American Airlines (oneworld) announced a transaction totalling US$5 billion involving TransWorld Airlines, US Airways and DC Air. With one swoop, American acquired:

- **TWA**: the majority of its assets, including 190 planes, most of its stowage rights and time slots at numerous airports, the St-Louis hub and the maintenance facilities at St-Louis, Kansas City and Los Angeles. TWA walks away with $500 million after handing its lease agreements over to American.

- **US Airways and United**: 66 planes, 20 leased planes, 14 stowage sites, 36 time slots and various other rights and slots associated with operating the Washington-New York-Boston shuttle with United. American paid United US$1.2 billion cash for the sale of its assets, and took over $300 million in leasing agreements.

- **DC Air**: 49 per cent of this young company that will be run out of Reagan National Airport in Washington. In return, DC Air gets $82 million cash and 11 leased planes from American.

Apparently, the deal with DC Air raises some issues. American and DC Air will operate out of Reagan National Airport in Washington, but US Airways is the principal carrier there, controlling 33 per cent of airport traffic, and United has its own hub at Dulles International Airport in Washington. Also, DC Air depended on United for its planes and crew, thus ensuring its control over local airports. However, with the new agreement, American will be in charge of planes and crew. It remains to be seen how these two "aggressive" giants decide who controls this important hub.

---

[19] Since the DOJ considers that this merger would violate antitrust laws, it is initiating legal proceedings in the courts.

Given the recent large-scale transactions, Delta, the third largest American carrier, is wondering if it should also get into the act and consider merging with another carrier or if it should simply play the game on its own. The people at Delta believe they can remain competitive without signing any mega-agreements. On the other hand, they are not opposed to considering any interesting offer that might improve the company's market positioning. At the end of January 2001, Delta entered into negotiations with Northwest and Continental. Continental would be an interesting choice for Delta, since the two companies' routes are in some ways complementary. Northwest, on the other hand, has a marketing agreement and veto rights on Continental's sale. Also, it seems that Delta and Northwest executives are not on the best of terms. In the end, Northwest was not interested in a Delta/Continental merger, and asked an exorbitant price. The latest news is that there might be a turnaround in which Continental would absorb Delta. If Delta were to clinch such a deal, the three American giants could control up to 85 per cent of the current market. In 1998, Delta already held a 27 per cent interest in Atlantic Southeast Airlines, a 21 per cent share in Comair and 15 per cent of SkyWest.

Some experts believe Delta should continue to fly solo to maintain its good track record, competent management and reputation as one of the best carriers. If Delta concluded a hasty agreement, the increased debt burden would force it to enter into a merger, with all the possible changes to its corporate culture and attendant employee disputes. Other analysts believe that Delta should react in some way to the recent transactions in the American market. There are also numerous obstacles to be overcome before these agreements can be finalized. In fact, Carl Icahn, former owner of TWA, is contesting the terms of the agreement and may try to set himself up in competition, either solo or with other partners. The businessman could also force American to pay millions of dollars in compensation for non-respect of contract — he signed a contract with TWA that expires in September 2003.

In Canada, since acquiring Canadian International at a cost of C$92 million, Air Canada controls 90 per cent of the Canadian market and operates most of the flights formerly covered by Canadian and its partners. Shortly after this transaction, Air Canada announced the consolidation of its affiliated regional carriers, Air Nova, Air Ontario and AirBC, to give itself greater operational flexibility. Since then, Air Nova has been providing service on regular routes within Quebec, increasing the number of flights, the number of seats available, and its cargo capacity in many Quebec communities. By deploying a large fleet, Air Nova is now targeting the lucrative market of same-day round-trip business travel, going head-to-head with the small regional carriers.

The competition has decided to fight back against Air Canada's virtual monopoly and discount carriers want to increase their market share. Virgin Atlantic Airways (a British company) has entered the Canadian market by offering non-stop flights between London and Toronto since summer 2001[20].

The European market
The trend towards consolidation is also well established in Europe. When Swissair increased its holdings in Sabena in April 2000, the move opened up the possibility of a new regulatory outlook on the key question of who can own route rights, an issue that had until then been hindering the creation of true cross-border alliances. Swissair was guaranteed ownership of its rights in the European Union, regardless of the nationality of its shareholders. This transaction has opened the door to other airline mergers involving companies from different countries. British Airways, looking for a partner with a strong presence in Western Europe, discussed the possibility of taking over KLM, of the Netherlands. However, these talks fell apart in September 2000 because the development potential of Shiphol Airport, the Amsterdam hub, was of primary importance in the negotiations.

Following its departure from the Wings alliance, Alitalia began discussing the possibility of merging with Swissair and American Airlines (AA). However, unable to reach an agreement with them, Alitalia began negotiating an exclusive bilateral agreement with Air France and Delta to solidify a strong commercial partnership and ensure its entry into the SkyTeam

---

[20] Last year, Toronto became the 4th most popular long-distance destination for flights leaving London, receiving 1.3 million passengers.

alliance. These negotiations led to the signing of an agreement on July 27, 2001. Alitalia's entry into SkyTeam will take effect as soon as the Italian company brings its services, procedures and frequent flyer program in line with the alliance's standards. These conditions should be met by November of 2001. As for the agreement, it should remain in effect until at least October 2011 and help encourage co-operation among the Roissy-Charles-de-Gaulle, Milan-Malpensa and Rome-Fiumiuni airports.

In other developments, Iberia broke off negotiations to purchase Air Europa in January 2001, due to disagreements over the sale price and lay-offs. Air France, KLM and SAirGroup withdrew their offer to purchase Malaysian Airline System, leaving Australia's Qantas Airways the only potential buyer of the national carrier. British Airways and American Airlines restarted discussions aimed at reviving their business agreements. British Airways put its discount carrier, GO, up for sale but as yet has found no takers. Apparently KLM has shown some interest.

The Asia-Pacific market

Most Asian countries were initially uninterested in alliances because the carriers always tried to efficiently exploit the exploding Asian market on their own. However, many Asian governments are now easing their policies to improve access to the most promising markets and offer the flexibility needed if their national carriers are to join major international alliances and reduce their operating costs. Cathay Pacific, Thai Airways, Singapore Airlines, Qantas, Air New Zealand and, in June 2000, Korean Airlines have all become members of large airline alliances. Other legislative changes could strengthen this trend: open skies accords, industry deregulation, more privatized carriers, etc.

Asian carriers tend to focus their operations on the hubs at either end of the most travelled routes, which enables them to increase the number of flights and use larger aircraft, thereby cutting the cost per passenger. However, they can only do this if the most convenient landing and take-off slots are available, which is not the case in certain airports. This focus on hubs leads the major carriers to seek alliances with smaller, "feeder" carriers to ensure their planes are filled to capacity.

The Middle East market

In the Middle East, the Arab Air Carriers Organization (AACO), founded in 1965, is an association of some twenty carriers[21] from 25 countries[22] in the region. In October 2000, at a convention held in Beirut, Lebanon, the AACO launched a code-share marketing alliance of member carriers on specific medium and long-distance routes, principally those to Asia and Africa. This agreement will likely be extended to other regions. The association also intends to start discussing possible avenues of co-operation with the major international alliances.

I.2.6 THE FUTURE OF ALLIANCES

The alliance waltz: Choose your partner!

In some respects, the trend towards equity investment could weaken the five existing major alliances. For example, discussions between Qantas Airways (oneworld) and New Zealand and Australian authorities aimed at convincing the governments to allow Qantas to purchase a major share in Air New Zealand (Star) in place of Singapore Airlines, which is already a majority shareholder in the Ansett Group, an Australian carrier, could weaken Star's position on the Asian market. Furthermore, Thai Airways is re-assessing its place in Star Alliance since the arrival of Singapore Airlines–its primary competitor with respect to connecting traffic.

---

[21] EgyptAir (1932), Saudi Arabian Airlines (1945), Middle East Airlines (1945), Iraqi Airways (1945), Syrian Arab Airlines (1946), Sudan Airways (1946), Tunis Air (1948), Gulf Air (1950), TransMediterranean Airways (1953), Air Algerie (1953), Kuwait Airways (1954), Royal Air Maroc (1957), Yemen Airways (1962), Royal Jordanian (1963), Libyan Arab Airlines (1964), Emirates (1985), Qatar Airways (1993), Oman Air (1995), Palestinian Airways (1995), Trans Arabian Air Transport.

[22] Democratic Republic of Algeria, Morocco, United Arab Emirates, Bahrain, Republic of Iraq, Republic of Yemen, Kuwait, Libyan Arab Jamahiriyah, Lebanon, Arab Republic of Egypt, Qatar, Syrian Arab Republic, Hashemite Kingdom of Jordan, Republic of Sudan, Kingdom of Saudi Arabia, Tunisia, Oman, Palestine, Somalia, Mauritania, Djibouti and Comoros.

Towards a common identity

In light of all this global consolidation, it is easy to imagine that the super-alliances will eventually further integrate their members, replacing individual partner codes with alliance codes on the screens of computer reservations systems (as is already the case with the Star Alliance) as well as on the tail wings of the planes themselves. Of course, major obstacles do remain such as the integration of information systems and the resistance of unions and personnel.

Increased surveillance

The market concentration taking place in the U.S. airline industry and around the world is a concern of antitrust officials, who are rather reluctant to lend their approval. They do, however, intend to examine the impact of this consolidation on consumers. Since travellers already complain about poor service and high prices, it is entirely appropriate to wonder whether they will benefit from the growth of alliances and consolidation of carriers.

I.2.7 ALLIANCES WITH OTHER SECTORS

For a number of years, the big international carriers have been setting up subsidiaries directly related to the air transport industry such as charter airlines, cargo services, catering, ground services, aircraft maintenance, and pilot and flight crew training. However, in recent years there has been an intensification of the business relationships between airlines and other suppliers of travel services such as car rental companies, hotels, wholesalers, railways, cruise operators, and even credit card and financial service companies — MasterCard, Citibank — and certain retailers. The alliances mainly involve joint promotions and the exchange of air miles, although some carriers have subsidiaries in the distribution network and hotel industry, as the three sectors are closely connected.

Star Alliance in Partnership with the SNCF

Star Alliance has entered into co-operative agreements with the French national railway, SNCF, for high-speed train links such as Paris–Lyon, enabling it to stream customers into Paris and onto planes with just one ticket, as has traditionally been done with planes. United Airlines and Lufthansa are the originators of this strategy.

I.3 THE DISTRIBUTION NETWORK

I.3.1 THE DOMINANCE OF CONGLOMERATES

Since the distribution network is the last sector of the travel industry to move towards consolidation and integration, it is only natural to speculate on the motivations behind the current merger mania. For many players, consolidation is a wise course, made all the easier by the financial community's view that leisure has become a leading industry. Little by little, major players are divesting themselves of some of their traditional activities to concentrate more on tourism and travel, considered more profitable because of their ability to attract capital investment.

To better understand the extent of this consolidation, we are presenting an overview of the major conglomerates that make up the distribution network; their primary activities, characteristics and associated brands are listed in greater detail in Part 4 of this document.

I.3.2 PORTRAIT OF THE MAJOR CONGLOMERATES

Table 5 ranks the major conglomerates according to the most recent operating results available (2000) and notes the relative importance of their travel-related activities. However, it is important to note that the Proportion — travel (in %) column does not necessarily refer only to the company's tour operator activities. In the case of Accor, for example, the group's hotel activities account for 68 per cent of its total sales.

Table 5
Major Global Travel Conglomerates in 2000

	Company	Headquarters	Sales (in billions US$)	Proportion — travel (in %)	Sales — travel (in billions US$)
1	Carlson Companies[23]	United States	31.4	-	-
2	American Express	United States	22.1	79	17.4
3	Japan Travel Bureau[24]	Japan	14	100	14
4	Preussag	Germany	19.2	48	9.3
5	Airtours	United Kingdom	6.5	100	6.5
6	Accor	France	6.6	94	6.2
7	C & N Touristik	Germany	4.2	100	4.2
8	Rewe (Touristik)	Germany	35.5	10	3.7
9	First Choice	United Kingdom	2.7	100	2.7
10	Groupe Kuoni	Switzerland	2.5	100	2.5

Source: Chair in Tourism, Université du Québec à Montréal, based on financial data from the companies. These amounts were converted into U.S. dollars at the exchange rate in effect at the end of the fiscal year. Some apparent inconsistencies may be due to exchange rate fluctuations.

Preussag

German group Preussag is the leading European tour operator, although as recently as 1997 it was completely absent from the travel market. Having divested itself of its shipbuilding and mining activities, Preussag has invested heavily to refocus on the travel industry in the last few years. The push began in 1997, when Preussag purchased TUI, the top German tour operator. The company then acquired Thomas Cook and Carlson U.K. of Great Britain in December 1998. Finally, in May 2000, Preussag took over Thomson Travel, the number one British agency, for US$2 billion. However, for this purchase to receive EC approval, Preussag had to promise to sell off Thomas Cook. In France, Preussag acquired a 6 per cent interest in Nouvelles Frontières in November 2000; this share should gradually increase to

---

[23] 1999 sales. It was impossible to determine what proportion of sales was related solely to the travel sector.
[24] 1999 sales.

34 per cent by March 2002[25]. Preussag is also interested in Accor and Club Méditerranée and many experts see it as ready to take over Nouvelles Frontières.

In other transactions, Preussag purchased GTT[26], the number one Austrian tour operator, in February 2000. In Spain, after gaining a foothold with the RIU hotel chain, Preussag planned to acquire Viajes Marsans in April 2001. That same month, it acquired all remaining shares of TUI Belgique, thereby becoming sole proprietor. In May 2001, it purchased a 10 per cent interest in Alpitour, Italy's number one tour operator.

In February 2001, Preussag (through its subsidiary, TUI), Maritz Travel Company (U.S.), Internet Travel Group (Australia), Protravel (France) and Britannic Travel (U.K.) joined forces to create a global business travel network: TQ3 Travel Solutions. Sales should reach $9 billion.

Preussag is now making travel the company's chief sector of activity and the source of half of its sales[27]. This percentage should rise to 77 per cent by 2002. The group has three divisions: travel (50%), logistics and industry (see the table in Part 4 of this document).

Condor & Neckermann Touristik AG

C & N Touristik AG was founded in 1998 when Germany company Karstadt Quelle decided to create a major tour operator by merging its travel division, NUR Touristik GmbH (Germany's number two tour operator), with Condor Flugdienst GmbH, Lufthansa's charter airline. Each founding company holds a 50 per cent share in the new group. Karstadt Quelle is Europe's largest retail and mail-order corporation. Its new business activities include travel services, e-commerce and over-the-counter business.

C & N Touristik AG has made several successful acquisitions in France, notably Aquatour, Albatros and the leisure travel activities of Havas Tourisme, in April 2000 (American Express acquired Havas Voyage Affaires, the business travel side). However, C & N's efforts in Great Britain have not been as successful: failed take-overs of both Thomson Travel and Airtours. In December 2000, it did acquire Thomas Cook for 885 million euros when Preussag was forced to divest itself of this tour operator as a condition of acquiring Thomson Travel (see above).

In other developments, in early May 2001, the number two German tour operator[28] abandoned the off-putting name of C & N to adopt the name of Thomas Cook, a brand within the group that enjoys a higher international profile.

Japan Travel Bureau

Founded in 1912, Japan Travel Bureau (JTB) is one of the largest travel groups in the world. A member of the JTB Foundation, the company focusses primarily on organizing group tours of Japan, planning travel and accommodations for conventions and events held in Japan, and putting together incentive and business travel packages. In fact, domestic travel generates two-thirds of JTB sales.

Carlson Companies

An American conglomerate, Carlson Companies serves two distinct client groups: corporations and consumers. The company offers corporate clients integrated marketing solutions and business travel services. Its consumer services include restaurants, hotels, cruise ships and branded travel agencies.

---

[25] J. Maillot, President and CEO of Nouvelles Frontières, will then hold a 38 per cent interest and other shareholders will have the remaining 28 per cent.

[26] GTT (Gulet Touropa Touristik).

[27] It is estimated that travel will account for approximately 77 per cent of Preussag's sales once the Thomson Travel Group's activities are fully integrated.

[28] In Belgium, C & N is the leader with its Neckermann, Sunsnacks, Pegase and All Season brands (*The Tribune*, April 5, 2000, p. 10).

Major Players in the Corporate Travel Sector

American Express continues to be recognized as one of the world leaders in corporate travel account management. In addition to adopting several new programs aimed at delivering more personalized services, Amex is working to develop a digital business-to-business marketplace through partnerships with dozens of e-commerce firms. Amex has global annual sales of US$22.1 billion.

Carlson Wagonlit Travel, a subsidiary owned 50-50 by Carlson Companies and Accor, is also a leader in the corporate travel sector. With more than 3,000 offices in 140 countries, the company generates annual sales of more than US$11 billion. To expand its services to the Japanese market, on January 1, 2001, Carlson Wagonlit Travel entered into a joint venture with Japan Travel Bureau, creating JTB-CWT Business Travel Solutions. This firm will offer corporate clients travel services better suited to their needs.

Rider-BTI Travel is a major corporate travel specialist in Canada. Originally called the Rider Travel Group, the company became Rider-BTI in 1998 when Hogg Robinson, a British conglomerate offering financial services and corporate travel account management, acquired a 51 per cent share. Hogg Robinson is now the sole owner of Rider-BTI, known as BTI-Canada since April 2001. Formed as a joint venture with Hogg Robinson, which is now managing partner and majority shareholder, Business Travel International Worldwide is the largest corporate travel solutions provider in the world (sales: US$20 billion).

Rewe

Based in Cologne, German conglomerate Rewe owns a chain of supermarkets. In the past two years, this group has developed an interest in travel. In 1999, it created Rewe Touristik, its travel subsidiary, by purchasing German tour operator DER for approximately US$400 million. The group acquired a 51 per cent interest in LTU Touristik, the third largest German tour operator, in August 2000 when LTU's primary shareholder, Swissair, was experiencing financial difficulties[29]. Three years ago it had no interest in the travel sector and now Rewe[30] ranks third among German[31] tour operators with an impressive distribution network throughout the country.

Accor

Accor is a European leader and global player in the world of tourism and services. It has three main sectors of operations: hotels (68%), complementary travel activities like travel agencies, casinos, restaurants and rail onboard catering (26%) and corporate services (6%).

Airtours

Airtours, a world leader in all-inclusive packages, has adopted a vertically integrated structure even as it extends its operations geographically[32], making a number of acquisitions in the last few years. In 1997, it purchased an 80 per cent interest in Sun. In 1998, it took over the top Scandinavian tour operator, invested in German tour operator FTI[33] and took over Costa-Paquet in association with Carnival. In June 1998, it purchased Direct Holiday. In September 2000, it purchased a 50 per cent share in Spanish group Hotetur and in early 2000, purchased U.S. tour operator TSI[34].

---

[29] Swissair had acquired it in November 1998.

[30] Rewe enjoys a preferential relationship with Club Méditerranée. The Club strengthened its distribution agreement with the German tour operator and enjoys access to Rewe's airline network through its charter airline subsidiaries, ITS and LTU. Club products are marketed by both Atlas and Dertour, two Rewe subsidiaries.

[31] Rewe used to be the number 2 operator in Germany until it was recently pushed out by C & N following the purchase of Thomas Cook.

[32] Airtours has an extensive distribution network (800 agencies under the Going Places brand).

[33] FTI (Frosch Touristik).

[34] TSI (Travel Services International).

In fiscal year 1999-2000, despite the losses incurred by its German subsidiary, FTI, Airtours enjoyed a steady increase in earnings thanks to the sale of its shares in Italian cruise operator Costa[35]. However, the British group is somewhat weakened by the fact that Carnival, the world leader in cruises, would like to sell its 25.1 per cent share in Airtours.

<u>First Choice Holidays</u>
Founded in 1973, First Choice Holidays is now the third largest British tour operator, behind Thomson and Airtours, and the fifth largest in Europe. In October 1998, the company's directors adopted a vertically integrated structure and announced a new distribution strategy. The group reorganized and defined four new divisions: Tour Operator–United Kingdom and Ireland; Tour Operator–International; Distribution–United Kingdom; and Air Transportation. The group's primary sectors of activity are all-inclusive packages, charter flights, retail sales via travel agencies and yachting and water sports holidays. In France, First Choice already owns Marmara-Etapes Nouvelles and in June 2001 took over Tourinter as part of its acquisition strategy. France, Italy and Spain are currently its target markets.

Courted in succession by Kuoni and Airtours, First Choice is currently a target of various tour operators, including C & N Touristik AG (known as Thomas Cook since May 2001) and Spanish tour operator Barcelo. First Choice has already entered into an alliance with Barcelo that covers various fields, notably lodging. Under this agreement, Barcelo has the option of increasing its share in the British tour operator[36] to 21 per cent by 2001. First Choice has another heavyweight among its shareholders: RCCL[37] (U.S./Norway), the world's number two cruise operator, acquired 20 per cent of First Choice with an option to increase its holdings to 29.9 per cent.

Chart 5
Sales Volume of Top 10 European Tour Operators
(in billions of French francs)

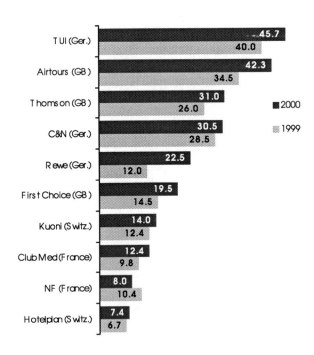

Source: *L'Écho touristique*, June 29, 2001

---

[35] Airtours used to own 50 per cent of Costa and Carnival held the other 50 per cent. Following its purchase of Airtours' shares, Carnival became the sole owner of Costa.

[36] Barcelo gave First Choice its 400 Turavia travel agencies in return for a 15.75 per cent stake in the British group.

[37] RCCL (Royal Carribean Cruises Ltd).

Kuoni

Swiss travel group Kuoni is maintaining its position as one of the largest tour operator groups in Europe. It operates three business sectors: leisure travel, business travel — through a joint venture with Business Travel International (BTI) — and inbound services. Leisure travel activities account for 85 per cent of Kuoni's activities. The company has had to recover from an unsuccessful merger with First Choice Holidays. In July 2001, it sold its 51 per cent interest in Austrian tour operator NUR to Thomas Cook, which already held the other 49 per cent.

The U.S. market

The U.S. distribution network differs from the European network in a number of ways. Unlike Europe, the United States has very few vertically integrated groups. Carlson Companies is one exception, offering a complete array of travel services: restaurants, hotels, cruises and branded travel agencies.

The U.S. network is also characterized by the dominance of the airlines. Given the high volume of domestic air traffic, the airlines are constantly deploying various strategies to maintain or increase their market shares. The major U.S. airlines are represented by giant corporations capable of exerting pressure on the entire distribution network. This is why the American Society of Travel Agents (ASTA) is wary of certain airline initiatives, such as the creation of Orbitz[38], an e-commerce travel site controlled by several airline companies.

Strategies involving the electronic distribution network are of crucial importance in the United States where this market has reached maturity faster than anywhere else in the world. These conditions helped favour strong market entries of exclusively electronic distributors such as Travelocity.com and Expedia. Table 6 illustrates their rapid ascent to the heights of the U.S. distribution market.

The U.S. market is also noteworthy because of the importance of specialized services for small businesses and business travellers. Companies like American Express, Carlson and Rosenbluth devote a considerable portion of their activities to developing this lucrative market, which explains why they are among the top American travel services groups. Industry associations like the American Society of Travel Agents (ASTA) and the American Bus Association also play a key role, acting as powerful lobbies for their members, much like the influence wielded by associations of franchisees.

Table 6
Largest U.S. Distributors of Travel Products

	Agency	Sales — 1999 (in thousands US$)	Rank 1998
1	Amex	13,700	1
2	Carlson Wagonlit Travel	11,000	2
3	WorldTravel	4,300	4
4	Rosenbluth Int.	4,200	3
5	Navigant[39]	3,300	6
6	Maritz Travel	1,740	5
7	Liberty Travel	1,390	7
8	Sato Travel	1,200	8
9	Travelocity.com	1,200	19
10	Expedia	832	25

Source: L'Écho touristique, June 30, 2000

We are now starting to see the first signs of consolidation in the U.S. distribution network. Although existing companies have not yet adopted vertical integration to the extent seen in

---

[38] For more information about Orbitz, see section I.4.4.

[39] This does not reflect the October 2000 acquisition of Toronto-based GTS Global Travel Solutions.

Europe, the situation seems to be changing. In the last year, several major European tour operators have attempted to penetrate the U.S. market. British company Airtours is one such example, strengthening its North American presence with the acquisition of Travel Services International (TSI) in May 2000. This merger will enable Airtours to unite its cruise, air transportation, car rental, travel agency and resort services under a single brand. At the time of the transaction, TSI's estimated sales were approximately US$1.1 billion.

Airtours began its assault on the U.S. market in 1997 by acquiring Suntrip. It then took over Vacation Express in a 1998 deal carried out by its Canadian subsidiary, North American Leisure Group (NALG).

In other developments, in October 2000 Navigant International, the fourth largest U.S. travel solutions company, acquired Toronto-based GTS Global Travel Solutions, which has estimated sales of nearly C$145 million. The deal helped Navigant strengthen its presence in Canada and position itself as one of the top distributors of plane tickets. It sells more than US$3 billion in plane tickets yearly through its 635 travel bureaux in the United States, Canada, the United Kingdom and South America.

Many experts wonder whether deals such as these signal the beginning of a North American wave of consolidation like that seen in Europe. However, no one seems certain as yet.

The Canadian market

Canadian travel agency revenues come primarily from the domestic market (40% in 1997)[40]. Among the provinces, Ontario and Quebec take in 63 per cent[41] of all the revenues generated by Canadian travel agencies.

Transat A.T.: Leading distributor in Canada

Transat A.T. Inc. is a flagship company in Canada's travel industry. Employing a vertical integration strategy, Transat is active in every sector of holiday travel organization and distribution: retail sales via travel agencies, package-tour organization and distribution via tour operators, air transportation and hotel management.

Air Transat, a wholly-owned subsidiary of Transat A.T., has a fleet of 22 planes, the largest of any Canadian charter airline. Serving Canada's major cities, it offers 90 destinations in 27 countries and transported 3.5 million passengers in 2000. Transat's goal is to maintain its leading position in Canada and be a leader in mass market holiday packages in Europe. Transat's activities are split between North America and Europe, with sales representing 60 per cent and 40 per cent, respectively.

Transat is very active in acquisitions and is slowly positioning itself as a global leader. After closing a number of transactions in the French market–Look Voyages (99.2%), Brok'Air, Star Airlines (51.4%), Anyway, Club Voyages-France, Clubs Lookéa and Vacances Air Transat-France–, in November 2000, Transat A.T. announced it had acquired Jonview Corporation, the largest inbound operator in Canada. In early January 2001, Transat A.T. acquired Toronto's Marlin Travel. In March of the same year, Transat A.T. pursued its goal of becoming an increasingly visible presence on the international scene by acquiring Rêvatours, a tour operator specializing in upmarket tours of Asia, Eastern Europe, North Africa, Greece and Turkey. Several days later, Transat increased its share in Toronto's World of Vacations from 35 per cent to 100 per cent. The next to join Transat's ranks was the Greek company Tourgreece, with French subsidiary Look Voyages acting as intermediary. Transat now holds a 40 per cent interest in this Athens-based inbound operator.

At the same time, Consultour–Transat's distribution network–unveiled its strategy for expanding into Ontario. Its long-term goal is to have 400 travel agencies in English-speaking Canada by 2003. Consultour's Canadian expansion is happening in tandem with a campaign of acquisitions in France where the company intends to double its current network and sales figures. Finally, Transat has entered the U.S. market by selling Caribbean holiday packages.

---

[40] Canadian Tourism Commission, *Annual Survey of Travel Agencies and Wholesalers, 1997*, Research Report, 1999-2.

[41] Ibid.

Other players on the Canadian market
British tour operator Airtours is a major player in the Canadian holiday market. In 1995, this group entered the North American market by purchasing three Canadian companies, Sunquest Vacations, Alba Tours and Sunquest West, to create the North American Leisure Group (NALG). In November 2000, Airtours acquired franchiser Algonquin Travel. As for First Choice, another British group active in the Canadian market, its subsidiary tour operator, Signature Vacations, continued the company's vertical integration strategy in Canada by purchasing Sun Holidays, a network of 36 travel agencies, in December 2000. It then struck again, buying 23 American Express travel offices in February 2001.

The mergers and acquisitions wave hits Canada
The Canadian distribution network has not been exempt from the wave of mergers and acquisitions. In the first half of the 1990s, more than 1,000 of the 5,000 agencies existing in 1990 went out of business. Many smaller ones were integrated into larger companies, either through franchising or in the form of consortia. In a research report, the Canadian Tourism Commission noted that in 1997, 63 per cent of all travel agencies were somehow affiliated with a chain and 43 per cent held a franchise[42]. Travel agencies are vulnerable to large integrated groups because of their small size. In 1996, more than half of all travel agencies recorded sales under C$2 million. Independent agencies face the prospect of a forced merger or else major pressure from the competition.

Table 7
Changes in Canadian Travel Agency Groups

Group	Points of sale		
	1996	1998	2000
Gem Travel[43]	754	841	---
Giants Travel	790	756	800
Thomas Cook	280	300	120
Uniglobe	226	230	152
TravelPlus[44]	210	210	---
Travel T-COMM	205	205	201
Consultour	200	200	200
Carlson Wagonlit	148	200	295
CAA	135	141	129
INTRA[45]	121	135	---

The largest Canadian group, Gem Travel, is now part of U.S. giant Vacation.com, which owns a total of 8,500 travel agencies. Vacation.com also includes GEM Cruiselink, SPACE, AURA, Crown Travel Group, TIME, The Consortium and Consolidated Travel Services.

The Asia-Pacific market
The distribution network is extremely fragmented in the Asia-Pacific region, which has approximately 20,000 travel agencies. Of these, some 9,000 are members of the IATA. The recent surge in tourists from China, which opened its first travel agency in 1995, is largely responsible for the explosion in the number of independent agencies in this part of the world.

[42] Canadian Tourism Commission, *Annual Survey of Travel Agencies and Wholesalers, 1997*, Research Report, 1999-2.
[43] In August 1998, GEM Canada became part of Travel Associates Network (TAN), a Washington-based firm that, in turn, merged with Vacation.com, a Boston-based U.S. group, in June 1999.
[44] Part of Carlson Wagonlit since January 1999.
[45] Part of Carlson Wagonlit since January 1999.

Table 8

Changes in the Number of Travel Agencies in the Primary Tourist-generating Countries in the Asia-Pacific Region

Country	Points of sale		
	1995	1997	1999
Australia	1,628	2,322	2,247
China	11	110	2,136
Hong-Kong	294	253	242
India	967	1,367	711
Indonesia	230	322	332
Japan	734	812	792
Malaysia	516	727	679
New Zealand	648	795	649
Philippines	202	213	217
Singapore	180	201	200
South Korea	437	500	397
Taiwan	210	279	261
Thailand	275	364	391
Total	6,332	8,265	9,254

Sources: International Air Transport Association (IATA) and Travel Business Analyst (TBA)

It would seem that the Asia-Pacific region is not yet ripe for consolidation, although the number of new travel agencies has stagnated in most countries in the area, with the exception of China. Table 8 illustrates the changes in the number of travel agencies in the primary tourist-generating countries of the Asia-Pacific region from 1995 to 1999. While China is the primary source of the overall increase in agencies in the area, Japan has the most concentrated market: the top three tour operators share over 60 per cent of the market held by the eight largest tour operators in the country.

I.3.3 ELECTRONIC TOURISM: A NEW DISTRIBUTION CHANNEL

The entire travel industry is experiencing an unprecedented period of change. The development of information technologies and telecommunications plus the boom in e-commerce have had a major impact on travel marketing by offering new channels for distributing products. Over 84 million Internet users around the world visited travel sites in June 2001.

Tourism is, moreover, the dominant industry in retail e-commerce, far ahead of books, music and computers. Many experts believe that 33 per cent of all on-line transactions are related to travel and that on-line travel sales will be worth more than US$50 billion by 2004, with just over US$20 billion of this amount generated by business travel[46].

However, the first challenge facing on-line travel agencies is convincing Web users that the tools for shopping on the Internet are effective since more and more consumers are using the Internet to research travel information. The Travel Industry Association (TIA) reports that 59 million U.S. travellers consulted the Internet in the year 2000 to plan their trips. The trick now is for agencies to convince these lookers to purchase products on line. For U.S. leaders Travelocity and Expedia and new arrival Orbitz, the conversion rate of lookers into bookers for

---

[46] Forrester Research (2001).

the month of June 2001 was 3.2 per cent, 1.5 per cent and 1.3 per cent, respectively. According to Forrester Research, only 20 per cent of lookers actually buy on line, for the reasons listed below.

Reasons why consumers do not purchase travel products on line:

- They prefer the services of a travel agent.
- The information found is incomplete.
- They do not trust virtual agencies.
- Someone else organizes their travel plans.
- They do not know any good travel sites.
- They do not know how.
- They are neophytes on the Internet.

Source: Forrester Research, 2000

The various tourism sectors that have embraced the Internet revolution have developed numerous alliances with IT companies such as IBM, Logibro and ITA Software. These companies have, in turn, created customized services to meet the needs of the tourism sector.

The North American market

Electronic tourism will experience tremendous growth in the next few years in North America. According to Gomez, 30 million Americans purchased a travel product on the Web in 2000 and this number should reach 48 million in 2001. On-line travel sales totalled US$6.9 billion in 1999 and should rise to just over US$40 billion in 2003. However, despite an annual growth rate of 42 per cent, the on-line travel market will still represent only 17 per cent of total travel industry sales. Leisure travel, which currently accounts for 82 per cent of all on-line sales, will account for 84 per cent in 2003[47].

Chart 6
Market Shares of U.S. Travel Sites

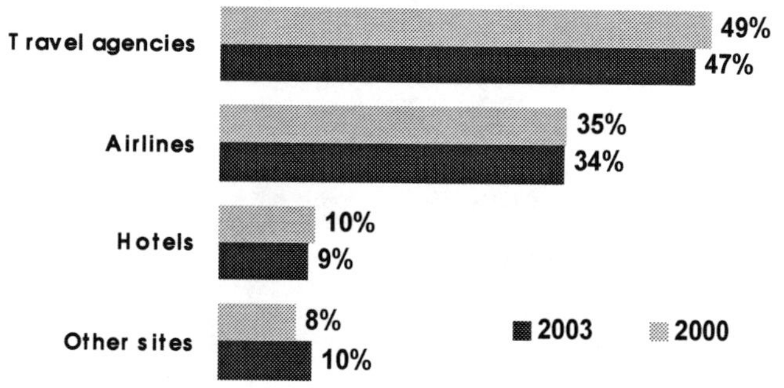

Source: PhoCusWright (2001)

Many firms are now building their strategies around the Internet. The large majority of on-line players offer consumers complete information on air transportation, accommodations and car rental. In 2000, plane tickets accounted for 62 per cent of the products sold on line. However, the range of products offered has widened to include cruises, tour packages, bed and breakfasts, adventure tourism, and so on. In the future, more complicated products will fight for consumer dollars. For example, packages and cruises, which only represented 2.8 per cent of sales in 2000, will account for 6 per cent in 2003. These products are attractive to sell because of their high profit margin (see Chart 6).

---

[47] Forrester Research (2001).

In 2000, a little less than half (49%) of Internet travel sales were made on travel agency sites, 34 per cent on airline sites, 10 per cent on hotel sites and 7 per cent on other sites.

In Canada, the on-line travel business is growing slowly, but it is nothing compared to the U.S. industry. According to Forrester Research, Canadians spent $790 million in 2000. Sales should reach $1.1 billion in 2001 and $2 billion by 2004. Moreover, 59 per cent of Canadians with Internet access looked up travel information and one in five made on-line reservations[48].

The European market

The on-line European travel market is expanding rapidly. Like North Americans, Europeans are turning to the Internet in increasing numbers to seek travel information and purchase travel-related products. Last year, Europeans spent US$2.9 billion in the on-line travel sector. According to U.S. company PhoCusWright, sales in 2002 will more than triple to just under US$11 billion. The United Kingdom, France and Germany are the three largest markets, accounting for more than 66 per cent of all on-line travel sales. On-line reservations, which represented US$869 million in 2000, should reach $5.3 billion by 2005 in the United Kingdom[49].

> **The Internet of growing importance to the French travel industry**
>
> After a slow beginning, the Internet is carving out a place for itself in the French tourism sector. According to Benchmark Group, travel was the most popular sector for on-line shopping in 2000.

A significant characteristic of the European market is that airlines are most popular with 28 per cent of all on-line travel sales, followed by tour operators with 27 per cent, on-line travel agencies with 26 per cent and railway companies with 9 per cent.

Developing regions

Latin America is one of the least developed markets in terms of retail e-commerce. In 2001, on-line travel recorded sales of US$200 million. According to Jupiter Research, Brazil will be the dominant market in the region with 50 per cent of all on-line travel sales in the next five years.

For Despegar.com, the region has amazing potential. For this reason, the agency has signed an alliance with Yahoo! to become the exclusive supplier of the U.S. portal's Latin American version. Despegar.com currently serves Brazil, Argentina, Chile, Colombia, Mexico, Uruguay, Venezuela, Spain and the United States.

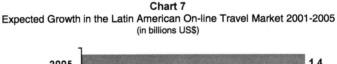

Chart 7
Expected Growth in the Latin American On-line Travel Market 2001-2005
(in billions US$)

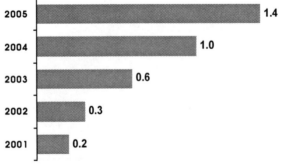

Source: Jupiter Research (2000)

---

[48] IPSOS-REID (2001).
[49] Forrester Research (2001).

The Asia-Pacific region, particularly Japan and Australia, is also attracting attention. According to a study published by Taylor Nelson Sofres Interactive, 4 per cent of all the goods and services purchased on-line in Australia are related to leisure travel, and this percentage jumps to 10 per cent in Japan.

Mobile telephony is of primary importance in this part of the world. After the United States, China and Japan are ranked second and third, respectively, for the greatest number of subscribers. By the end of 2000, 85.3 million Chinese and 66.8 million Japanese owned mobile phones[50].

I.3.4 GLOBAL DISTRIBUTION SYSTEMS: THE PIONEERS OF ELECTRONIC DISTRIBUTION

Global distribution systems (GDS) still dominate the distribution of travel products. After a number of mergers and acquisitions, four major systems emerged: Sabre (United States), Amadeus (Europe), Galileo (Europe) and WorldSpan (United States). These systems operate in a business environment that has changed enormously over the last few years. The advent of new distribution channels has forced the GDS to broaden their range of services and diversify their sources of revenue.

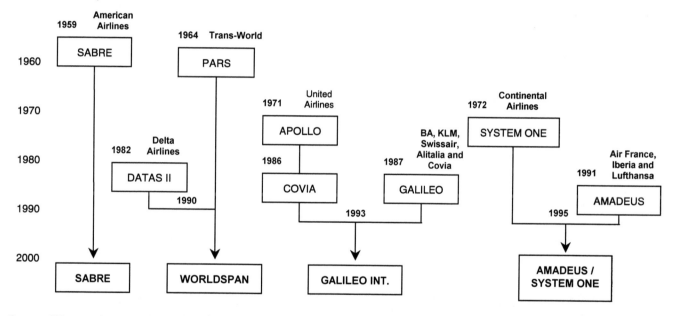

Source: O'Connor, Peter. *Electronic Information Distribution in Tourism and Hospitality*, CABI Publishing, 1999

In October 1996, the Sabre Holdings Corporation was the first GDS to venture into the on-line travel business by launching Travelocity.com, a virtual travel agency. Today, Sabre holds a 70 per cent interest in what has become the largest on-line travel agency. Sabre is also a leader in business travel e-commerce since it acquired GetThere.com in August 2000 for US$757 million. This deal helped Sabre better diversify its revenues since more than 50 per cent of GetThere.com's sales stem from hosting numerous airline Web sites. In August 2000, Sabre also acquired Gradient Solutions Inc., which provides the same type of service, among others. Today, Sabre hosts a total of nearly 700 Web sites.

Amadeus Global Travel Distribution — which had, like Galileo International, publicly promised to avoid direct competition with the travel agencies that are its clients — launched Amadeus.net in 1997. This on-line reservations provider is used primarily in Europe.

---

[50] International Telecommunication Union (ITU) (2001).

In July 2001, **Amadeus** acquired e-travel, an Oracle subsidiary specialized in business travel and reservation management. With the purchase of Vacation.com and Onetravel in November 2000, Amadeus is pursuing its attempt to penetrate the U.S. market to compete directly with Sabre, Galileo and Worldspan.

With Iberia (18.28%), Lufthansa (18.28%) and Air France (23.26%) as its majority shareholders, the European firm is planning to spend over US$220 million on acquisitions between now and the end of the year.

The third player, Galileo International, was more hesitant to enter the Internet. Its strategy was to focus on its chief activity and invest in researching and developing the best on-line reservations tools used by on-line travel agencies. In light of Sabre's success, Galileo Int. was recently forced to modify its business strategy. In February 2000, the firm purchased TRIP.com, one of the top on-line business travel agencies, for US$269 million.

Finally, WorldSpan, the fourth GDS, is basically a supporting player for travel agencies with Expedia and Travelprice.com among its major clients. The commercialworld.com Web site is used primarily by travel agents.

In June 2001, U.S. group **Cendant**, a world leader in hotel franchises and time-shares (RCI) and owner of the Avis car rental corporation, acquired the electronic reservations system Galileo for US$2.9 billion. In mid-August of the same year, it purchased Cheap Tickets, the fifth largest virtual agency, for US$425 million.

Part 4 of this document contains a table describing each of the major global distribution systems.

I.3.5 ALLIANCES, MERGERS AND ACQUISITIONS IN THE DISTRIBUTION NETWORK

Although the distribution network was the last tourism sector to move towards alliances, mergers and acquisitions, it is now undeniably a very concentrated sector where the primary players hold major market shares. Many corporate entities have changed and managerial structures themselves have evolved, creating a trend towards brand-name products.

Vertical integration: Necessary for profitability
Despite sales growth, travel wholesalers are having a hard time increasing their profit margin, which tends to hover somewhere under 5 per cent and, in certain cases, under 1 per cent. Tour operators seeking to ensure profits are using vertical integration to better control the

Chart 8
Average Profit Margin of 1 per cent for Top 5 Specialists - France

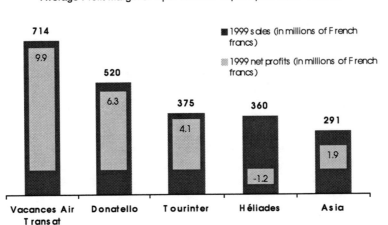

Source: *L'Écho touristique*, June 1, 2001

various links in the chain of distribution. An operator can more easily produce and distribute its vacation packages when it exercises some control over a fleet of planes (like Airtours, the largest British tour operator), a network of agencies, cruise lines or an impressive number of hotels. World leaders like German tour operators Preussag and Condor & Neckermann Touristik control elements throughout the entire chain of distribution and are constantly increasing their market share. Independent operators still offering vacation packages with no specific niche are finding the major players provide stiff competition. It is nearly impossible to compete in price while there is no comparison at all in marketing efforts. Even though consumers remain attached to and appreciate the services of independent travel agencies, they do look primarily for the low prices offered by major operators.

The domination of Germany and the United Kingdom

Efforts to expand and take over the entire chain of distribution really took off in Europe where almost all the major markets are now controlled by a handful of tour operators. The five largest European groups account for more than 67 per cent of total tour operator sales, estimated at US$30 billion. The industry is largely dominated by colossal German and British companies. In Germany, five wholesalers control 76 per cent of the market, while in Britain, the four largest companies generate nearly 80 per cent of travel package sales[51]. By using charter flights, these tour operators rack up significant profits because they are not subject to the pricing policies of regular carriers.

The race to consolidate continues

The push towards acquisitions should continue as the British market has achieved maturity and consolidation has reached a peak in Germany. The major tour operators, in particular the British and German conglomerates, are absorbing major losses in the pursuit of an intensive market penetration strategy to solidify their future hold on Europe. Integration is also taking place in other European countries such as France where the industry is less structured.

France has no large conglomerates and the companies there make few foreign acquisitions. French tour operators are not truly powerful and are more likely to be bought out by other companies. Family-run firms are often targeted first by large integrated foreign groups looking to expand.

Club Méditerranée–whose largest shareholder is the Italian family, Agnelli–purchased JetTours in June 2000. Club Med is a desirable target and, despite the presence of heavyweight investors (21% for the Agnelli family, 6.4% for the Caisse des Dépôts et Consignations, etc.), the group is still vulnerable to a take-over bid due to its watered capital[52]. As for Nouvelles Frontières, as we saw earlier, Preussag will own a 34 per cent share by 2002 and holds an option to significantly increase this percentage. This means that, in the end, Nouvelles Frontières will be under foreign control. Fram, the third largest French tour operator, is still independent but coveted by Airtours. Accor purchased 40 per cent of Go-voyages, took over Frantour–the SNCF tour operator–and is itself vulnerable to a take-over bid. Look was purchased by Canadian firm Transat; Marmara was bought by First Choice; and Paquet was acquired by Italian company, Costa, which was, in turn, bought out by Carnival. Finally, British firm LastMinute acquired Dégriftour. Havas Tourisme was handed over to American Express, which held onto the business travel division, while the leisure travel division went to German conglomerate C & N Touristik. As for Carlson Wagonlit, it is owned, 50-50, by Accor and Carlson.

For the time being, the United States and Japan are seeing fewer acquisitions because vacation packages are less popular among consumers there than they are in Europe. However, these countries are likely to be targeted by the expansionist designs of a few major players, notably the German companies Preussag — the leading European service provider — and C & N Touristik.

Chart 9 illustrates the market shares of the top five tour operators in the primary European tourist-generating countries.

---

[51] *L'Echo Touristique*, March 3, 2000, No. 2494.
[52] *Le Figaro Économie*, March 31 and April 1, 2001, p. 43. *Le Figaro Entreprises*, May 14, 2001, p. 89.

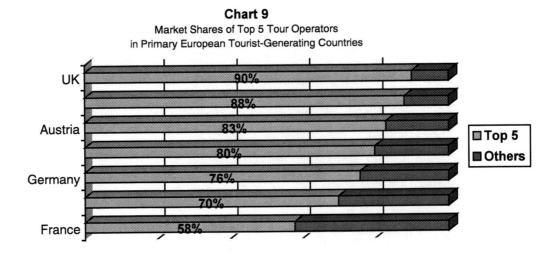

Chart 9
Market Shares of Top 5 Tour Operators
in Primary European Tourist-Generating Countries

Source: *L'Écho touristique*, No. 2494, March 3, 2000

Club Med, First Choice and Kuoni are not expected to remain independent much longer because all are very desirable targets. An eventual alliance between Accor and a major European tour operator also appears increasingly likely. It is in a company's best interest to find the best partner among those still available before it runs out of options.

In fact, acquiring companies are often willing to pay an inflated share price rather than see a company go to a competitor. This is exactly what happened when Preussag purchased Thomson Travel. Since Preussag wanted at all cost to prevent Thomson from becoming part of Karstadt Quelle (Condor & Neckermann Touristik A.G.), the price negotiated was equal to twice the earnings per share traditionally found in the travel sector[53].

It is difficult to accurately predict who will come out on top in this frantic rush to consolidate. For the time being, consumers should enjoy some benefits due to an emerging price war that could well persist. One thing is certain: the main winners at the moment are the shareholders of the companies purchased who are seeing their stock values skyrocket.

---

[53] *Economist Newspaper Ltd.*, May 20, 2000.

I.4 THE ON-LINE TRAVEL SECTOR

I.4.1 OVERVIEW OF THE TOP PLAYERS IN ON-LINE DISTRIBUTION

The North American market

In the United States, many travel agencies have taken advantage of the development of new technologies to modify their distribution channels while new companies have sprung up. Chart 10 illustrates the top agencies in the on-line travel industry.

Chart 10
Major On-line Travel Agencies - 2000

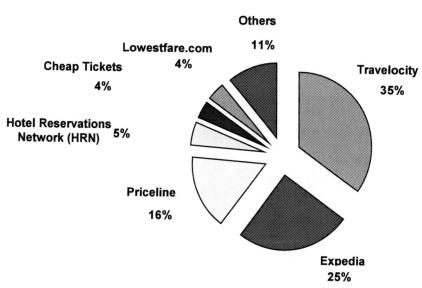

Source: PhoCusWright (2001)

In less than three years, Travelocity.com and Expedia have become major companies. In 2000, they were among the ten largest U.S. distributors of travel products, ranked by revenue. The jump in on-line travel sales and the numerous acquisitions within the industry explain this rapid ascent.

At a glance	At a glance
NAME Travelocity	**NAME** Expedia
YEAR FOUNDED 1996	**YEAR FOUNDED** 1996
HEADQUARTERS Fort Worth, TX, United States	**HEADQUARTERS** Bellevue, WA, United States
OWNER Sabre Holdings Corporation	**OWNER** USA Networks
REVENUES - 2000 US$192.7 million	**REVENUES - 2000** US$222 million
RESERVATIONS - 2000 US$2.5 billion	**RESERVATIONS - 2000** US$1.8 billion

The European market

Launched in September 1999, eBookers, now the largest European on-line agency, recorded sales of US$150 million in fiscal 2000. Its chief British competitor, Lastminute.com, conducted transactions worth nearly US$116 million in fiscal 2000.

The year 1999 was notable for the arrival of Travelprice.com. This agency quickly established itself and has already recorded sales of US$51 million for the year 2000.

At a glance	At a glance
NAME eBookers.com	**NAME** Lastminute.com
YEAR FOUNDED 1999	**YEAR FOUNDED** 1998
HEADQUARTERS London, England	**HEADQUARTERS** London, England
OWNER Dinesh Dahamija	**RESERVATIONS - 2000*** US$116 million
RESERVATIONS - 2000 US$152.6 million	* Fiscal year 2000 ended on September 30, 2000.

I.4.2 NEW METHODS OF ELECTRONIC DISTRIBUTION

"Click-and-mortar" agencies

As we saw earlier, consumers still hesitate to purchase travel products on-line because they prefer the services of a travel agent. For this reason, on-line travel agencies feel obligated to add a "human" touch to their services. The creation of "click-and-mortar" agencies (on-line players supported by a network of traditional travel agencies) are a response to this concern. While numerous traditional travel agencies hasten to establish themselves on the Internet, some virtual agencies are trying to develop off-line sales and support infrastructures. Hotel Reservations Network, Cheap Tickets and Lowestfare.com offer customers the option of reserving plane tickets or hotel rooms through a call centre.

Often criticized for their absence from the Web, traditional agencies are now developing the infrastructures needed to offer customers the option of on-line transactions. The strategies differ. Many are setting up their own sites, like the Carlson Wagonlit group (carlson-travel.com, August 1999) and American Express, who announced in the summer of 1999 that it would be investing US$250 million in its Web site. In early 2000, French travel groups Nouvelles Frontières and Club Méditerranée launched their Internet subsidiaries, NF Online and Club Med Online.

Other agencies have decided to acquire or establish partnerships with firms already established on the Web. For example, in August 1999 Rosenbluth International purchased Biztravel.com and created Rosenbluth Interactive. French group Accor purchased a 2.5 per cent interest in U.S. agency WorldRes.com for US$23 million and Cendant acquired Cheap Tickets for US$425 million.

Partnerships are Proving to Be Viable Solutions

There is more co-operation between the old and the new economy. Large chains and traditional brands are increasing their Internet presence. According to the most recent figures, 11 of the 15 most popular on-line retail sites during the 2000 holiday season were **"click-and-mortar"** companies, in other words, companies using both on-line and off-line distribution. On March 5, 2001, the Sunday Times announced that Wal-Mart and on-line bookstore Amazon.com would be signing a strategic alliance within six months.

Name-your-price systems: New business models

E-commerce today is powered by new business models that go beyond the traditional consumer-vendor relationship. The latest technologies enable customers to play a more active role in finding information and making decisions. Some examples of these new ways of doing business are auctions, name-your-price systems and group purchasing.

On April 6, 1998, Jay Walker presented consumers with a new way of purchasing products and services on the Internet: the "name your price" on-line system. It is a sort of reverse auction, in that the potential consumer tells the supplier what he is looking for, for example, the desired destination, travel dates and price he is willing to pay. In return, the agent, or in this case the Web site, transmits the offer to the supplier who can either accept or reject it. The system was an instant success with 1.5 million unique visitors in its first month of operation. Following the lead of Priceline.com, other distribution companies developed similar business models, negotiating contracts with suppliers to offer consumers an attractive array of discount products and services. The mechanism between supplier and consumer can take various forms, but in the case of Priceline.com, inventory is purchased only when the consumer closes the deal. Lowestfare.com, Cheap Tickets and Travelscape.com are among the companies who have used the Priceline.com model to sell their on-line travel products.

I.4.3 VIRTUAL CONSOLIDATION

New methods of on-line communication have reduced the access barriers to the travel market, leading to a flood of new players. Hundreds of Internet sites have sprung up in the last few years, looking for a share of this expanding market. According to Bear Stearns investment bank[54], there are approximately 1,000 virtual travel agencies. These start-ups are founded on new ideas and supported by investor confidence in the new economy. They have significant financial resources at their disposal, enabling them to serve both national and international markets.

The value of Internet company mergers and acquisitions for 2000 totalled US$87 billion, an increase of 84 per cent over 1999. Upwards of 900 transactions were recorded, with 83 per cent of them taking place in the United States. According to Webmergers.com, this strategy is showing signs of slowing down: as of June 30, 2001, the value of transactions was US$29 billion, or barely one-third of the value for the year 2000. However, there has been an increase in the number of transactions; 726 agreements were signed in the first six months of 2001.

Table 9 Value of Initial Public Offerings (IPO) (in US$)		
March 1999	Cheap Tickets	48 M
March 1999	Priceline.com	160 M
September 1999	GetThere.com	75 M
September 1999	Expedia.com	75 M
November 1999	eBookers.com	61 M
March 2000	Lastminute.com	169.5 M

On the other hand, the consolidation trend that has been occurring specifically in the on-line travel sector over the past few years is showing no signs of slowing down. Two recent transactions involving Cendant Corp. and USA Networks were worth US$ 4.4 billion, or more than double the total recorded in the year 2000. The number of transactions this year should rise as the highly competitive market squeezes out smaller companies and financing opportunities become increasingly rare. The following table lists the most recent major transactions recorded.

---

[54] BEAR STEARNS, *Point, Click, Trip: An Introduction to the Online Travel Industry*, 2000.

Table 10
Most Recent Major Transactions in On-line Travel

	Buyer	Acquisition	Amount (US$)
August 2001	Cendant Corporation	Cheap Tickets	425 M
July 2001	USA Networks	Expedia	1,500 M
July 2001	Amadeus	e-travel	n/a
June 2001	Cendant Corporation	Galileo International	2,900 M
Jan. 2001	Hotel Reservations Network (HRN)	TravelNow.com	47.4 M
Nov. 2000	Amadeus / Terra Lycos	OneTravel.com	n/a
Oct. 2000	Amadeus	Vacation.com	90 M
August 2000	Lastminute.com	Dégriftour	88.4 M

Source: PhoCusWright (2001)

The outcome of all these mergers and acquisitions is becoming clear: according to PhoCusWright, the top five industry leaders control more than 57 per cent of the on-line travel market in the United States.

In July 2001, New York-based USA Networks purchased Expedia, the second largest U.S. on-line agency, for US$1.5 billion and the National Leisure Group, a virtual agency specialized in holiday packages and cruises. This move illustrated how the travel industry is converging with the technology of interactive television.

USA Networks owns five TV networks: USA Network, SCI FI Channel, TRIO, NWI and Studios USA. It plans to take advantage of this technology by launching the USA Travel Channel before the end of the year 2001. Despite the fact that interactive TV is still not available to a mass market, various initiatives indicate that this type of service is moving beyond the stage of trials and prototypes. The simplest way to make a television interactive is to use the Internet and add some television content, thus creating what will likely be a new way to combine TV with shopping.

Despite the global economic slowdown, the year 2001 is supposed to symbolize the emergence of on-line business travel specialists. A study done by the National Business Travel Association in late April 2001 showed that 59 per cent of the businesses surveyed are now looking for better value and will not hesitate to seek out new hotels or airlines offering lower prices. A stagnant economy should attract even more bargain-hunters to the Internet. U.S. companies spend nearly US$185 billion on business travel.

The largest travel sites attract a significant proportion of this kind of clientele: last year, American business travellers accounted for 25 per cent of Expedia's sales and 30 per cent of Travelocity.com's. Launched in November 2000 and marketed in January 2001, Egencia is a European on-line travel agency devoted exclusively to business travel. The people behind Egencia estimate that this market will be worth more than US$1.5 billion in 2001, with France alone accounting for 20 to 25 per cent of the entire European market.

Table 11
Ranking of U.S. Business Travellers' Favourite Web Sites (%)*

1.	Travelocity.com	35.3
2.	Southwest Airlines	27.6
3.	Priceline.com	25.3
4.	Expedia.com	21.3
5.	Delta Airlines	21.2
6.	American Airlines	19.3
7.	Holiday Inn	16.7
8.	United Airlines	16.6
9.	Marriott	16.3
10.	Budget	14.6

* Respondents could name more than one site

Source: Gomez, 2001

American domination

Despite the boom in the number of on-line players, activity is still concentrated in a dozen major American agencies who together account for 89 per cent of the US$7.1 billion in revenues. In 2000, three of these companies, Travelocity.com, Expedia and Priceline.com, earned more than two-thirds of all on-line revenues.

Consolidation of Virtual Agencies on European Market

In August and September 1999, British agency eBookers.com acquired La Compagnie des Voyages, the first French on-line agency, and German agency Teletravel Flugreisen GmbH. Almost four months later, it announced the purchase of three other players: Lloyd Tours, Finland's largest discount agency (revenues of US$9 million), and two German players, Take-Off Reisen and Cosmos. eBookers.com is now present in eleven European countries: Denmark, Finland, France, Germany, Ireland, the Netherlands, Norway, Spain, Sweden, Switzerland and the United Kingdom.

On August 15, 2000, Lastminute.com acquired the top French agency, Dégriftour, for US$88.4 million. This deal made Lastminute.com the third largest e-commerce site in Europe. The transaction was motivated primarily by Dégriftour's expertise at marketing travel in France. The company enjoys a high recognition factor (45%) in the country.

I.4.4 THE AIRLINES AND ON-LINE TRAVEL DISTRIBUTION

The airlines too have recognized the importance of e-commerce, using it to establish direct relationships with their customers and reduce the cost of issuing tickets. It is, in fact, much cheaper to issue a confirmation number and a receipt rather than print up a properly completed paper ticket. According to the carriers, they save $30 for every ticket purchased on-line.

Airlines are taking an increasingly large share of the U.S. on-line travel market. The number of tickets sold through airline Web sites is growing steadily. Although airlines are subject to the same rules as travel agencies, they often offer exclusive rates and special promotions to consumers who visit their sites, thus motivating them to purchase their tickets directly rather than from a travel agent. In the United States, the on-line sale of plane tickets is expected to climb 21 percentage points between 2000 and 2005, growing from US$8.7 billion and 10 per cent of sales in 2000 to US$32.7 billion and 31 per cent in 2005[55].

Discount carrier **Southwest Airlines** dominates the U.S. on-line market with estimated sales of over US$1.4 billion, or 26 per cent of their overall sales. The seventh largest carrier in the U.S., Southwest has succeeded where other carriers have not because the average volume of reservations on airline sites is 3 to 8 per cent of total revenues.

In Europe, British carrier EasyJet records 86 per cent of its airline reservations on-line. Plane ticket sales top US$1.4 million per day.

Not to be left behind in the on-line travel boom and to further reduce the cost of selling and distributing tickets, the top carriers in the world have recently begun launching their own virtual travel agencies. Their goal is very clear: compete head-to-head with the major virtual agencies.

Orbitz stirs up controversy

Several months behind schedule, American, Continental, Delta, Northwest and United Airlines–five airlines that control 75 per cent of domestic air travel in the United States–officially launched Orbitz.com. This new portal sells tickets for 455 airline companies, including 35 "partners," makes hotel reservations and arranges car rentals. A few days after its launch, the site announced that it was selling 10,000 plane tickets per day. After one

---

[55] International Data Corporation (2001).

month of activity, Orbitz.com was ranked the sixth largest travel site with just over four million visitors.

The announcement of this site sparked controversy and generated a lot of press. Given the somewhat monopolistic nature of the alliance behind Orbitz, the entire traditional distribution network is seriously wondering whether Orbitz will violate anti-competition regulations. Its competitors fear that member airlines will be able to offer discount tickets on Orbitz that will not be available to other intermediaries. To prevent this form of collusion, the U.S. Department of Justice, at the request of the American Society of Travel Agents (ASTA), examined the new competitive environment created by the arrival of Orbitz. Despite an apparent competitive edge, Orbitz has not yet won the e-commerce war, where the major on-line travel agencies are waging a tough fight. Travelocity.com, Priceline.com and Expedia already enjoy impressive market shares, which means Orbitz will have to invest heavily in marketing to attract and retain consumers. Orbitz will also face the problem of respecting the individual interests of all the partners who, after all, are still competitors who want to attract customers to their respective flights.

Hotwire: Discount portal
Following the announced creation of Orbitz, Hotwire entered the distribution network in October 2000 as an initiative of U.S. carriers America West, American, Continental, Northwest, United and US Airways. This business portal offers discount flights, accommodations and car rentals. Hotwire was started with an initial investment of some US$75 million from the partner carriers and the Texas Pacific Group. Technology partners include Eland Technologies, Sabre and Scient. Paradoxically, Sabre, which owns a 70 per cent interest in Travelocity.com, a competing on-line travel agency, will be a distributor for Hotwire. Hotwire's structure differs from that of Orbitz: the partner carriers hold no voting shares in the company.

> July 18, 2001, Orbitz and Hotwire signed an agreement to share information about airfares and hotel rates. This will facilitate their customers' access to all airfares and hotel rates.

Opodo takes off
Two months after the launch of Orbitz, nine airline companies launched Opodo. Aiming to become the European leader of the on-line travel market, this portal will start up in December 2001 for the German, British, French and Italian markets. Air France, British Airways and Lufthansa each hold a 22.8 per cent interest in the company, Alitalia, Iberia and KLM each hold a 9.14 per cent share and Aer Lingus, Finnair and Austrian own the rest. The site will use Amadeus technology and offer a wide variety of products: 480 airlines, 55,000 hotels and 23,500 car rental companies.

Reduced commissions
On February 28, 2001, Northwest Airlines and KLM announced that as of March 1, sales commissions to on-line agencies would be eliminated. This decision came at a time when the sales of airline tickets through virtual agencies were taking off. In fact, 42 per cent of all airline tickets sold on line (representing US$3.6 billion) are sold through Internet travel agencies. The decision to cut commissions could have a significant impact on the industry, particularly the small independent travel agencies. In early March, Southwest announced that its tickets could no longer be purchased at Travelocity.com. This move was intended as a response to customer service issues.

The question now is whether other carriers will follow suit. Forrester Research has forecast that all airline companies will have eliminated their commissions to on-line agencies by the end of 2001, leaving them with the choice of either passing on service costs to their customers or seeing their profit margins shrink.

I.4.5 THE HOTEL INDUSTRY IN THE ERA OF ON-LINE RESERVATIONS

Technology has entered all areas of the hotel sector and the transition to electronic tools is well under way. New technologies are important instruments for enhancing a company's performance and efficiency, improving customer service, offering avant-garde products, facilitating operations and, finally, offering new marketing tools and distribution channels.

Concerned with improving its competitiveness, the hotel industry has adopted a technological plan to progressively eliminate traditional reservation methods in favour of electronic solutions. In 2000, Internet hotel reservations accounted for sales of US$2.6 billion, an increase of 136 per cent over 1999.

Although hotel owners recognize the importance of marketing associations, they want to make their own sites attractive to better compete with on-line travel agencies and maintain better relations with their clients. Therefore, some large hotel groups are developing their own reservations systems to represent all their brands; Hilton, Marriott, Choice, Best Western and Bass are leaders in this field. In June 2000, hotel giants Starwood, Accor, Hilton and Forte created an alliance to develop a Web site to serve the Asia-Pacific region. Other partners will join them later. In December 2000, Bass, Hilton, Hyatt, Marriott and Starwood began discussing the possibility of developing a standard distribution system and adopting a common technological platform. The Honest Broker project, as it has been dubbed, would allow the companies to distribute a total of 1.4 million rooms on-line. The hotel companies deny developing a common Web site, but there has already been some speculation in the industry, fuelling rumours about a mega-site. Traditionally linked with global distribution systems like Sabre and Galileo, the five hotel companies are anxious to reduce the fee of $3.50 per reservation charged by these systems and improve the customer's experience.

The Accor Vision

Accor has long been a symbol of pride to the French. A major player in the global hotel industry (3,500 hotels and nearly 400,000 rooms in 88 countries), the distribution network and the restaurant business, Accor is ranked the 38th largest corporation in France. Contrary to other large hotel groups, particularly Cendant and Bass, Accor is the only global player in 2000 to own or manage more than 80 per cent of its total number of rooms: 15 per cent of the rooms are franchised, 19 per cent are under management contracts and 65 per cent are owned or leased.

Although its Sofitel chain is positioned in an upscale market, Accor's strength lies primarily in its economy and mid-class brands like Etap'Hotel, Ibis, Formule 1, Motel 6, Studio 6 and Red Roof Inns. Having sold its shares in car rental company Europcar in November 1999, the company recently began focussing its activities on the hotel business and its network of agencies — Carlson Wagonlit — that it owns 50-50 with Carlson Companies.

Accor management announced in 2001 that it intends to make the company a leading player in the Internet-based hotel industry. This new strategy focusses on offering a complete product and making information on all its hotels available on a single site. To ensure its products are present at all levels of on-line distribution, Accor is deploying a vigorous e-commerce penetration strategy. To support this strategy, Accor purchased a 2.5 per cent interest in WorldRes.com Inc. in June 2000, along with a 19 per cent share in its European subsidiary, WorldRes Europe. Since early 2001, Accor's Web sites have recorded more than 15 million visits, generating sales of over one million rooms throughout the hotel company's network. Accor expects this number to double by the end of 2001.

At the same time, in August 2000, Accor signed a partnership agreement with Bass, GranadaCompass, Hilton International and Whitbread to create a virtual marketplace built on a business-to-business on-line purchasing structure. The strength of this alliance lies in its ability to provide a wide range of services enabling industry buyers and suppliers to achieve significant operating earnings. The site should be launched by the end of 2001.

To offer a more comprehensive product, hotels will hold more and more room inventory on their own sites to make up for the fact that travel agencies often suggest a similar category competitor when the brand requested is unavailable. Although experts predict that it will be more advantageous to use the services of an on-line travel agency because these sites are growing exponentially, hotel owners are still determined to build customized sites to attract and serve their loyal customers. In December 2000, Hyatt announced that its hotel accommodations could be combined with flights or car rentals.

According to Yesawich, Pepperdine & Brown, the existence of the Internet means hotel owners in both the United States and Canada can no longer hope to make the kind of profits they saw in the middle of the previous decade; high prices are also a factor in low hotel occupancy rates. For the new consumer, brand loyalty is being replaced by price loyalty. The Internet is the perfect search tool and the "value" of a vacation is now determined by its convenience. In other words, travellers want a full itinerary before departure, so hotels will have to work harder to position their brands as both convenient and predictable.

PEGASUS SOLUTIONS

Pegagus is the leader in the field of e-commerce and transaction-oriented systems. It provides a wide range of marketing services and distribution channels to both large hotel groups and independent hotels.

Pegasus Solutions is:
- the leading technological partner of the hotel industry
- more than 40 million Internet reservations in 2000
- sales of US$161.5 million in 2000
- a partner to nearly 100,000 travel agencies, processing monthly commissions of over US$40 million
- 40,000 hotels around the world
- thousands of Web sites
- the owner of REZsolutions, the most popular hotel reservation system in the world
- a Web site, TravelWeb.com
- a company with more than 2,000 employees

Accor, Hilton and Forte join forces to conquer the European on-line hotel industry

Announced in October 2000, andbook.com was launched in April 2001. The site represents the 4,000 hotels of the founding groups as well as 50,000 others, accessible through the intermediary of the Amadeus system. Management plans to offer airline reservation and car rental services by the end of 2001, making it a competitor of European virtual travel agencies.

I.4.6 ELECTRONIC PROCUREMENT: A NEW TYPE OF ALLIANCE

Business-to-business (B2B) e-commerce and virtual marketplaces are slowly developing. For businesses, there are many advantages to using these Internet sourcing systems: access to a large supply of products and services, competitive prices, economies of scale and reduced order processing, just to name a few. Forrester Research estimates the B2B market is worth over US$6.3 trillion. The travel industry, particularly the airline and hotel sectors, will benefit from this boom, which has already created a number of alliances and partnerships.

On Air Canada's initiative, 13 of the world's biggest carriers announced the creation of the largest B2B e-commerce site for the airline industry. Launched in the fall of 2000 under the name Aeroxchange, this Web site will offer airlines the world's largest selection of airplane parts, services and general supplies. It is expected to process purchases worth more than US$50 billion a year for various items, especially airframes, aircraft assemblies and engine components, as well as maintenance contracts and a wide range of aeronautical goods and services. In addition to the founding members, airlines who do not belong to the Star Alliance, other firms with industry ties and their suppliers will be invited to use the services of the site, which will be administered independently of the carriers themselves.

I.5 THE HOTEL INDUSTRY

Over the past several decades, market globalization has led to unequalled growth in the lodging industry. In 1998, the World Tourism Organization (WTO) reported the existence of 15.4 million hotel rooms worldwide, compared to less than 8 million in 1980. In 1998, Europe had the most rooms of any other region (38.5% of the total number) followed by the Americas (33.5%).

From 1990 to 1998, South Asia posted the strongest growth rate (54.3%) with the number of rooms rising from 111,146 to 171,462. The East Asia and Pacific region was next with 3.5 million rooms, or a 45.3 per cent increase. From 1997 to 1998, the Middle East led with a 6.9 per cent increase while Africa's number of rooms actually dropped 0.4 per cent. At certain times of the year, demand even outstrips supply in cities like Amsterdam, Barcelona, São Paulo and Seoul.

I.5.1 A GUIDE TO THE VARIOUS TYPES OF HOTEL-RELATED ACTIVITIES

The hotel industry comprises a multitude of varied and complex activities: ownership/leasing, management, franchising and consortium, or a combination thereof. For example, some companies outsource the management of their hotel facilities, while others administer the property themselves. Some manage their own hotel business in addition to managing hotel facilities owned by another party. Some are shareholders (majority or otherwise) in hotels, sell franchise rights and also own consortium-based properties. Still others are involved in only one activity, such as management or franchise development. For example, the Marriott Château Champlain in Montreal is owned by Ocean Properties and Thibault, Messier, Savard and Associates; managed by the Atlific Group, a division of Ocean Properties; and operated under the Marriott franchise, granted by Marriott Hotels of Canada, a division of Marriott International Inc. The advantages and disadvantages of each type of hotel-related activity are outlined in Table 35 in Part 4 of this document.

I.5.2 REITS: ANOTHER WAY OF DOING BUSINESS

Over the course of the last decade, real estate investment trusts, or REITs, have played a key role in the success of large hotel groups, particularly in the United States and Canada. Combined with other means of financing, REITs have fundamentally changed the structure of hotel-related activities by dividing ownership and management. The introduction of this new means of financing has created a new kind of hotel owner.

Hotel owners used to be "hoteliers"; today they are "in real estate." This has created two different kinds of hotel executives: hotel owners who are in business, and businesspeople who work in the hotel industry. This difference gives rise to two unique orientations: the first group develops long-term strategies and focusses on customer satisfaction, while the second group makes decisions based primarily on short-term financial considerations and focusses on investors[56]. Although REITs seemed to be losing their popularity[57] due to a less-than-stellar stock market performance, market volatility has shown them to be relatively stable investments.

---

[56] *Hotel & Motel Management* editorial, as quoted by Horwath Consultants.
[57] Arthur ANDERSEN, *Hospitality 2000: The Capital.*

REIT–Real Estate Investment Trust

In the early 90s, the American hotel industry created a new kind of financing called REITs, or Real Estate Investment Trusts. This name designated a business corporation that had beneficial tax rates with regard to ownership. *The Real Estate Investment Act* was passed in order to allow small investors to invest in a variety of real estate properties, such as office buildings, shopping centres, apartment buildings, spas and hotels. In 1993, the first hotel REITs were formed and soon became prolific financial vehicles for their investors, as well as providing a quick source of income for REIT companies to acquire new properties. The *Tax Relief Extension Act of 1999*, signed in December 1999 and effective as of January 1, 2001, modifies the rules governing REITs in several ways. The most significant provision, however, is the opportunity to create a new type of corporation—a Taxable REIT Subsidiary—which will allow REITs to create new incremental income streams.

Starwood Hotels & Resorts is an American REIT made up of real estate investors; Starwood Hotels & Resorts Worldwide is the management company which the REIT has hired to manage its real estate developments.

Although legislation varies depending on the country, this method of financing has spread to Canada. Royal Host Hotels & Resorts, CHIP Hospitality and Legacy Hotels are the top three Canadian REITs.

While many investors around the world have already discovered that REITs can offer a good rate of return and help diversify one's portfolio, several Asian governments are starting to consider them as a way to raise public capital and ease the crushing debt that followed the Asian financial crisis. However, various attempts to create REITs have ended in failure because of poor investments or a lack of desirable assets on the market.

In May 2000, the Japanese government passed legislation adopting the J-REIT. This closely resembles the Australian model (Australian LPT), which was, in turn, based on the American REIT (U.S. REIT). The J-REIT offers tax transparency but also allows foreign firms to manage the hotels–unlike the U.S. REIT. At the same time, with economic growth boosting real estate prices and demand, the Monetary Authority of Singapore (MAS) drafted guidelines for a REIT without providing for tax breaks, a move that could inhibit the creation of the new market. These developments spurred both Korea and Indonesia into seriously considering REITs. There remain other obstacles before the Asian markets will fully recover but certain lessons can be learned from the U.S. REIT experience[58].

In Europe as well, some real estate companies are entering the market and pension funds are buying hotel properties according to contracts similar to U.S. REITs. In several recent large-scale transactions, banks have also played a major role in financing.

I.5.3 LARGE INTERNATIONAL GROUPS: DOMINATED BY THE U.S.

The size of a hotel group is often determined by the number of rooms. Given that criterion, the large American hotel groups dominate the international picture (see Table 12). As shown, 8 of the 10 largest companies are located in the United States and more than half of the 50 biggest hotel groups are based there. It is also interesting to note that only nine countries are represented on the list of the 50 largest hotel groups: the United States is listed most often, followed by the United Kingdom with seven major companies and then Spain and Japan, tied with four companies each. As for brands, once again, 8 out of the 10 largest chains are U.S.-based and the two others belong to the English.

There were very few transactions in 2000 so the rankings closely resemble those of the year before. European companies Bass, Accor and Sol Meliá continue to compete with the Americans. Between 1998 and 2000, the top ten companies consolidated their positions by boosting their number of rooms by 13.7 per cent and significantly increasing their international exposure.

---

[58] Arthur ADLER, "Real Estate Investment Trusts," *Smart Structures in Hotel Investment*–JONES LANG LASALLE Hotels 2000. [http://www.joneslanglasallehotels.com/].

TABLE 12
The 15 Largest Global Hotel Industry Players,
Ranked by Number of Rooms (2000 vs. 1999 vs. 1998)

Rank (no. of rooms)	GROUP	Rooms	Hotels	Rank (no. of hotels)
2000 1999 1998		2000 1999 1998	2000 1999 1998	2000 1999 1998
1 1 1	Cendant Corp. Parsippany, NJ, United States	541,313 542,630 528,896	6,455 6,315 5,978	1 1 1
2 2 2	Bass Hotels & Resorts London, England	490,531 471,680 461,434	3,096 2,886 2,738	5 5 4
3 3 3	Marriott International Washington, DC, United States	390,469 355,900 328,300	2,099 1,880 1,686	6 6 6
4 4 6	Accor Evry, France	389,437 354,652 291,770	3,488 3,234 2,666	4 4 5
5 5 4	Choice Hotels International Silver Spring, MD, United States	350,351 338,254 305,171	4,392 4,248 3,670	2 2 3
6 7 11	Hilton Hotel Corp. Beverly Hills, CA, United States	317,823 290,000 85,000	1,895 1,700 250	7 7 19
7 6 5	Best Western International[59] Phoenix, AZ, United States	307,737 313,247 301,899	4,065 4,037 3,814	3 3 2
8 8 7	Starwood Hotels & Resorts Worldwide White Plains, NY, United States	227,042 217,651 225,014	738 716 694	9 9 8
9 9 9	Carlson Hospitality Worldwide Minneapolis, MN, United States	129,234 114,161 106,244	716 616 548	10 10 10
10 10 12	Hyatt Hotel / Hyatt International Chicago, IL, United States	86,711 85,743 82,224	201 195 186	28 26 26
11 12 13	Sol Meliá S .A. Palma de Mallorca, Spain	82,656 69,178 65,586	338 260 246	14 20 22
12 14 14	Hilton International Watford, Herts, England	64,647 61,889 54,117	223 217 170	25 22 33
13 11 10	Wyndham International Dallas, TX, United States	62,262 73,215 100,989	242 303 472	21 17 11
14 15 16	Compass Group (Forte)[60] London, England	59,928 58,636 48,407	453 449 249	12 11 20
15 13 17	Société du Louvre Paris, France	53,083 65,970 37,630	868 990 601	8 8 9

Source: *HOTELS' Corporate 300 Ranking*, HOTELS, July 2001 (www.hotelsmag.com)

[59] Best Western is an exception among the largest global players because it is not a franchiser as is commonly assumed, but a non-profit organization that markets the independent members of the brand.
[60] When this ranking was compiled, Compass Group had not yet sold off its Posthouse, Heritage and Le Méridien brands—these transactions took place in 2001.

I.5.4 THE TITLE OF "BIGGEST INDUSTRY PLAYER": A DIFFICULT CHOICE

It is difficult to compare the major players in the hotel industry with the data available, since each one has a distinctive profile. For example, in 2000, Cendant emerged as the frontrunner in three categories: number of rooms, number of hotels and number of franchises. Bass, however, had the highest worldwide penetration rate, and Marriott took the lead in number of hotels managed. Sales figures are hard to compare, since these vary depending on the various types of activities and market segments the company is involved in.

Thus, although large hotel groups are expanding more and more, no company can boast that it has achieved full, horizontal integration. No single group has acquired every class of hotel in every market segment, nor have any of them established a base in every country, or in every sphere of the hospitality industry. Practically speaking, no group aspires to such diversification. Instead, they strive to achieve a certain critical mass, establish a brand in a new market, convert hotels to one of their brands or simply purchase an existing chain. It is rare to simply create a new brand since there are already a lot brands and it is relatively difficult to enter the market.

Table 13
Various Statistics on the Global Hotel Industry (2000)

Most rooms	Cendant Corp.	541,313 rooms
Most hotels	Cendant Corp.	6,455 hotels
Presence in the most countries	Bass Hotels & Resorts	100 countries
Most hotels franchised	Cendant Corp.	6,455 hotels franchised
Most hotels managed	Marriott International	806 hotels managed
Biggest brand	Best Western	307,737 rooms
Largest marketing service provider	UTELL / Pegasus Solutions	1,139,708 rooms

Source: *HOTELS' Giant Survey 2000*

I.5.5 ALLIANCES, MERGERS AND ACQUISITIONS IN THE HOTEL INDUSTRY

Following the lead of the airline industry and distribution network, the hotel industry has also been swept up in a powerful wave of consolidation. By entering into acquisitions, mergers and partnerships of various types, hotel groups are showing unparalleled growth in the number of rooms, annual sales, and worldwide presence on five continents. And even though the number of deals per year is beginning to slow, from 830 in 1998 to only 300 the following year, it would appear that the consolidation of the sector is an ongoing process and not a passing trend.

A brief look at the statistics confirms this market concentration: in the year 2000, the ten largest chains accounted for a total of 3.23 million rooms. Although these groups have a powerful influence on the hotel industry due to their evolving products and strong brand image, particularly in the business travel segment, they only account for a small part of the world supply (18.4% in 1998). Furthermore, only 26 per cent of all hotel rooms are marketed under the brand names of the top 50 global companies. International growth has not prevented the emergence of new companies, some of which have done quite well, nor has it inhibited the development of domestic groups (Dorint and Maritim in Germany, Jolly in Italy, Fujita Kanko in Japan, Southern Sun Hotels in South Africa, Scandic Hotels in Sweden, etc.). Therefore, although the hotel sector is indeed experiencing consolidation, the industry remains fragmented with independent hotels in the majority.

Hotel groups, large and small, get bigger

In 1999, the United Kingdom was the most active European country with 63 per cent of the total number of transactions, followed by France with 10 per cent. In 2000, Spain captured first place with 40 per cent, while the U.K. fell to second place with only 19 per cent[61]. The title of "second-largest Spanish group" was a hotly contested one as activity within the Spanish

---

[61] Insignia Hotel Partners, London.

hotel industry boosted the global rankings of a number of groups: Barcelo jumped from 48th largest to 36th, NH Hoteles rose from 82nd to 39th, Occidental Hotels from 59th to 47th and Princess Hotels from 161st to 127th.

The year 2000 was relatively free of large-scale transactions. The most exciting developments came from Spain where Sol Meliá acquired the TRYP chain and NH Hoteles entered a new market–Benelux–by purchasing Krasnapolsky.

The pace seems to be picking up quite a bit in 2001, with a dozen or so acquisitions worth more than US$8 billion being signed in the first quarter alone. The Asians and British set the pace for consolidation. The most notable transaction was the sale of Forte by the Compass group. Having failed to find a buyer for its entire hotel portfolio, Compass decided to put each brand on the market separately. Heritage was purchased by MacDonald Hotels, Posthouse by Bass Hotels & Resorts and Le Méridien by Nomura. Raffles International from Singapore acquired Swissôtel from SAirGroup and Hilton International walked off with Scandic, a major Scandinavian chain. FelCor Lodging, an American REIT, merged with MeriStar Hospitality, creating the largest U.S. REIT. Finally, Starwood has decided to sell its prestigious CIGA hotels, a transaction that will be probably be worth more than US$1 billion.

Six Continents Hotels

On July 30, 2001, Bass Hotels & Resorts changed its name to Six Continents Hotels. The new appellation clearly identifies the reach of its global hotel activities–100 countries and counting–and enables it to make a clean break with its former activities and focus on its primary sector, the hotel industry.

Table 14
Recent International Mergers and Acquisitions

BUYER	YEAR	TRANSACTION	HOTELS / ROOMS	AMOUNT (US$)
Accor France	1999	Red Roof Inns–United States	322 hotels 37,005 rooms	1.1 billion
Bass H & R (Six Continents Hotels) United Kingdom	1998	Inter-Continental	167 hotels 65,000 rooms	2.9 billion
	2000	Southern Pacific Hotels (SPCH)–Australia	59 hotels	315 million
	2001	Posthouse (Forte)–United Kingdom	79 hotels 12,300 rooms	1.2 billion
Cendant Corp. United States	2000	AmeriHost Inn and AmeriHost Inn & Suites–acquisition of brands franchise rights		n/a
	2001	Fairfield Communities–time-share properties	324,000 contracts	635 million
FelCor Lodging Trust United States	2001	MeriStar Hospitality–United States Merger	113 hotels 30,000 rooms	2.7 billion
Hilton Hotels Corp. United States	1999	Promus Hotel–Doubletree, Embassy Suites, Hampton Inn and others	approx. 1,400 hotels 200,000 rooms	3.7 billion
	2001	Hoteles Camino Real–Mexico	14 hotels	n/a
Hilton Int. United Kingdom	2001	Scandic Hotels–Sweden	152 hotels	881 million
Macdonald Hotels plc United Kingdom	2001	Heritage Hotels (Forte)–United Kingdom	48 hotels 3,110 rooms	approx. 330 million
Marriott Int. United States	1997	Renaissance Hotels & Resorts (Renaissance, New World and Ramada)	220 hotels	approx. 1 billion
NH Hoteles SA Spain	2000	Krasnapolsky–Benelux	64 hotels 10,002 rooms	743.9 million
Nomura Int plc Japan	2001	Principal Hotels–United Kingdom	17 hotels 2,750 rooms	370 million
		Le Méridien (Forte)–United Kingdom	150 hotels 40,000 rooms	2.63 billion
Raffles Int. Singapore	2001	Swissôtel Hotels & Resorts–Switzerland	23 hotels	243 million
Starwood H & R Worldwide United States	1997	Westin Hotels & Resorts	108 hotels 47,800 rooms	1.57 billion
		ITT Corporation (including Sheraton and Caesars World)		10.2 billion
Sol Meliá S.A. Spain	2000	TRYP Hotel–Spain	60 hotels 9,700 rooms	216-243 million

Source: Compilation of the Chair in Tourism, Université du Québec à Montréal (2001)

Unexpected vertical integration

Cendant's acquisition of Galileo, the global distribution system (GDS), sent a shock wave through the industry. The first supplier other than an airline to own a GDS, Cendant purchased Galileo as part of its vertical integration strategy. In August 2000, Cendant announced an agreement to acquire the name and franchise rights of the AmeriHost Inn and AmeriHost Inn and Suites brands. In November 2000, it purchased the remaining shares of car rental company Avis for US$935 million (it already owned an 18% share). In March 2001, Fairfield Communities was taken over by Cendant subsidiary RCI in a transaction worth $635 million. In June 2001, Galileo was purchased for the sum of $2.9 billion and in August 2001, Cendant acquired Cheap Tickets. The last two acquisitions give Cendant access to the airline industry and position it to seize the growing opportunities afforded by the travel industry. However, Cendant will be subject to scrutiny to ensure that its control over the distribution network does not unfairly favour its brands. Having received the approval of U.S. federal authorities, the Galileo purchase must still be approved by authorities and shareholders outside the United States.

Table 15
Overview of Cendant and Galileo

Cendant, New York, U.S.	Galileo, Illinois, U.S.
Primary activities • **Real estate**–Century 21 (on average, one property bought or sold every minute) • **Travel** **Car rental**–Avis (fleet of nearly 700,000 vehicles. One car is rented every two seconds) **Hotel franchises**–Days Inn, etc. (541,313 rooms, 6,455 hotels, 8 brands) **Time-shares**–RCI (2.8 million members, 3,750 affiliated resorts in over 90 countries) • **Misc. services** • Presence in over 100 countries	**Electronic distribution services for the travel industry–client list:** • 43,000 travel agencies • 505 airlines • 37 car rental companies • 47,000 hotels • 368 tour operators • major international cruise companies • Presence in 109 countries

Consolidation through market globalization

Travel & Tourism Analyst recently established an arbitrary yardstick for defining a "global" company: presence in 125 countries, 250,000 rooms and 1,000 hotels. The only groups truly positioned to achieve this status in the coming years are Accor, Bass, Best Western, Carlson, Marriott and Starwood. With the exception of Carlson, Accor and Cendant, the giant groups focus their activities primarily on the hotel sector and their development strategies are essentially geared towards brand acquisitions, franchising and geographic expansion. Each brand targets a specific market segment and the stronger the chain, the greater the benefits.

In terms of global distribution, Cendant is number one in North America. In South America, Bass is number one and Sol Meliá is number two. In Europe and the Middle East, Accor is the leader with Bass as number two. In the Asia-Pacific region, it is the opposite, with Bass as number one and Accor as number two[62].

As a whole, the hotel industry was doing well on all continents when suddenly, within a year, everything changed: the U.S. economy began to stagnant, dragging the global economy and

---

[62] Simon COOPER, *Conference Proceedings–Tourism and the Trend Towards Consolidation*, Montreal, November 2000, p. 14.

travel industry down with it; the Israeli-Palestinian conflict flared up, sharply reducing the number of tourists; British tourism was shaken by the outbreak of foot-and-mouth disease; and finally, the tragic events of September 11, 2001.

The North American market

The North American market took a sharp turn downwards and is heading straight for a recession, especially since the events of September 11, 2001. Historically, when the economy slows down, hotels suffer the consequences. Nevertheless, many experts are confident that the slump will be short-lived and have a limited impact on the hotel industry. In fact, after studying the last 30 years, Stephen Rushmore of HVS Int. observed that economic recessions do not significantly affect occupancy rates; generally speaking, although people may curb their spending and length of stay, they still travel.

While American hotel groups enjoy a clear advantage in terms of market share, they are also very concentrated domestically and have the most brands in the world. Faced with a market that has reached maturity, the vast majority of American chains are seeking to expand beyond the continent. A few years ago, Choice announced its intention to reach 10,000 hotels and one million rooms by the year 2010. To achieve their goals, some large hotel groups are buying small independents to create some pressure on the market and incite other independents to request franchises. In today's difficult economic climate, the chains compete for new members by offering financial incentives: reduced membership fees, first-year royalty exemption, partial refund of capital invested, etc.

Table 16

North America

Largest Hotel Group in Each Country Listed on Corporate 300 Ranking (2000)

Country	Group	Rooms	Hotels	Global Rank
United States	Cendant	541,313	6,455	1
Canada	Canadian Pacific H & R	30,100	71	27
Mexico	Grupo Posadas Management	12,569	63	63

Experts are predicting a decline in hotel development and fewer transactions in the U.S. market. Among the main reasons cited is the fact that buyers and sellers are having trouble finding common ground, especially on prices. Lenders are also showing reluctance to invest in this market. According to HVS International, the consolidation movement is nearly at an end and hotel companies will start splitting up in the next ten years.

European companies trying to penetrate the U.S. market, which is already saturated with brands, are simply purchasing U.S. chains instead of trying to set up their own, which is exactly what the Accor group did when it acquired Red Roof Inns in 1999.

The European market

As a whole, the European hotel industry is stable and exhibits steady growth. The question now is whether the U.S. recession will continue, which could weaken the sector's performance without necessarily curbing the consolidation phenomenon. Forecasts for the year 2002 are still positive. In Europe, the hotel industry is generating record profits and enough cash to enable companies to pay off their debts and easily access capital. This is why PricewaterhouseCoopers, a consultant on 21 transactions in Europe alone, has predicted that, in the short term, major players will be purchasing smaller ones. This scenario is all the more likely since hotel chains hold less of the market than they do in the United States.

As long as the major groups are buying out chains or entering into mergers, independent hotels are hardly affected. However, with the growth of franchising, which offers quick opportunities for expansion with a minimal capital investment, more and more brand hotels are likely to set up shop near a small independent and take away customers. To expand in a given geographic area, some large companies are even adopting the "hub-and-spoke" strategy developed by the airlines: build a luxury brand hotel in a major urban centre and then move out into the surrounding area with secondary brands to compete with independent hotels. Marriott, for example, wants to penetrate the Russian market, so it is targeting Moscow and St. Petersburg as strategic hubs and the cities of Nizhni Novgorod, Samara, Kazan and Yekaterinburg as secondary markets.

Table 17
Europe
Largest Hotel Group in Each Country Listed on Corporate 300 Ranking (2000)

Country	Group	Rooms	Hotels	Global Rank
England	Bass	490,531	3,096	2
France	Accor	389,437	3,488	3
Spain	Sol Meliá	82,656	338	11
Germany	TUI Group	49,801	204	17
Sweden	Scandic Hotels AB	26,459	154	30
Poland	Orbis Company	10,200	56	84
Norway	Rica Hotels	9,700	81	88
Switzerland	Mövenpick H & R	7,415	36	117
Italy	Jolly Hotels	6,874	50	124
Hungary	Danubius Hotel and Spa	6,440	42	134
Ireland	Jurys Doyle Hotel Group	6,389	33	135
Finland	Restel	6,085	39	139
Scotland	Macdonald Hotels	5,731	77	145
Cyprus	Louis Organization	4,976	26	168
Malta	Corinthia Hotels Int.	4,859	24	170
Portugal	Pestana (GP) Hotels	4,395	23	180
Austria	Austria Trend H & R	3,567	26	204
Denmark	Helnan Int. Hotels A/S	2,680	13	253
Turkey	Dedeman A.S.	2,311	13	276

Although the tendency to consolidate and create brands was largely absent from Europe in the last decade–nearly 70 per cent of European hotels are independently-run–, Europe is currently the primary target of hotel groups seeking to expand. Of 83 European chains surveyed[63], only 16 held more than 100 hotels in their portfolio. The largest chain is Ibis (438 hotels) followed by Mercure, Campanile and Formule 1.

France is the country with the most branded hotels while Austria and Italy are those in Western Europe with the fewest. The continent boasts a wide variety of hotels and there is no uniform chain image in each country.

Nine hotel groups make up 71.6 per cent of the entire supply of European chain hotels[64], with Bass and Accor at the head of the list. The consolidation movement in Europe has been particularly active in Spain with Spanish groups making a number of acquisitions. Sol Meliá is easily the largest group in the country, is currently ranked 11th globally, and is now looking to North Asia. East European countries located next to richer countries are showing more development and, along with those in Northern Europe, are attracting hotel companies seeking regional markets. Having already acquired 20 per cent of Polish chain Orbis (56 hotels) in 2000, Accor announced it will purchase the remaining 80 per cent in 2002. Hilton International has bought Swedish chain Scandic, which includes 150 hotels, 133 of them in the north.

The Asia-Pacific market
The Asia-Pacific region seems poised to attract the major global groups because 75 per cent of its hotels are independently owned and operated. Four hotel giants–Bass, Marriott, Accor

[63] Chains with more than 10 hotels and a minimum of 500 rooms.
[64] COACH OMNIUM, "L'Hôtellerie Économie – Chaînes hôtelières intégrées en Europe," *La Revue*, 1999 / 2000, p. 1-4.

and Starwood—manage only 8 to 12 per cent of the total number of rooms. An attractive option for those wishing to develop this market is to create partnerships with major local operators like Asia Pacific, Mandarin Oriental Hotel Group, Shangri-La, etc. However, the region does present certain risks: the high tax rates, fragile banking system, the impact of oil prices on domestic demand and political instability in certain countries.

Despite the lack of investor activity in the Asia-Pacific region in 2000, Australia was a point of departure for several foreign operators because of its strong economy. After two relatively quiet years, there were a number of acquisitions, with Accor and Bass quickly boosting their respective portfolios. In this frenzy, Bass improved its position the fastest, rising from 10th place in 1999 to 2nd place in 2000. However, Accor held onto to the number one position. Economic ties between Australia and Asia are expected to strengthen in the future.

Table 18
Asia-Pacific
Largest Hotel Group in Each Country Listed on Corporate 300 Ranking (2000)

Country	Group	Rooms	Hotels	Global Rank
Japan	Prince Hotels	24,674	71	31
China	Shangri-La H & R	19,202	37	46
India	Taj Hotels, Resorts & Palaces	7,784	62	109
Singapore	Meritus H & R	6,303	14	136
Australia	Rydges Hotel Group	5,960	32	142
Thailand	Dusit Thani Company	5,133	20	162
Malaysia	Hotel Equatorial Group	3,883	9	196
Korea	Hotel Lotte Company	3,419	5	215
Indonesia	Sahid Group of Hotels	2,800	17	244
New Zealand	Stamford H & R	2,472	11	264

Southeast Asia continues its efforts to improve its situation but few markets show much potential, except Phuket, Thailand, and Siem Riep, Cambodia. Indonesia, the Philippines and Malaysia are trying to deal with an oversupply of hotels and the problems in Jakarta. However, the economic climate will likely change and Bass has entered the market anyway.

Experts and hotel owners alike agree that China and India show tremendous potential for growth. Hotel chains, in particular, are attracted by India's economic recovery and improved hotel performance. Since domestic travellers tend to be more price-sensitive, major players like Accor, Carlson, Bass and Hyatt have begun entering the market with mid-range brands, hoping to then bring in their upscale chains. To facilitate its access to this market and overcome cultural, political and economic barriers, Cendant has set up partnerships with local businesses. Such partnerships are proving to be the most effective means of growth in this region.

China is the subject of intense speculation because of its large population, imminent entry into the World Trade Organization and its role as host of the 2008 Olympics. Bass has entered the Chinese market with a bang by purchasing the coveted Regent Hotel in Hong Kong for US$346 million. Accor has already set up nine Sofitel and Novotel hotels there and announced a partnership with Zenith Hotels International, manager of eight hotels in China. Starwood is also on the lookout for potential acquisitions or partnerships in the country. In Beijing, brands enjoy a significant competitive advantage for their ability to attract foreign tourists and free-spending domestic travellers[65]; Marriott is planning to set up shop there as it is one of the country's primary ports of entry.

The major chains will be increasing their presence in Asia in the next few years and new financing vehicles must be created to support these transactions.

---

[65] Christopher KHOO, Research Director, Hospitality and Leisure, Asia Pacific, PricewaterhouseCoopers, Singapore.

The Middle East market

The Middle East is developing new destinations. Prices are still low and countries are working to diversify their tourism products. In 1998, this region recorded the highest growth rate in the number of rooms, compared to the year before: 6.9 per cent for a total of 221,000 rooms. Although the hotel market will support substantial future development, certain locations run the risk of creating an oversupply. Dubai is continuing to consolidate its position as a major Middle East destination by pursuing mega-projects such as hotel construction; 12 hotels and 4,500 rooms will be built in the next three or four years, despite the fact that occupancy rates are falling.

Despite some uncertainty, most of the growth in hotels can be traced to major U.S., European and Asian hotel brands—led by Bass, Accor, Starwood and Marriott—determined to increase their presence in the region. However, the giants are competing with several regional hotel chains like Dubai-based Rotana Hotels.

Table 19
Middle East
Largest Hotel Group in Each Country Listed on Corporate 300 Ranking (2000)

Country	Group	Rooms	Hotels	Global Rank
Syria	Cham Palaces & Hotels	4,200	18	187
Tunisia	Abou Nawas Hotels	4,195	18	188
Israel	Dan Hotels Corp	3,300	12	219
United Arab Emirates	Rotana Hotels	2,551	15	259
Egypt	Orascom Hotel Holdings	2,097	9	287

The African market

With some areas of Africa experiencing political conflict, international firms, although present, are hesitant to engage in an intense market penetration. Hotel statistics show that the number of rooms actually dropped by 1,000 between 1997 and 1998, reaching 428,000. Africa was the only continent to register a decrease that year while the average global growth rate was 3 per cent.

Table 20
Africa
Largest Hotel Group in Each Country Listed on Corporate 300 Ranking (2000)

Country	Group	Rooms	Hotels	Global Rank
South Africa	Southern Sun Hotel Interests	13,483	81	58

North Africa is remarkable for the number of resorts that have been developed there. Since this part of the continent is becoming more stable and improving its image, upscale destinations are emerging and attracting foreign investors. In the east, Kenya is recovering from a crippling recession and the future is looking brighter. Rebuilding its image in the upscale market has helped spur resort development. South Africa continues to increase its market share on the continent, as that of the north declines, and two regional hotel companies—Southern Sun and Protea, who held a total of 26,000 rooms and nearly 200 hotels in 2000—are starting to compete with Bass, Accor and Club Med.

The Latin American market

Latin America is showing encouraging signs such as increased domestic and intra-regional demand due to the Mercosur economic agreement. However, some countries suffer from uneven economic development, poverty remains a problem, many travellers still harbour concerns about personal safety and certain infrastructures are deficient. On the other hand, authorities in countries like Brazil have taken steps to improve their tourism products, such as investing in infrastructure improvements.

From 1995 to 1998, South America registered the highest average annual growth rate, worldwide, in the number of rooms: 11.9 per cent. Globally, the average annual growth rate was only 3 per cent. Its 773,000 rooms make up 5 per cent of the world's total supply. Spanish hotel groups are well established in the Latin American market and although all the international chains have invested in the most strategic areas, none of them have launched a major market offensive. The Posadas group from Mexico is very active in this market and is ranked one of the major hotel chains.

Table 21

Latin America

Largest Hotel Group in Each Country Listed on Corporate 300 Ranking (2000)

Country	Company	Rooms	Hotels	Global Rank
Cuba	Cubanacan SA	10,859	46	77
Jamaica	SuperClubs	3,990	14	194
Brazil	Blue Tree H & R	3,419	17	216
Dominican Republic	Viva Resorts	2,096	6	288

Bigger giants

In the next few years, hotel giants are expected to get even bigger, primarily through a significant rise in franchising. This trend will likely benefit American players, who already dominate in this sector. However, in the United States, the consolidation movement seems to be taking a different route: real estate investment trusts (REITs) and management companies are merging, American hotel groups are merging with international groups, various brand hotels are joining forces, etc.

In Europe, the major players are eager to expand by setting off a new wave of consolidation. Bass, for example, is selling off its breweries so it can double and diversify its hotel activities in the next five years.

There will always be small companies who will emerge and expand by filling specific niches. Their success will then attract the attention of larger companies, making them targets for takeover. The distinct trend towards consolidation will continue and produce increasingly powerful global giants. According to some experts, gigantic companies will eventually be so global that the geographic location of their headquarters will not matter. In other words, there will no longer be major American or European players, but genuine world players.

Associations: A way to compete with the giants?

Marketing associations of independent hotels are designed to give individual members the kind of market visibility enjoyed by chain hotels. The phenomenon began in Europe before spreading to North America. Rather than succumbing to market pressures to franchise, some independent establishments prefer to affiliate themselves with a type of voluntary association such as Relais & Châteaux. These associations are usually based on members having a common strategy and image. Best Western in the United States is the largest such association in the world. In France, as of January 1, 2000, there were 26 voluntary associations, the largest of which, Logis de France, boasted 3,650 hotels. In the coming years, in addition to a brand image that accurately targets specific market segments, voluntary associations will have to offer their members a high recognition factor and access to all the latest technologies[66].

Associations can also take the form of marketing and reservations providers. The largest such company in the world is UTELL in the United Kingdom, a subsidiary of Pegasus in the United States. A brand-new addition to the list of top groups and currently ranked 23rd globally, U.S.-based Design Hotels has successfully established itself by offering clients a hotel experience typical of the city visited. When in Rome...

---

[66] Robert GAGNON, *Conference Proceedings–Tourism and the Trend Towards Consolidation*, Montreal, November 2000, p. 16.

The number of associations has grown over the years and the phenomenon is now subject to the trend towards consolidation. In 2000, Relais & Châteaux (France) and Leading Hotels of the World (United States) joined forces to create the Luxury Alliance. In 2001, Pegasus sold off its three independent hotel chains: NH Hoteles purchased Golden Tulip (337 hotels) for US$2 million and IndeCorp increased its holdings by acquiring Summit and Sterling (see box). In July 2001, five Asian hotel chains–Dusit Hotels & Resorts (Thailand), Landis Hotels & Resorts (Taiwan), Marco Polo Hotel Group (Hong Kong), Meritus Hotels & Resorts (Singapore) and New Otani Hotels (Japan)–came together in a single marketing association called the Asian Hotels Alliance (AHA) to focus on building a quality reputation based on Oriental-style service.

IndeCorp

In September 2000, Preferred Hotels & Resorts Worldwide set up a new holding company called IndeCorp. IndeCorp is an umbrella organization for numerous independent hotel brands to help them compete with the big chains by providing a critical mass, sharing resources, realizing economies of scale and facilitating marketing and access to technology. While Preferred Hotels & Resorts was the 17th largest marketing provider in 1999, IndeCorp rose to 6th place in 2000.

In January 2001, IndeCorp paid Pegasus, the world leader in hotel reservations systems, US$12 million for Summit Hotels & Resorts (167 independent hotels in 45 countries) and Sterling Hotels & Resorts (141 independent hotels in 30 countries). These brands will now join Preferred Hotels & Resorts Worldwide (110 independent hotels), IndeCorp's first subsidiary.

I.5.6 THE KEY TO SUCCESS

In short, it is increasingly difficult for businesses to survive alone. Regardless of the strategy adopted to respond to an increasingly competitive business environment, it is important to develop local partnerships to bring in complementary strengths and thereby offer an attractive product representative of the location. It is indeed possible to promote consolidation on a smaller scale and ultimately succeed in this industry.

Too often, a co-operative agreement is seen as a transitional step to give a business time to restructure and respond to competition and market globalization, rather than as a long-term arrangement. In fact, 60 per cent of the alliances studied[67] did not endure more than four years and fewer than 20 per cent lasted at least ten years. Generally speaking, alliances form and fall apart so quickly because strategic goals are often not clearly defined at the outset.

The first prerequisite for a successful alliance is that it must benefit all members: if this is not true, the alliance is bound to fail. Alliances are usually very successful when members have complementary aims and abilities, such as management expertise or resources, which helps create compensating strategies. Other factors like economies of scale and maintained or even improved customer service–which is not very common thus far–also contribute to successful alliances, mergers and acquisitions.

Resource investment: A step towards stability
Experience has also shown that the stability of an alliance increases with the amount of resources (time, money, personnel) invested: the most stable alliances are those in which members are most involved in all areas of operations, including customer service. In the case of the airline industry, this is especially true when two carriers enjoy anti-trust immunity that enables them to harmonize pricing, schedules and fleets, gate access, service levels, baggage handling and frequent flyer programs. Each carrier's activities complement the other's so fully that passengers feel they are on one continuous flight, which is a powerful marketing tool for attracting prospective customers. Customers sometimes don't even notice

---

[67] T.L. Doorley, "Teaming Up for Success," *Business Quarterly*, No. 57, 1993, p. 99-103.

a difference between flying with one carrier or the other because both offer the exact same service.

Partner confidence

The more that partners are willing to co-ordinate and integrate their resources, the more evident it is that the success of an alliance is directly proportional to the level of trust between the partners. Moreover, since alliances are often formed among various types of businesses from different sectors, they will tend to function more smoothly if the partners share similar cultures, both corporate and general.

Success in proportion to the cost of leaving the alliance

Alliances with equity investment involve substantial financial resources and often require complex interactions at the highest decision-making levels. Partners in such alliances can easily encounter a number of problems when it comes to integrating management systems, corporate cultures, business philosophies, etc. However, the high level of financial involvement is a strong incentive for the partners to make the alliance work. Consequently, this type of alliance is the most successful.

PART 2: THE EFFECTS OF CONSOLIDATION

II.1 IMPACTS OF ALLIANCES IN THE AIRLINE INDUSTRY

Trying to define the impacts associated with the development of alliances in the airline industry is not easy. On one hand, the airlines claim that the alliances are the natural outcome of new economic and technological realities, and that they will help improve services to consumers. On the other hand, consumer associations see them as nothing more than a way for the big airlines to get richer at the consumer's expense. Some people even think that consumers would benefit more if smaller carriers entered the market.

II.1.1 FROM FIERCE STRUGGLE TO NEW MONOPOLIES

The appearance of new companies, combined with the rapid expansion of the large existing carriers, has provoked unprecedented competition in the airline industry. Despite bankruptcies and mergers, the biggest ones are still around and competing ferociously on all markets to expand their range of destinations. This is the case of Star Alliance and oneworld, in particular, who faced off in the fight for Canadian Airlines.

May the Best One Win!

Canadian Airlines, one of the founding members of oneworld with American Airlines and British Airways, had rationalized its operations with major financial support from AMR Corporation, the parent company of American Airlines, when Air Canada, a member of the Star Alliance, wanted to buy it in November 1999. But American Airlines and British Airways made a better offer. United Airlines and Lufthansa, both core members of Star Alliance, then backed Air Canada with substantial financial support, and managed to bring both major Canadian airlines into their group. We all know what happened after that. Star Alliance has been well rewarded in terms of destinations and itineraries offered.

To deal with the new situation, the carriers have developed increasingly powerful alliances that amount to rebuilding the monopolies that predated deregulation. The rebuilding of monopolies limits passengers' freedom of choice and may thus compromise free competition. Although European case law has set 40 per cent of market share as the point at which a company is deemed to be dominant and liable to abuse its power, the big five alliances — Star, oneworld, Qualiflyer, Wings and SkyTeam — already control 60 per cent of world traffic.

The Struggle Continues

Similarly, Star Alliance got a bargain when Lufthansa bought out 20 per cent of British Midland, which ranks second after British Airways among the chief holders of landing and takeoff slots at Heathrow. The purchase had one condition, that British Midland join the Star Alliance. And that is how United Airlines and Lufthansa are now able to offer strong competition to British Airways on transatlantic routes (using United's hubs in the U.S. and Midland's slots at Heathrow), on European routes (using Lufthansa's Frankfurt hub), and on Midland's regional routes in the U.K.

II.1.2 DOMINATION OF HUBS

These alliances also dominate the main airports. Chicago O'Hare, one of the busiest American airports, is 87 per cent controlled by United and American. At London Heathrow, the busiest airport in Europe, British Airways and American control 80 per cent of the peak-hour slots.

The heavy traffic at hubs can cause delays. Waits for connecting flights are increasingly long: in Europe, for example, more than a quarter of flights in the summer of 1999 were delayed by over 30 minutes and the situation was no better in the summer of 2000. Similarly, in the U.S., 30 per cent of flights out of Chicago were more than 15 minutes late. These delays are estimated to cost consumers and airlines US$5 billion[68].

Table 22
Nine U.S. Airports with Most Flight Delays

Airport	%	Average minutes of delay
New York, La Guardia	42	26.4
San Francisco International	35	21.9
Boston, Logan	33	19.6
Chicago, O'Hare	33	20.0
Los Angeles International	30	16.3
Philadelphia International	30	16.9
Newark International	29	18.0
New York, Kennedy	29	16.8
Atlanta, Hartsfield	27	15.4

* percentage of flights arriving at destination airport 15 or more minutes late

Source: Federal Aviation Administration

Also, many accidents serve as a reminder that safety is always a problem and that ensuring safety is more complex in an alliance.

II.1.3 IMPACT ON PARTNERS' REVENUE

Any increase in sales is largely dependent on how integrated the alliance is: the greater the integration, the greater the impact on revenue, because it helps create economies of scale and reduces the operating costs associated with shared resources (e.g., flight crews, fleets, ground crews and technology). A study published in January 2000 by Airline Business and Gemini Consulting estimated that membership in a major alliance could bring a carrier an additional US$100 to 200 million in revenues per year and cut costs 1.9 to 11 per cent, depending on the degree of integration. However, the first few years of an alliance can actually increase a carrier's costs as it must harmonize its reservation system, frequent flyer program, etc. For example, Austrian Airlines had to pay US$42 million when it switched from Qualiflyer to Star Alliance, with 40 per cent of this money used to integrate its technology with that of Star.

---

[68] *Les Affaires* (newspaper), April 15, 2000, p. 51.

Table 23
Increase in Sales Directly Associated with Alliances

Alliance	Year	Impact on revenue (in U.S. dollars)
Northwest / KLM	Per year	+175 million to KLM
Varig / Delta Airlines	Per year	+44 million to Varig
Varig / Japan Airlines	Per year	+21 million to Varig
American Airlines / South African Airways	Per year	+2 million each
Delta Airlines / Virgin Atlantic Airways Delta / Air France	1997 2000	+100 million to Delta +150 million to Air France
Air Canada / Star	2000	+ 600 million
Lufthansa / Star	Per year	+273 million
Austrian Airlines / Star	2000	+25 million
United Airlines / Austrian Airlines	2001	Not specified +14 million +25 million (estimated)
Air France / SkyTeam	2000	100 million

Sources: General Accounting Office (1995) and ICAO (1996), *Air Transport World News*, www.atwonline.com, and FRENCH, Trevor. "British Airways and the new airline economy", *Travel & Tourism Intelligence*, No. 6, 1999, p. 13.

II.1.4 IMPACT ON TRAFFIC AND MARKET SHARE

Alliances provide opportunities to grow through new market development and geographic expansion as well as through increasing shares of existing markets. They increase a carrier's number of destinations and cities and add seamless flights without requiring an investment in new aircraft. Since they can offer consumers a huge system of routes around the world, carriers in an alliance have a definite marketing advantage. The more integrated the operations of alliance members — co-ordinated flights, check-in, baggage, maintenance, frequent flyer plans — the more air traffic increases because passenger service improves. Yet this increase in traffic is at the expense of airlines that are not alliance members, which lose traffic to alliance partners.

II.1.5 IMPACT ON COMPUTER RESERVATIONS SYSTEMS (CRS)

Computer reservations systems (CRSs) are the key component of the airline ticket distribution system, both for the airlines themselves and travel agents,[69] because they allow people to look for satisfactory travel options and book tickets in real time.

Multiple listings of a flight as a result of code sharing between partners in an alliance causes a problem known as "screen stuffing." For example, an Air Canada flight from Thunder Bay to London, England, could be displayed as two intra-company connections, as well as one or more interline connections. These multiple listings of the same flight may push travel options offered by competitors down onto secondary screens. Imposing a requirement that flights may not be displayed more than twice could prevent screen stuffing and increase competitive options. Such a rule has been imposed in a number of European jurisdictions.

By providing greater visibility on CRSs,[70] a code-share alliance gives members a definite advantage. Very aware of this clear marketing advantage, the Star Alliance was the first to announce, in July 1999, the introduction of an alliance display accessible through CRSs.

---

[69] In the last few years, airlines have been substantially reducing their equity in CRSs by reselling to other carriers or publicly trading shares. The list of major shareholders in the main CRSs is given in Part 4 of this document.

[70] A study has found that 90 per cent of bookings made by a travel agent involve direct flights or connecting flights on the same carrier.

Star Alliance: World Premiere on CRSs

The Star Alliance is the first air carrier group to establish CRS alliance display parameters. It now has an alliance display accessible through computer reservations systems, allowing travel agents to consult Star Alliance flight timetables and availability from a single screen showing only direct routes and connections provided by allied carriers on a given itinerary. From a single display screen, travel agents can access a combination of flights offered by Star Alliance and thus offer optimal itineraries. The new display helps allied carriers heighten public awareness of the Star Alliance brand. CRSs still display the different codes of the allied carriers, however.

II.1.6 IMPACT ON PASSENGER SERVICES

The confusion and lack of transparency associated with code sharing can be major inconveniences to some passengers, which can decrease the airlines' customer satisfaction ratings (Chart 11). In fact, passengers are not always informed that they will be changing airlines mid-trip. As we have seen, it becomes even more complicated when some companies in a specific alliance maintain code-share agreements with non-member carriers. Better co-ordination of flight timetables, and thus shorter waits between connecting flights, compensate to some extent for the inconvenience, however.

Chart 11
Degree of Customer Satisfaction with Airlines
1994 - 2000

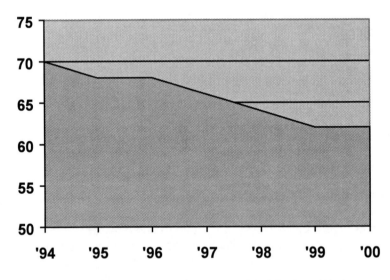

Source: BRADY, Diane. "Why service stinks," *Business Week*,
October 23, 2000, p. 116-126.

Code-share flights are considered connecting flights. With code sharing, an interline connection is displayed as a connecting flight in the CRS, giving it a higher display priority than competing interline flights, even if they have a shorter flight time than the one with shared codes. Seat availability may be distorted as well. A carrier may say that there are no more seats on a given flight, but its partner may still have some left.

The development of extensive customer loyalty programs is one of the most positive aspects for consumers, especially very frequent flyers, who are also those who benefit most from the alliances.

II.1.7 IMPACT ON RATES

Theoretically, alliances can easily influence demand for air transportation services by reducing plane fares, since alliance partners enjoy reduced operating costs. That is what we have seen, especially on routes with greater competition: fares are often lower, if certain conditions are met, such as a Saturday night stay, booking at least three weeks ahead, or flying on certain days or at certain times of day. Furthermore, carriers are also competing to provide discount seats. Once again, alliances increase the possibility that a carrier can offer cut-rate seats.

In reality, even though alliance fares are often lower for routes or markets where there is more competition, the monopoly and position of strength engendered by alliances on certain routes may lead carriers to restrict their capacity, cut flight frequency, or even raise fares. This is particularly true in the case of business flights. On the European market, business class fares rose significantly between 1994 and 1999 (see Table 24). In the States, they went up by 38 per cent between 1996 and 1998.

Consumers may also wind up paying more because of the way the computer reservations systems work. They display direct flights first, in increasing price order. Next come intra-company flights with connections, once again in increasing price order, then non-direct flights operated by various carriers. Code-share flights are listed by the system as intra-company flights, so they come at the top of the list on screen. This means that a code-share itinerary requiring a change in planes, or even airports, may be higher on the list than a cheaper flight with a connection! Similarly, the flights of a new competitor — which might have only a small network of routes or offer only one flight between several localities — will show up on the display as interline connections. This means they are listed lower than a big carrier's intra-company flights, even if the interline connection results in a shorter flying time.

Furthermore, depending on the pair of cities selected, travel agents may consult several screens of flight options, but they rarely do so. A study[71] actually found that travel agents made 80 per cent of reservations from the first screen of options displayed and 50 per cent from the first line of the first screen. Display order is obviously a crucial factor in selling tickets.

Table 24
Change in Airfares from France and Europe, 1994-1999

	France	Europe
1st class	+17%	+35.1%
Business class	**+16%**	**+25.3%**
Economy class (full fare)	+9%	+12.9%
Economy class (reduced fare)	+9%	+13.2%
Excursion fare (high season)	-21%	-6.2%

Source: *L'Écho touristique*, No. 2501, April 21, 2000

II.1.8 IMPACT ON THE DISTRIBUTION NETWORK

Airline initiatives to cut costs and sustain the growth in air traffic have largely contributed to the changes that have occurred in the distribution network. Travel agencies, the chief distribution mechanism for selling plane tickets, have not escaped the efforts of the major carriers to cut production costs. As travel agent commissions are the fourth largest airline expense, after human resources, fuel and the purchase of aircraft, carriers have started reducing commissions and setting up their own Web sites to sell directly to consumers.

---

[71] "Computer Reservation Systems," *The Avmark Aviation Economist*, May 1987, p. 21.

General Drop in Commission Rates

- Air Canada reduced commissions to 5 per cent on the domestic market, while increasing the maximum to $60 for a round-trip ticket.

- Lufthansa, British Airways, Swissair and its Qualiflyer partners are cutting their commissions from 9 per cent to 7 per cent on the French market.

- In October 1999, United Airlines reduced its travel agency commission from 8 per cent to 5 per cent on the Canadian and American markets.

- In August 2001, American Airlines announced a 60 per cent reduction in travel agency commissions.

It remains to be seen if other carriers will follow suit. As a consequence, override commissions will become an even more important source of revenue to travel agencies. Override commissions are a strong incentive to agencies to deal with particular carriers.

Using these new distribution methods, airlines have found an efficient way to substantially lower their operating costs. Since 1995, American carriers have saved $4.3 billion this way, but at whose expense? In 1994, the American Society of Travel Agents numbered 33,000 members; by 2000, membership had dropped to just 26,000. The worst is yet to come: it is expected that about a quarter of these agencies will close their doors within the next few years.

II.1.9 IMPACT ON THE TOURISM INDUSTRY

Optimally speaking, the creation of alliances gives consumers access to many routes and destinations, stimulating demand and thus the development of air services, which in turn stimulates the growth of goods and services associated with the tourism industry. The equation could not be simpler: the creation of alliances engenders growth in tourism, which translates into more jobs, and more jobs lead to economic growth. To arrive at this equation, alliance partners must combine their efforts in a strategy that recognizes consistent, or even increased, customer satisfaction as its primary objective.

The tourism industry benefits from the competition in commercial aviation, since airlines try to stimulate consumer demand at home and abroad in order to sell seats that would otherwise be unoccupied by business travellers, who are more profitable passengers.

This competition within the industry is an incentive to air carriers to work with tour operators, travel agents and destinations to market travel to consumers, open new routes and increase capacity, while keeping in mind that leisure travellers are more sensitive to price than to travel time.

Business travellers look for quick and easy trips, which means plenty of available seats — even at the last minute — and some flexibility (possibility of making last-minute changes to itineraries, refunds without penalties, and so on). They will prefer a carrier that can offer what they are looking for. Often, a code-share alliance allows a company to increase the frequency and number of flights to a given destination in order to meet the needs of this type of traveller.

II.1.10 IMPACT ON NEW CARRIERS

The growth in alliances raises questions about the opportunities for a new carrier to enter a local market served by a large carrier from a hub that often has a high fare policy. The arrival on such a market of an air carrier offering low fares may benefit consumers enormously. Some examples demonstrate that traffic can triple when fares drop by half.

In any case, for some years now, small carriers and new arrivals have been complaining of overly aggressive attacks by dominant carriers in certain airports. The large carriers try to push the small carriers out of a route or the entire market by slashing prices and increasing capacity in the short term, with the intention of making up for these losses with long-term fare increases. Consumers seem to enjoy lower prices at first, but the end result is fewer choices and higher prices.

Limited access to airports and terminal facilities is also a source of concern on international markets. It is very difficult for new arrivals to start serving these airports because runway slots are few and often held by big carriers that belong to powerful alliances.

II.2 IMPACTS OF CONSOLIDATION IN THE DISTRIBUTION NETWORK

II.2.1 LARGE INTEGRATED GROUPS: THE GOALS OF CONSOLIDATION

Economies of scale

Grappling with incredibly slim profit margins and increasing pressure from the expanding Internet which threatens to cut these margins even further, large travel groups see economies of scale as the best way to protect themselves against future upsets. For example, the ability to negotiate a better price for airplane fuel gives one a major competitive edge when setting prices for one's services. For travel agencies, being part of a large group means taking advantage of the stronger buying power of the parent company, which can use the group's size to negotiate exclusive agreements with clients such as airlines and global distribution systems.

Increased visibility

Consolidation can help companies improve efficiency in activities such as reservations, accounting, marketing and advertising; it also helps attract many potential investors to this sector. Large groups can more easily carry out the major marketing efforts required to increase product recognition among consumers, which, in turn, contributes to the overall growth of the industry.

Market presence

Many tour operators opt to set up shop in a large number of countries to significantly minimize the risk of industry upheavals, since structural changes do not occur at the same rate everywhere. By concentrating their activities within a single conglomerate, partners have an advantage when it comes to distribution, which offers a wide variety of channels (travel agencies, the Internet, call centres, interactive TV, etc.). By integrating the Internet into their operations, tour operators find they can save time and money even if they continue to make most of their sales through traditional channels.

Controlling distribution and monitoring the competition

Companies working within a single corporate structure enjoy more flexible payment terms and better guarantees when it comes to making air travel arrangements. It is also much easier for an integrated group to follow its clients' needs because it controls each segment in the chain of distribution. It is easy to set up an efficient process for monitoring the competition by rigorously following up on sales, which is a major advantage over competitors who are not vertically integrated. By setting up yield management tools, a company can foresee the capacities required and quickly produce the relevant brochures.

II.2.2 IMPACTS ON INDEPENDENT AGENCIES

Differentiation strategies

Players in the distribution network who are not yet under the thumb of large conglomerates work to adopt individual differentiation strategies to enable them to compete where they can. Personalized service has always been very important in the travel industry. Small tour operators must therefore focus on specific niches and build on their firm's strengths. They also have the advantage of being able to quickly adapt to change, especially when it comes to consumer needs.

Price wars

However, small tour operators must deal with barriers that increase with industry consolidation, in particular price wars. Since they do not belong to an integrated group with its own fleet of planes, independent operators can be shut out of the market because of their inability to find cheap chartered seats. Since they are often obliged to resort to the regular airlines, they have to charge their clients more. Even worse, in addition to increasing their own sales, integrated groups can control, and indeed block, the distribution of certain competitive products because their agency networks also sell packages for other tour operators.

Be that as it may, direct sales are never enough, even for the largest groups. Thomson makes approximately 68 per cent of its sales through its distribution agency, Lunn Poly. Tour operators must turn to independent agencies and other competing networks to sell all their products. Competing tour operators must reach a certain market balance that enables them to sell all of each other's excess inventory.

II.3 IMPACTS OF CONSOLIDATION IN THE HOTEL INDUSTRY

II.3.1 IMPACT ON THE TOURISM INDUSTRY

By building resorts or developing a strong market position in a given area, major hotel groups can often attract enough tourists to benefit independent hotels. At the same time, their expansion projects offer independent hotels the attractive option of being associated with a brand.

II.3.2 IMPACT ON THE HOTEL INDUSTRY

The growth of national hotel groups has not slowed yet independent hotel owners are still in the majority. Considered primarily an urban phenomenon, the large number of brands sometimes leads to more aggressive competition in cities.

As for the debate over whether it is more profitable to belong to a chain, the numbers appear to be reversing[72]. Is belonging to a chain necessary for optimal performance? In a Smith Travel Research study of occupancy rates from 1994 to mid-2000, there was a drop in the chains' occupancy and rate advantage over independent hotels. In fact, in the mid-price and economy price categories, the independents even outperformed chains. And yet, chains enjoy "the marketing muscle, the technology to attract customers and the operational efficiencies to generate profit"[73].

Experts have came up with some possible reasons for this decline:

- weak independent hotels have joined chains, leaving only the strongest and most aggressive independents;
- the proliferation of brands has fragmented the market and confused consumers;
- independents now enjoy access to established GDSs and the Internet.

In 1999, a study by Horwath Consulting showed that, globally, chains perform better than independent hotels. However, in certain markets like Hong Kong, Singapore, São Paulo, Sydney, Budapest and Amsterdam, independents outperformed chains in one or more categories: price, occupancy rate and revenue per available room (RevPAR).

II.3.3 IMPACT ON THE CLIENTELE

The trend towards consolidation has meant hotel executives tend to think more in terms of financial performance than in terms of customer service. However, there are some advantages from the consumer's point of view. The increase in hotel brands worldwide makes for a more diverse product in addition to guaranteeing a certain level of quality. Also, since the consolidation of large hotel groups forces independent owners to develop niche markets, travellers are able to choose the product best suited to their needs. Finally, the increasing reliance on technology enhances hotel products, and the proliferation of distribution networks facilitates hotel reservations.

II.3.4 IMPACT ON ROOM AND OCCUPANCY RATES

Any attempt to determine the impact of hotel consolidation on room and occupancy rates is fraught with difficulty since these can vary depending on current events, the economy and the competition. For example, both the Sydney Olympics and the unrest in the Middle East have had a significant effect on the hotel industry. Supply and demand have a direct impact on the price of hotel rooms and occupancy rates. When the economy is doing well, consumers tend to spend more freely and the number of hotel rooms goes up. Also, room rates in a given area can fluctuate based on the region's tourism or economic development, the number of competing properties or the scarcity of accommodation.

---

[72] Fletch WALLER, "Chain Marketing Muscle? It Isn't Necessarily So," *HOTELS*, January 2001, p. 20.
[73] Jeff WEINSTEIN, "Chains Versus Independents," *HOTELS*, January 2001, p. 5.

II.4 THE EFFECTS OF CONSOLIDATION AND GLOBALIZATION ON TOURIST DESTINATIONS

Is tourism a blessing or a curse? This ongoing debate divides public and expert opinion on the intrusive impact of massive tourism on regions considered either naturally or culturally fragile. Economists see opportunities for development, while ethnologists see tourism as a threat to local culture.[74] Tourism is now considered an unavoidable social fact that must be understood, in all its negative and positive aspects, and intelligently developed.

In the race toward expansion, the large northern countries, the primary tourist-generating regions, have naturally developed formidable tourism-based businesses. Having developed their own markets, these businesses have engaged in a widespread movement towards consolidation, seeking new opportunities in markets that have not yet been exploited. In doing so, these companies are generating a mass movement that affects tourist destinations in a number of different ways.

II.4.1 EMERGENCE OF NEW DESTINATIONS

Developments in transportation both precede and stimulate the development of exchanges, whether they are economic or tourism-based. Although it is almost impossible to establish a direct link between the development of international airline alliances and the development of certain destinations, we can say that these alliances have led to better access to a growing number of destinations throughout the world, mostly through partner networks. These networks make business and leisure travel easier for more and more people who are unable to take advantage of the direct flights offered by charter airlines–which do not have sufficient volume to provide charters every day, for example, between Bangkok and Montreal. Global alliances make it possible to develop a significant tourist market. This section will attempt to establish the relationship between the increase in passenger air traffic and the growth in international tourist arrivals, and thereby illustrate the role of air transportation–and alliances– in the emergence of new destinations.

Changes in air traffic and international arrivals

In general, the main tourist-generating countries are those nations with greater buying power (United States, Germany, Japan, United Kingdom, France, etc.). By the same token, the top tourist-receiving destinations are also highly developed countries (United States, Italy, France, Spain, United Kingdom, etc.). Contrary to popular opinion, less economically developed regions like Africa, Eastern Europe and Latin America have hardly profited from the "manna of tourism" up until now.[75] This is confirmed by our analysis of changes in domestic and international air traffic.

Chart 12
Domestic and International Air Passengers
Breakdown of Global Market - 1985

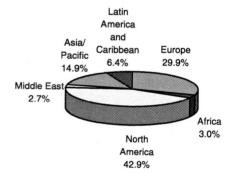

Chart 13
Domestic and International Passenger-Kilometres
Breakdown of Global Market - 1999

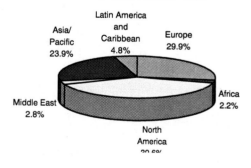

---

[74] Michel FRANK, "Des hôtes et des autres – tourisme et altérité," *Espaces*, no 171, May 2000, p. 14-15.
[75] Yves TINARD, "Les grandes tendances du tourisme mondial: l'émergence de l'Asie de l'Est?" *Espaces*, March-April 1997, pp. 36-44.

North America and Europe represent nearly three-quarters of the passenger-miles flown in 1999 by the air carriers of the ICAO member countries (see Chart 13). However, North America's share of global traffic has fallen in recent years as traffic in the Asia-Pacific region has risen, and this trend will probably continue over the next decade. Between 1985 and 1995, the Asia-Pacific region's share of global air traffic (domestic and international combined) rose from 14.9 per cent to 23.9 per cent and is expected to rise to 42.9 per cent by 2010, according to IATA estimates. If we look only at international travel, the share will likely reach 50 per cent by 2010, for a total of 1.1 billion passengers–almost equal to the total number of passengers around the world in 1995. The annual growth rate of passenger air traffic in this region is much higher than in any other region of the world, and by 2010 it will be double that anticipated in the other continents.

Like air traffic, international tourist arrivals are concentrated in Europe and the Americas and have lost ground to the Asia-Pacific region in recent years (Charts 14 and 15). While North America leads in air traffic, Continental Europe is the most visited area[76] and will remain so until 2020, according to the World Tourism Organization's most recent forecasts. However, Europe's global market share will diminish to around 45.9 per cent, while the Asia-Pacific region's share will continue to grow.

Chart 14
International Tourist Arrivals
Breakdown of Global Market–1980

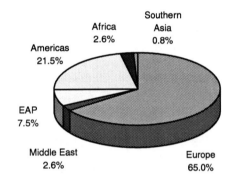

Chart 15
International Tourist Arrivals
Breakdown of Global Market–2000

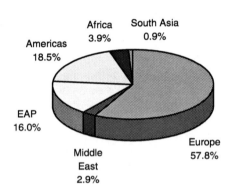

Chart 16
Average Annual Growth Rate, by Region, 1980-2000

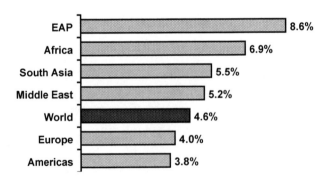

EAP: East Asia and the Pacific
Source: World Tourism Organization (WTO)

---

[76] This situation can be explained by the high rate of intra-European travel–which counts as international arrivals–and by the major role played by domestic transport in the United States, which increases air traffic without counting as international tourist arrivals.

The Asia-Pacific region also experienced the highest annual average increase–8.6 per cent–between 1980 and 2000 (see Chart 16), significantly above the world average of only 4.6 per cent. This impressive performance allowed the area to more than double its market share from 7.5 per cent to 16 per cent. Despite a troubled economy in Asia between 1995 and 2000, Northeast Asia–with China in the lead at 31.2 million tourists in 2000–is experiencing a period of strong growth. The area will continue its expansion in the coming years and will outstrip the Americas (282 million) to become the second most visited area with over 397.2 million international visitors in 2020 (Chart 17).

Chart 17
International Tourist Arrivals
Breakdown of Global Market–2020

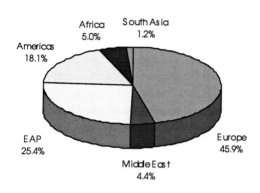

EAP: East Asia and the Pacific
Source: World Tourism Organization (WTO)

Forecasts of international arrivals suggest that the top ten destination countries will fall into a new order within the next few years. China–which currently stands in fifth place–will move into first place by 2020. Other Asian destinations, such as Vietnam and Thailand, will experience rapid growth. South Africa is also among the destinations expected to experience significant growth (from 6 million visitors in 2000 to over 30 million in 2020). Table 25 lists the top tourist-receiving countries according to their projected rank in 2020.

Table 25 Top Destinations Worldwide 2000-2020				
Destination	**Tourist arrivals (in millions)**			**Average annual growth rate**
	2020	**2000**	**Rank-2000**	
1) China	130.0	31.2	5	7.4%
2) France	106.4	75.5	1	1.7%
3) United States	102.4	50.9	2	3.6%
4) Spain	73.9	48.2	3	2.2%
5) Hong Kong (China)	56.6	13.1	15	7.6%
6) United Kingdom	53.8	25.2	6	3.9%
7) Italy	52.5	41.2	4	1.2%
8) Mexico	48.9	20.6	8	4.4%
9) Russian Federation	48.0	21.2	9	4.2%
10) Czech Republic	44.0	5.7	26	10.8%
World	**1,561.1**	**650.2**		**4.5%**

Sources: Chair in Tourism, Université du Québec à Montréal and WTO

Now we will look more closely at changes in air traffic and international tourist arrivals for each continent.

Europe

In Europe, air travel and international tourism have been following the same trend of continuous growth over the past few years. In 1998 and 1999, air travel grew faster than international arrivals (see Chart 18).

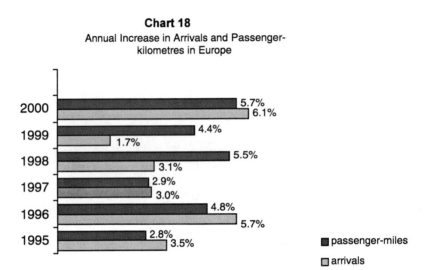

Chart 18
Annual Increase in Arrivals and Passenger-kilometres in Europe

According to the IATA, Europe's global share of international passenger air traffic is expected to decline slightly. Of all international passengers, 62 per cent travel on intra-European routes. As for other international markets, flights to and from North America show the highest volume of passengers. However, these flights are expected to demonstrate the lowest growth rate (4.4%), an indication that this market has reached maturity. Forecasts indicate that flights between Europe and the Middle East and Asia will show the highest growth rate (5.1%) between 1998 and 2015.

Asia-Pacific

Air traffic between Europe and the Asia-Pacific region makes up the largest share of the region's air traffic and will continue to do so. Japan, which ranked first among Asia-Pacific destinations in domestic and international air traffic until 1995, will be outstripped by China in 2010.

The Americas

The most popular destination in the Americas is the United States, followed by Canada and Mexico. However, Chile experienced the region's highest growth in international air passengers between 1985 and 1996. This trend should continue over the next decade, although at a slower pace. Peru, Argentina and Brazil are also expected to experience high growth. Also noteworthy is the growing popularity of Central America: its share of international arrivals to the Americas rose from 2.4 per cent to 3.3 per cent between 1995 and 1999.

The Middle East, Africa and South Asia

The Middle East, Africa and South Asia all experienced a period of significant growth in the late 1990s. In addition, the growth rate for international tourist arrivals in the Middle East is expected to remain markedly higher than the world average (6.3%) for the next two decades.

Middle East / Africa / South Asia			
Tourist arrivals (in millions)	1995	2000	Average annual growth rate
Middle East			
Egypt	2.8	5.1	12.8 %
Africa			
Morocco	2.6	4.1	9.5 %
Zimbabwe	1.4	1.9	6.3 %
South Asia			
Iran	0.5	1.7	27.7 %

Source: WTO

Changes in tourist receipts

Having attempted to explain the emergence of new destinations by examining air traffic and international arrivals, we will now look at how these changes have affected tourist receipts in the top ten world destinations, although it is difficult to impute these changes directly to the development of alliances.

It is interesting to note that despite capturing the most international arrivals, France ranks last among the top ten destinations in terms of receipts per international tourist, as shown in Chart 19. On average, a tourist spends approximately US$400 in France, or only one-quarter of the amount spent in the United States, which ranks first in receipts per international tourist, followed by Germany and the United Kingdom.

Chart 19
Top Ten World Destinations Ranked by International Tourist Arrivals–2000
Ratio of Receipts / International Arrival (in US$)

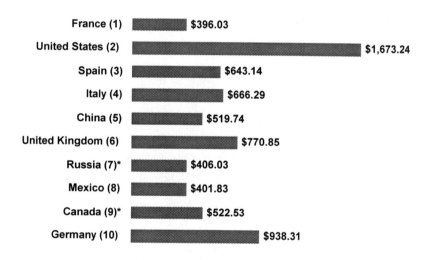

France (1) $396.03
United States (2) $1,673.24
Spain (3) $643.14
Italy (4) $666.29
China (5) $519.74
United Kingdom (6) $770.85
Russia (7)* $406.03
Mexico (8) $401.83
Canada (9)* $522.53
Germany (10) $938.31

* 1999 Data

Source: Chair in Tourism, Université du Québec à Montréal (2001)

Furthermore, average spending per international tourist in France has dropped approximately 14 per cent since 1995. Over the same period, Mexico, China and the United States have logged increases of 31.6 per cent, 19.2 per cent and 14.3 per cent respectively. Despite a 23 per cent decrease in spending per tourist, Germany still ranks second, with an average of US$938 (Chart 20).

Chart 20
Top Ten World Destinations Ranked by International Tourist Arrivals
Changes in Receipts / International Arrival 1995-2000

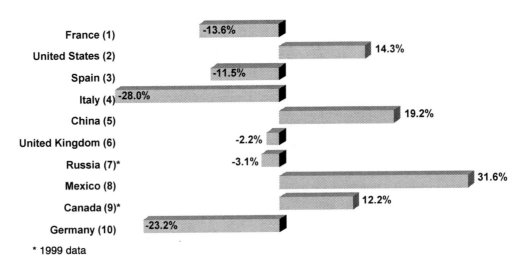

France (1) -13.6%
United States (2) 14.3%
Spain (3) -11.5%
Italy (4) -28.0%
China (5) 19.2%
United Kingdom (6) -2.2%
Russia (7)* -3.1%
Mexico (8) 31.6%
Canada (9)* 12.2%
Germany (10) -23.2%

* 1999 data

Source: Chair in Tourism, Université du Québec à Montréal (2001)

The role of alliances

The creation of large airline alliances has also helped new destinations to emerge. In fact, according to Ross MacCormack, Chairman of the Management Board of the Star Alliance, without an alliance between United and Lufthansa, links such as Frankfurt-Montreal would not exist. On the same note, Pascal Briodin, former Vice-President and Director General for Canada, Air France,[77] commented, "The fact that our networks–through SkyTeam–have a growing number of interconnections means that people from Eastern and Western Europe, Asia and the Middle East can travel under exceptional conditions. They enjoy accessible transportation at a good price because of our retail aggressiveness in markets we do not dominate." [78]

Furthermore, as we saw earlier, the members of a global alliance certainly benefit economically when they funnel the greatest possible number of passengers through their respective hubs, because operating costs drop when their planes are filled to the maximum. There has been a huge increase in the number of flights between Amsterdam, KLM's hub, and Detroit, Northwest's hub (both members of Wings), from 7 flights per week in 1992 to 28 in 2000. Traffic between Frankfurt and Chicago, the hubs of Lufthansa and United, respectively, has also grown significantly. Similarly, Austrian Airlines started a new Toronto-Vienna link five times a week with an Airbus A330 as soon as it joined the Star Alliance. This is definitely beneficial for the hub cities, but what about other destinations, those served by the secondary airports of these same carriers? The German city of Hamburg is currently asking this question. After joining the Star Alliance, Lufthansa dropped several direct flights to North America and Asia originating in Hamburg and based them in Frankfurt and Munich. To put it plainly, this means that the Hamburg population receives inferior service because it must now pass through Frankfurt.

---

[77] Vice-President, Air Transat Vacations, since September 1, 2001.

[78] Pascal BRIODIN, *Conference Proceedings–Tourism and the Trend Towards Consolidation*, Montreal, November 2000, p. 65.

II.4.2 ENRICHING DESTINATIONS AND CREATING NEW ECONOMIC CENTRES BY ENHANCING TOURISM PRODUCTS AND INFRASTRUCTURES

Economic globalization has led to the development of new economic centres, encouraged the movement of capital, and created certain business opportunities. Major global groups can "think globally" while acting locally. Airline, hotel and distribution network alliances contribute to the expansion of a destination's tourist activities and to the development of its tourism potential, giving even the world's less developed countries and regions the opportunity to join the global market.

The development of new hubs and airports: Economic drivers for the destination

Large air carriers are a case in point. Due to the expanding use of their respective hubs, the members of the major airline alliances have created such pressure on certain airports that they are now completely booked up, causing frequent delays, especially for passengers in Europe and North America. To counter this congestion, the airlines have encouraged the development of strategic airports such as Dallas, Denver and Atlanta in North America, which were not important hubs 25 years ago. The Atlanta airport is now the busiest airport in the world (see Table 26).

Table 26
The World's 50 Busiest Airports - 2000

Rank	Airport	Total number of passengers*	Variation (%) 2000 / 1999
1	ATLANTA, GA	80,171,036	2.8
2	CHICAGO, IL	72,135,887	0.7
3	LOS ANGELES, CA	68,477,689	5.1
4	LONDON, GB	64,607,185	3.8
5	DALLAS/FT WORTH, TX	60,687,122	1.1
6	TOKYO, JP	56,402,206	3.8
7	FRANKFURT, DE	49,360,620	7.6
8	**PARIS, FR****	**48,240,137**	**11.6**
9	SAN FRANCISCO, CA	41,173,983	2.1
10	AMSTERDAM, NL (AMS)	39,604,589	7.7
11	DENVER, CO	38,748,781	1.9
12	**LAS VEGAS, NV**	**36,856,186**	**9.5**
13	**SEOUL, KR**	**36,727,124**	**10.1**
14	MINNEAPOLIS/ST PAUL, MN	36,688,159	5.3
15	PHOENIX, AZ	35,889,933	7.0
16	DETROIT, MI	35,535,080	4.6
17	HOUSTON, TX	35,246,176	6.5
18	NEWARK, NJ	34,194,788	1.7
19	MIAMI, FL	33,569,625	1.0
20	NEW YORK, NY (JFK)	32,779,428	3.5
21	**MADRID, ES**	**32,765,820**	**18.2**
22	**HONG KONG, CN**	**32,746,737**	**10.2**
23	LONDON, GB	32,056,942	4.9
24	ORLANDO, FL	30,822,580	5.6
25	ST LOUIS, MO	30,546,698	1.2
26	BANGKOK, TH	29,621,898	8.5
27	TORONTO, OT, CA	28,820,326	4.0
28	**SINGAPORE, SG**	**28,618,200**	**9.8**
29	SEATTLE/TACOMA, WA	28,404,312	2.5
30	BOSTON, MA	27,412,926	1.3
31	TOKYO, JP	27,389,915	6.7
32	ROME, IT	25,921,886	7.5
33	PARIS, FR	25,399,111	0.2
34	NEW YORK, NY	25,233,889	5.9
35	PHILADELPHIA, PA	24,900,621	4.7
36	**SYDNEY, AU**	**23,553,878**	**9.4**
37	MUNICH, DE	23,125,872	8.7
38	CHARLOTTE, NC	23,073,894	7.6
39	HONOLULU, HI	22,660,349	0.4
40	ZURICH, CH	22,649,539	8.4
41	CINCINNATI, OH	22,537,525	3.5
42	**BEIJING, CN**	**21,659,077**	**9.1**
43	BRUSSELS, BE	21,604,478	7.9
44	MEXICO CITY, MX	21,042,610	2.9
45	**MILAN, IT**	**20,716,815**	**22.1**
46	OSAKA, JP	20,472,060	2.9
47	WASHINGTON, DC	19,971,449	1.6
48	SALT LAKE CITY, UT	19,900,810	0.1
49	PITTSBURGH, PA	19,813,174	5.5
50	**BARCELONA, ES**	**19,797,135**	**13.8**

*Includes arriving + departing passengers + direct transit passengers counted once. Results are preliminary.
**Airports listed in bold are those that experienced a major increase last year.
Source: Airports Council International, March 2001

In Asia, the phenomenal increase in international travel suggests that airports will soon reach their full capacity, especially in Japan where there are fewer airports than in most industrialized countries. The improvement of airport infrastructures is crucial if Japan is to play a key role in international connections.

Airport congestion and the ensuing need to increase airport capacity are development opportunities for cities and regions alike. The construction of new runways and new airports helps stimulate almost all sectors of the economy. According to a recent study by the Airports Council International (ACI), planned expenditures for the improvement of airport facilities (excluding new airport construction) totalled US$22 billion in 1999. If this spending is maintained for the next 15 years, total expenditures will surpass US$300 billion.

The development of new hubs and the improvement of airport capacity are also economic drivers for tourist destinations.

Positive Economic Impact of Airports: Brisbane, Australia, and Vienna, Austria

According to an economic impact study undertaken by Ernst & Young in 1998, the Brisbane airport represented 6.8 per cent of the Australian GNP and 5.2 per cent of the country's workforce in 1996-1997, that is, 16,400 people drew their income directly from airport operations and another 67,200 people had indirect links to its operations. In 2018, these figures will rise to 42,000 and 200,000 people respectively, according to estimates by the same company. The Air Transport Action Group (ATAG) predicts that revenues from goods and services and tax revenues will reach US$37 million and US$1.52 billion, respectively. Salaries are expected to reach US$3.5 billion.

Situated at the gateway between Eastern and Western Europe, the Vienna airport is on the way to becoming a driving force behind the Austrian economy and a major east-west traffic centre. Its economic impact is evaluated at US$695 million. It has created 10,500 direct and 9,800 indirect jobs. The ratio of jobs per million passengers is 2,200.

Furthermore, airports often attract many retail and industrial companies that frequently need air transport services and the land transport infrastructures that are often associated with airports, such as roads and highways and the railroads that provide transportation for their merchandise or raw materials. A case in point is Manchester, in the United Kingdom, which has drawn an impressive number of international companies because of its excellent air transport services. An economic impact study carried out by the Vancouver International Airport in 1997 suggested that Whistler/Blackcomb, a ski resort of international renown, would not have achieved such success without direct links between that destination and Japan and Europe.

Hotel chains as economic levers

Foreign hotel investors get involved in tourist destinations in a number of different ways. Table 27 lists the various options for investment in this field and the consequences for the destination. As project instigators or participants, large hotel groups contribute positively to the development of tourism products and the socio-economic development of the areas where they are located. The influx of capital combined with the renown of large hotel chains generates economic leverage that attracts other investors, ensures project viability and elicits interest in creating a variety of activities to help enhance the tourism product. The arrival of hotel groups helps create new business opportunities for smaller companies who can offer products that complement hotel activities. In addition, their financial assets encourage the development of an upscale industry that might otherwise have had trouble getting off the ground locally. A case in point is the arrival of the Intrawest real estate group in Mont Tremblant and Whistler, in Canada. Once Intrawest set up shop, other big hotel chains like Canadian Pacific (Fairmont and Delta), Westin Resort and Marriott Residence Inn decided to invest in these resorts, which have since earned wide renown (see box).

The numerous hotel brands, covering the entire range of market segments, contribute to the diversity of a destination's tourism product. The quality of the services and facilities offered by large chains also helps drive up standards at the destination, enabling it to satisfy international demand. A diverse, high-quality industry makes the destination more attractive and creates heightened interest among tour operators, whose distribution power helps the destination reach a large number of potential customers.

Table 27
Options for Investment in Hotels for Developing Countries
Costs and Benefits[79]

Types of investment	Benefits	Costs
Foreign ownership 100% ownership of equity by a foreign company	• No financial risk to the host country	• Large outflow of income from tourism (leakage) • Difficult to reflect government policy on tourism development
Joint venture Partial ownership of equity by foreign capital	• Access to extra capital • Access to international marketing networks • Lower social/political cost of FDI • Reduced income leakage	• Requirement for a certain base capital • Risk-sharing • Possibly unfavourable contracts due to limited bargaining power
Franchising Right to do business in a prescribed manner when existing brand is sold to a local company	• Transfer of managerial and marketing skills • Assured standard of quality • Brand image	• Management risk is with host country's firms
Management contracts Business is controlled and managed by a foreign firm without ownership by the latter	• Possible transfer of knowledge, skills and technology (e.g., GDS) through a co-operation agreement	• No control over finance, management and planning
Consortia Independent hotels pool resources in order to compete with integrated and franchised chains	• Joint national and international publicity campaign	• Small-size hotels may not be considered attractive to a consortium • Initial lack of brand reputation
National ownership Domestic investment without foreign links	• Reduced international leakage • Independence in adoption of corporate strategies	• Lack of international reputation • Higher marketing costs

[79] David Díaz BENAVIDES, "The Sustainability of International Tourism in Developing Countries," *Tourism in the least developed countries*, WTO–United Nations Conference on Trade and Development, 2001, p. 175.

Mont Tremblant, the Laurentians, Quebec, Canada

The Laurentians, a mountainous region situated just north of Montreal, have experienced unprecedented economic expansion since the Mont Tremblant ski area was acquired by the Intrawest real estate group in 1991. Investing nearly C$1 billion, Intrawest has transformed the ski area into one of the most prestigious four-season resorts in North America, if not the world. The main improvements were expanded slopes, the creation of condo-hotel villages, hotels, golf courses, a beach, restaurants, boutiques, tennis and horseback riding facilities, and the presentation of major events. Further investment on the same scale will probably be made over the course of the next few years. To successfully mount their project, Intrawest leveraged a regional vision and partnerships with the various levels of government, the local population, private industry and hotel chains.

Sizeable economic spin-offs for the region and facilities for the local community[80]

The resort has become the area's main economic driver and biggest employer. While the Mont Tremblant ski area employed 350 people during the high season in 1991-1992, it now employs some 2,300 and welcomes nearly two million visitors a year, in comparison with only 330,000 when it was first bought by Intrawest. From 1991 to 2000, Intrawest's investment created 19,780 jobs in construction alone, and 3,720 permanent jobs, bringing in C$222 million and C$140 million for the Quebec and Canadian governments, respectively, in addition to recurring revenues.

Since 1991, the number of jobs in the area has increased by 68 per cent; elsewhere in Quebec, this number has risen 7.4 per cent. The unemployment rate, which was approaching 15 per cent five years ago, was practically non-existent in 2000.[81] From 1991 to 2000, the population of the Laurentian regional county municipality increased by 22.6 per cent.[82] The expansion of the project is expected to have similar positive spin-offs.

The region's retail sector has exploded with grocery chains, pharmacies, hardware stores, restaurants, boutiques, etc. There are plans to re-open a disused military airport; real estate sales are skyrocketing; apartments are rented before the buildings are even built; and local expertise is growing. The road network has already improved and a new roadway is being planned that will provide a more direct link to another region, thus facilitating the movement of people and increasing the possibilities of economic spin-offs. The establishment of a public transport system between the resort and the surrounding municipalities and the construction of housing units for employees are just two of the infrastructures that benefit the local population.

II.4.3 THE INSTABILITY OF ECONOMIC SPIN-OFFS

Although the presence of international tourism-based companies contributes to the economic development of an area, it does not guarantee only positive effects. Income leakage casts a shadow over the economic data. Profits leave the country to return to the investors' head offices in many different forms: management fees, marketing, distribution system, advertising, etc. There are also the all-inclusive resort packages offered by tour operators that keep visitors "captive," carrying out all their activities in a practically closed economy. Some resorts even purchase their supplies in their country of origin. And we mustn't overlook agreements signed between multinationals–tour operators who only deal with an airline other than the country's national airline and an international hotel chain. These practices do little to stimulate the local economy and the destinations themselves get a very small piece of the pie.

---

[80] Gérard BÉRUBÉ, "La ville à la montagne: L'Expansion de Tremblant s'étirera jusqu'en 2010," *Le Devoir*, July 25, 2000, p. B 1.

[81] Martine TURENNE, "La montagne aux dollars," *Actualité*, Vol. 25, No. 8, May 15, 2000, p. 56.

[82] INSTITUT DE LA STATISTIQUE DU QUÉBEC, *"Population des MRC et des communautés urbaines, Québec, 1971-2000,"* [on line], January 30, 2001 [http://www.stat.gouv.qc.ca/donstat/demograp/regional/207.htm], July 18, 2001.

Likewise, tour operators, through a vertical integration strategy, manage to keep a significant portion of their customers' expenditures in their own coffers by buying inbound agencies and destination hotels, depriving the destination country of a significant stake in economic activities.

The strength of tourism groups gives them an advantage in negotiations with destination suppliers. If they are not completely satisfied with an offer, they can take their business to another area. Furthermore, their buying power allows them to acquire many local businesses, thereby exerting greater control over the market. Another point is that urban areas enjoy strong growth to the detriment of peripheral regions because international companies concentrate their investments in cities. Resorts are the exception.

II.4.4 PRESSURE ON THE NATURAL, SOCIAL AND CULTURAL ENVIRONMENTS

The constant growth of tourism brought on by economic globalization and the consolidation of major players in the tourism industry encourages mass tourism, which exerts considerable pressure on local environments.

To meet the high demand and fulfil certain imperatives related to profitability, tourism groups have developed products that cater primarily to this mass market, meaning the products are standardized. If they want to mass market their products, tour operators cannot customize them; to conform to their brand image, hotel chains offer a similar product in all their establishments around the world; and airline alliances schedule their flights to the most popular destinations and drop less lucrative routes. Although standardization has the merit of lowering prices, enabling more people to travel, it nevertheless creates a concomitant negative pressure on destinations. Standardization means homogeneity and the risk of reducing the tourism product to the banal. In travel brochures, we could easily substitute one seaside resort for another, the products are so similar. Mass marketing also means the overuse of certain tourist sites and negative pressure on all sorts of environments, which could in the long term lead to the deterioration and abandonment of the destination, if no measures are taken (see box).

Overuse–Negative Pressure on the Environment

In 1954, California's **Yosemite Park** welcomed its first million visitors. Today, it receives more than four million annually. On a typical summer day, about 7,000 vehicles drive through. This large flow of tourists affects the balance of the ecosystem–fauna, flora and air–as well as the tourist experience itself.

Tourist traffic can pose a danger to archaeological sites: dust raised by circulating pedestrians, carbon dioxide from their breath, and the increase in heat and humidity are all factors that can significantly alter the colours, materials and topography of a site. On a larger scale, the vibration of motor vehicles and widespread hotel construction present similar dangers such as sanitary drainage systems, which increase subterranean water volumes.

Although the tourism industry provides access to the world market, its growth has nevertheless disturbed local communities in a variety of ways: expulsion from their land or milieu, disruption of the economy, reduced access to natural resources, deterioration of traditional values and the natural environment, and social degradation arising from the commercialization of their culture and the influence of foreign communities.

Because of standards that must be respected or the needs of the invading clientele, some receiving countries are forced to adapt their services to the detriment of their cultural identity. Watering down the culture leads to a standardization of cultures and can even wipe out regional specificities. For example, the construction of large hotel complexes may disfigure the natural and historical environment and create an architectural landscape completely unrelated to the region. Likewise, food can lose its "local colour" in favour of so-called "international" cuisine.

While some cities want to increase tourism, others are trying to stem it. This is particularly true for some historic cities of international reputation that have to deal with growing numbers of tourists who disturb the quality of life for the local population–traffic jams, congestion, noise, invasion of local space and tranquillity. Nevertheless, without this tourist traffic, the local population may not have access to various services they now enjoy: restaurants, boutiques, etc.

II.4.5 HUMAN RESOURCE DEVELOPMENT AND CULTURE SHOCK

The arrival of a tourism mega-business has a direct impact on the labour market: new jobs, training, industry expertise, and management support all help increase the qualifications of the local workforce and the quality of tourism services. The presence of experienced, more highly qualified workers means the destination can develop its tourism products locally.

However, in terms of job quality, there are sometimes questionable hiring practices that end up exploiting cheap local labour, offering only positions that require few qualifications and offer little responsibility. There is also the whole notion of the hiring company's corporate culture, which may clash with the economic and cultural values of the destination country.

II.4.6 DISINTERMEDIATION AND ACCESS TO A POWERFUL DISTRIBUTION NETWORK

Multinationals help market destinations in many ways. Technological advancements, multiple distribution channels (call centres, global distribution systems, transactional Web sites, traditional and on-line travel agencies), the development of the communications network, access to a sizeable client base and the drawing power attraction of the groups themselves all help promote a destination and market it on a larger scale.

The advent of the Internet and its use as a distribution channel for retail activities gives consumers better access to information and makes their research more efficient. This heightens the competition among organizations offering products and services to the same market segments. The global character of the Internet has radically modified the dynamics of competition since on the Web, the competition is always only a few clicks away. There are no borders to limit the export of on-line products and services, which complicates the development of strategies for managers.

To remain competitive, players such as airlines and hotels have developed electronic solutions to reach their customers directly and bypass the traditional distribution chain. Technological advancements have therefore compromised the survival of certain intermediaries. With their very existence and cost no longer justified in the new reality, many of them have had to review their market position, especially travel agents.

> According to an Ipsos-Reid poll, 92 per cent of Canadians who have made a travel reservation on line confirmed that they used the services of a traditional travel agent less often.

With new technologies have come a flurry of new arrivals in the travel industry, some of which currently dominate the market. Certain on-line agencies are clearly aiming to position themselves in several geographic markets by creating subsidiaries adapted to each one. Expedia.com was a pioneer in this respect, entering the Canadian market in 1997 with Expedia.ca. Two years later, it launched a British version and, in 2000, a German version. Its chief rival, Travelocity.com, launched a British version in November 1998 and a Canadian site a few months later. This method of positioning oneself is also used by European players. Lastminute.com, for example, includes Australian, German, Swiss and French versions on its site. A second market penetration strategy is to acquire players already established in the target markets. The vast financial resources of the companies allow them to enter the on-line travel market. The absence of destination management organizations only serves to encourage this virtual domination.

At the same time, there is no doubt that brands have a major influence on many travellers because they suggest security and guarantee a certain level of quality. In the United States, 84 per cent of business travellers[83] and 74 per cent of tourists[84] prefer to stay in branded establishments. This means that these businesses have a definite advantage in terms of positioning the destination–when Marriott markets its hotels or a Preussag subsidiary develops a package tour for a certain destination, this helps develop or enhance the destination's reputation and image in the customer's mind. However, by increasing the ties between them or establishing their own offices in the destination, certain groups control the distribution channels, thereby cutting out local businesses. By integrating vertically with travel agencies and consolidating amongst themselves, tour operators are becoming an increasingly limited group of intermediaries, insinuating themselves between the destination and the consumers. Their power produces negative pressure on local markets and destinations–in terms of competition, negotiation of commissions, more extensive promotion of particular destinations, etc. We must examine the extent to which tour operators and airlines are able to control the number of tourists visiting one destination instead of another.

---

[83] YESAWICH, Pepperdine & Brown and Yankelovich Partners, *The YP&B Yankelovich Partners 2000 National business travel monitor*, Orlando, April 28, 2000, p. 27.

[84] Ibid, p. 24.

PART 3: OPPORTUNITIES PRESENTED BY CONSOLIDATION

The tourism industry is evolving in a constantly-changing business environment. Globalized markets, the concentration of economic power, technological developments and a highly competitive marketplace, combined with the increasingly sophisticated needs and expectations of tourists, are defining the new parameters of tourism-based businesses. In this context, we believe that destinations need to develop new strategies if they want to remain competitive and ensure increased tourist traffic. As we have seen, the trend towards alliances, mergers and acquisitions is "being driven by the economic demands of global markets, the costs of keeping up with fast-changing technologies, and the opportunities provided by government deregulation and liberalization initiatives."[85]

The majority of companies operating in the tourism industry are small and medium-sized businesses; decision-makers must employ creativity and innovation to differentiate their products from the competition and target the right niches. We will attempt to discern the new opportunities created by economic globalization by looking at current practices in the main tourism sectors. Which strategies will best exploit a destination's tourism potential and enhance the competitiveness of its businesses, while still meeting the requirements of a more discriminating clientele?

III.1 OPPORTUNITIES IN THE AIRLINE INDUSTRY

III.1.1 FRANCHISING: AN OPPORTUNITY FOR NEW CARRIERS

The franchising concept has been used in the airline industry in various countries around the world, but not in Canada. Under this system, the franchisee owns some assets but uses the franchiser's name, marketing system, frequent flyer program and operations manual. Instead of operating unprofitable flights, a carrier could allocate these flights to franchisees.

For example, certain domestic routes may not be profitable for a major airline with a fleet of very large planes poorly suited for the low traffic generated by such flights. However, regional carriers with smaller planes could most likely obtain a more efficient passenger load factor and thereby earn an acceptable financial return. Franchising could strengthen the marketing plan of a new or existing business since the franchiser assumes responsibility for marketing the flight. In return, the franchisee pays access rights and remits a percentage of its earnings to the dominant airline.

Under this formula, the franchisee does not compete directly with the dominant carrier; instead, the two carriers complement one another. The smaller carrier benefits from the larger one's reputation, while the larger one receives additional revenue at no extra cost. Franchising not only seems to satisfy both parties, as far as the consumer is concerned, it also helps maintain a well-serviced domestic network.

III.1.2 DISCOUNT CARRIERS

Discount carriers compete with dominant carriers on regional markets and are proliferating due to the high volume of business travel.

There are currently a number of discount no-frills airline companies: WestJet Airlines, in Canada; Southwest, JetBlue and AirTran in the United States; and EasyJet, City Bird and Ryanair in Europe. Moreover, discount airlines are a relatively new phenomenon in Europe, having developed in response to the myriad opportunities offered by airline deregulation, which has stimulated demand by creating new routes. The growth of low-cost carriers is all the more important for the future because currently only 5 per cent of European passengers use these carriers, while in the United States the proportion is around 25 per cent.

---

[85] OECD, *International Strategic Alliances: Their Role in Industrial Globalisation*, July 2000.

Many discount or charter companies could also offer regular flights at peak times from major cities to fill the void created when certain carriers join an alliance. Such a strategy would mean better service for destinations that were abandoned when an alliance was formed or even better service for new destinations.

On-line distribution is increasingly popular among discount carriers: EasyJet sells 40 per cent of its tickets through its Internet site while Southwest Airlines sells 25 per cent. Furthermore, Southwest sells the most electronic tickets of the ten largest U.S. carriers. On-line distribution is a natural in this era of e-commerce because it conforms with the discount carrier approach of reducing operating costs to a minimum.

III.1.3 CO-OPERATIVES

Another way to set up airline service with low operating costs is by creating a co-operative. By forming a network to collectively negotiate the best prices possible from suppliers of products and services like fuel, group insurance, plane and equipment insurance, and spare parts, carriers can realize major economies of scale. The co-operative formula's main strength is that it enables members to pool their capital and expertise while sharing risk, which in turn helps them expand and develop structures to compete with the competition.

III.1.4 INTERLINING: DEVELOPING STRATEGIC RELATIONSHIPS WITH LARGE INTERNATIONAL CARRIERS

When an alliance is created or two carriers merge, many companies lose their access to certain destinations. For example, ever since Air Canada acquired Canadian International, many international carriers, particularly those who belong to oneworld, Canadian's former alliance, have found it very difficult to serve the Canadian market and have considered signing agreements to regain access to certain Canadian cities.

One such company is Australia-based Qantas Airways, who used to transport passengers from Australia to Vancouver, via Honolulu, where Canadian International would take over the final leg to Vancouver. However, since being acquired by Air Canada, Canadian has cancelled its Honolulu-Vancouver route, forcing Qantas itself to continue the flight all the way to Vancouver at a substantially higher cost and consequently smaller profit margin. If Qantas signed an interlining agreement with a new carrier, its passengers could connect to a Vancouver flight in Los Angeles, Qantas' North American hub.

Like Qantas, several members of oneworld are very interested in signing interlining agreements with new carriers that would enable them to offer better connections to Canadian destinations at a lower price, with simplified ticketing and more seamless baggage handling.

Interlining agreements would be a first step that could eventually lead to other agreements such as code sharing or shared technology, which could ensure the survival of a new carrier.

III.1.5 FREQUENT FLYER PROGRAMS

Frequent flyer programs are key to attracting and keeping business travellers. Alliance members can offer more attractive programs because travellers have more opportunities to earn points and exchange them for travel to enticing vacation destinations. New carriers targeting business travellers find it difficult to compete because they are do not have a large network. Although they can try offering more generous terms for obtaining or cashing in points, they still lack a wide array of destinations.

Following the lead of the European Commission, governments could require national carriers to sell points in their frequent flyer programs to a new carrier or existing competitor for a reasonable price.

There is a widespread tendency to combine frequent flyer plans with loyalty plans in other industries like financial services (i.e., credit cards). This means consumers can obtain points when purchasing things other than airline tickets and sometimes exchange air miles for other goods and services, like hotel rooms. Such loyalty programs more adequately reflect the complexity of the tourism industry, particularly the needs of the business traveller.

III.2 OPPORTUNITIES FOR THE DISTRIBUTION NETWORK

The threat posed by a consolidated distribution network is very real to small independent businesses. These companies must exhibit ingenuity and adaptability if they want to hold their own against major industry players and the airlines who have steadily lowered travel agent commissions and reduced the cost of issuing tickets by relying increasingly on electronic ticketing. The travel agencies who are increasing revenues and surviving are those who are diversifying their products and services while charging consumers service fees to issue plane tickets. The waves of consolidation have also created new opportunities for operators in the form of new market niches.

III.2.1 DIVERSIFICATION OF PRODUCTS AND SERVICES

To offset the impact of consolidation, networks of independent agencies must develop effective strategies for exploiting the inherent weaknesses of large conglomerates. After all, since larger companies have trouble attracting niche markets or specialized products like eco-tourism, educational tours or exotic locales, they must focus their efforts on creating packages for the mass market. Wholesalers who carefully select a well-defined niche market can compete with the major players by fulfilling the specific requirements of the target clientele. Another option is to target a specific market segment, such as young people, business travellers or senior citizens. To more effectively deploy its strategy for penetrating these market niches, an agency or wholesaler must seek out partners who can enhance the product. The added value will create the profitability needed for the agency to survive, despite a much lower sales volume. Savvy consumers are, in fact, prepared to pay more for high-quality experiences that better meet their needs.

III.2.2 NETWORKING

Agencies who make alliances with local businesses can very effectively improve the products they offer and even develop theme tours. For example, a tour operator specialized in adventure tourism could create a varied and satisfying tourist experience by joining forces with a sled dog breeder, a restaurant serving local gourmet cuisine, an outfitter and a few other regional businesses. This type of complementary alliance among players in a given region or between neighbouring regions could produce a synergy effect that could even exceed the expectations of the target clientele. Some examples of high-potential niches are health tourism, eco-tourism, religious tourism, agricultural tourism, sports tourism, native tourism and adventure tourism.

III.3 OPPORTUNITIES FOR THE HOTEL INDUSTRY

Independent hotels have certain options for countering the growth among major hotel groups and the accompanying threat to their market segment.

III.3.1 AFFILIATION WITH MAJOR HOTEL GROUPS

Affiliating oneself with a brand name does have some obvious benefits: the drawing power of the chain's reputation and brand image, increased marketing power, insured product quality stemming from established standards, managerial assistance, ease of financing, and so on. However, there are also certain drawbacks to joining a hotel chain: a long-term contract, royalties, the inflexibility of having to observe pre-set standards and management formulas, etc. It is also important to remember that a brand name does not automatically guarantee customers; there is still a lot of work to do. According to some experts, an increasing number of independent hotels will opt to join recognized chains in the coming years.

Before joining a chain, a hotel must also consider the expectations of its target clientele. For example, if the hotel is trying to penetrate the American market, a brand name can be a definite advantage since 83 per cent of Americans tend to consume brand products. In France, chains are relatively popular with travellers and hold more than a 45 per cent market share. On one hand, brand names are more appreciated than certain rating systems (stars) because they are established around the world and have a standardized image. On the other hand, an increased number of chains on the market could simply confuse consumers.

III.3.2 THE CREATION OF SPECIFIC NICHES

With tourists exhibiting more and more individualism, there has been a marked shift in the hotel industry away from standardized products to niche products. Since the major hotel groups basically offer standardized products, they have left a vacuum when it comes to niche markets. One promising niche is that of luxury products. New products are being developed to meet the demands of this market, products such as boutique hotels (the five Malmaison hotels in the United Kingdom have already successfully targeted this niche), time-shares, retirement homes, and so on. As we saw with the distribution network, the development of partnerships with complementary businesses may well be the most effective way of creating a distinctive high-quality product since creativity and networking are often the hallmarks of a successful product.

III.3.3 ASSOCIATION MEMBERSHIP

From a marketing standpoint, membership in an association offers important visibility and leverage while preserving the hotel's managerial autonomy. It often enables an independent hotel to compete with the large chains, something it is unable to afford on its own. Contracts are short-term and flexible and the goals can vary: promote an image of prestige (Relais & Châteaux), become part of an association of theme products (Hôtellerie Champêtre), or simply facilitate distribution (Pegasus). Commercial associations are expected to take place at all levels, locally to internationally. Moreover, associations can always choose to offer more than just marketing support: group purchases of products and services; institutional partnerships and programs enabling business-owners to prepare for the changes in technology affecting all management activities; networking among key technology firms and local tourism-based businesses; etc.

III.4 CHOICES AND STRATEGIES FOR DESTINATIONS

More than any other economic activity, travel and tourism offer developing countries a chance to benefit from economic growth and market globalization. However, before opening up their borders to tourists, there are certain conditions new destinations (especially those in less developed countries) have to fulfil: remove the psychological barriers of potential visitors (risks associated with language, climate, medical system, food, safety, etc.), develop physical infrastructures (airports, roads, water supply system) and provide accommodations and attractions that meet tourist requirements. Lastly, a destination must make a name for itself with industry players from tourist-generating countries so that flights will be scheduled there, tour operators will package it and travel agents will distribute it effectively.

It is a destination's responsibility to lay the foundations of its tourism industry and promote its growth through concerted action by various categories of players–airlines, hotel owners, distribution networks, attractions, activities, etc.–thereby striking a balance between tourism growth and the needs of both travellers and the local population. In the current climate of globalization and free trade, destinations should welcome companies whose policies conform to the destination's goals. As it co-ordinates its activities, the destination must consider factors such as the pursuit of sustainable development, the removal of obstacles to growth (such as security and taxes) and the liberalization of markets.

Ultimately, a destination's most significant challenge will be to take advantage of the opportunities offered by globalization, rather than approaching it fearfully and hesitantly. To this end, the next section outlines several strategies that destinations could adopt to deal with globalization.

III.4.1 TOURISM AND INTERNATIONAL AGREEMENTS[86]

The numerous trade agreements in existence (NAFTA, APEC, Mercosur, the EU and the prospective FTAA) are proof of countries' willingness to open their borders and encourage trade. Moreover, it is up to economic alliances and national governments to impose regulations to make their markets more accessible and ensure that their legislative framework encourages healthy competition and a level playing field for all parties. Investment incentives, business permits for foreign interests, freedom of movement, the standardization of certain business practices and the abolition of visas are all measures, permanent or otherwise, that help move the country towards greater liberalization.

Also, given tourism's economic impact and dominant position in the service sector, it must be a party to the multilateral trade negotiations co-ordinated by the World Trade Organization (WTO) and, more specifically, to the General Agreement on Trade in Services (GATS). However, a study group has found serious deficiencies in the GATS. These include a failure to address strategic factors, notably traffic rights and reservation systems in the airline industry; an absence of regulations to curb anti-competitive practices resulting from globalization; a lack of measures to stimulate sustainable development; and, for certain countries, an inequitable distribution of the benefits resulting from a liberalized market. To mitigate the effects of these deficiencies, some developing countries–with the technical assistance of the WTO's Working Group on Liberalization, together with the WTO and the UNCTAD[87]–have begun developing a formula to be included in the GATS. This formula, a "proposed Appendix to the GATS on Tourism," would measure the unique value of tourism services. Whether in its current form or somewhat modified, the Appendix would be a way to monitor the effects of globalization on the tourism sector, specifically with regard to anti-competitive practices or those running counter to the principles of sustainable development.

---

[86] Henryk HANDSZUH, "Seminar on globalization and its challenges and opportunities for tourism development in the Middle East and North Africa", Cairo, Egypt, May 20, 2001.

[87] United Nations Conference on Trade and Development.

The Tourism Satellite Account (TSA)

The Tourism Satellite Account (TSA) has become an essential instrument for producing consistent and comparable statistics that make it possible to measure the economic importance of tourism in the national and international economy. This tool may also be used to more accurately estimate the economic spin-offs of investments.

III.4.2 NEW LEGISLATIVE FRAMEWORKS: A STEP TOWARDS ALLIANCES AND OPEN BORDERS

As previously mentioned, a country's courts must ensure that its legislative bodies encourage healthy competition and provide a level playing field for all those involved in the sector. The role of national governments should therefore be to facilitate partnerships among local companies or encourage networking with foreign ones. These partnerships will help develop and promote the destination.

The Case of the Island of Malta: A Profitable Partnership

In November 1997, Air Malta and Accor formed a joint venture: the Accor Air Malta Company Ltd, 60 per cent owned by Accor and the rest by Air Malta.

Between 1998 and 1999, the casino division of the Accor Group negotiated a deal to acquire shares in the Dragonara Casino in Malta. Once the transaction was completed, a new company was formed: Dragonara Casino Limited, with BCW (owners of three 5-star hotels) and Stake Holding Ltd (comprising Accor Casino and Accor Air Malta Limited) as equal partners in the venture. Dragonara Casino Ltd's aggressive marketing strategy created such demand that Air Malta had to schedule new flights, mainly to the Middle East and Northern Italy.

At the same time, the Accor-Air Malta alliance encouraged tour operators to promote the destination in trade publications. Malta also benefited from the fact that Accor is one of the principal shareholders of Carlson Wagonlit, a chain that owns approximately 3,000 travel agencies around the world, an excellent distribution network to promote the destination.

The first step is to enable all sectors–tourism, transport, environment, finance, legislation, national heritage, etc.–to communicate effectively and deal efficiently with the various ministerial levels involved in order to achieve concerted action. Legislation designed to open borders to visitors and trade and help set up large tourism-based businesses can also be introduced. These legislative measures can take the form of tax cuts, waived import duties, investment incentives, cost-sharing, rescinding of visa requirements, tax exemptions, simplified administrative procedures, subsidies, etc. In fact, it may be helpful to create a legislative body specifically to promote foreign capital investments in tourism-related projects and to facilitate the importation of the goods and services needed to develop the tourism infrastructure.

- *Open skies agreements*
  To take advantage of the international alliances' ability to develop global markets, destinations such as Asia and the Middle East should provide the most promising potential markets (i.e., the primary tourist-generating countries) with greater access to their territory by introducing new legislation such as open skies agreements. The agreement signed by the U.S. and South Korea in 1998 should put some pressure on Japan to completely open its airways to the United States. Also, if these regions open

up their borders to one another, they will attract more tourists. New Zealand and China seem to have grasped this concept as they have begun discussing ways to liberalize the current bilateral agreement governing air travel between them. In anticipation of significant numbers of Chinese tourists, New Zealand has even suggested an open skies agreement similar to the one it recently signed with Australia. And in Thailand, the government has ended the monopoly of the national carrier, Thai Airways, on domestic routes, with the goal of gradually liberalizing the entire industry.

The liberalization policies adopted by some regions in Africa have paved the way for air travel between various African countries, resulting in a 13.2 per cent increase in 1998 in the number of travellers over the previous year. The trend will likely gather momentum when even more liberalization initiatives are implemented at the regional and continental level.

Decreased air traffic restrictions and increased competition notwithstanding, airlines in African and South American countries and certain parts of Asia are anxious to ensure their financial survival through partnerships or involvement in large international airline alliances such as Star, oneworld, etc.

- *Privatization of national carriers*
  Another potential means of facilitating and promoting tourism-based trade is for governments to privatize carriers and increase the percentage of shares that foreign companies may hold in national airlines. This strategy is gradually being implemented in Asia. In Thailand, the ceiling for foreign-owned shares been raised from 10 per cent to 30 per cent and the government's interest in Thai Airways has decreased from 79.5 per cent to 49 per cent. The South Korean government has raised the limit on foreign-owned shares–formerly set at 7 per cent for individuals and 26 per cent for groups–to 50 per cent. These changes mean that national carriers may now participate in existing international alliances, which can, in turn, expand their markets. For destinations such as Thailand or South Korea, the access to new markets provided by their involvement in international alliances can only benefit their local and regional economies. Other destinations such as Africa and the Middle East may want to consider privatizing their carriers to increase the tourist flow and thereby boost local economies.

- *Development of charter flights*
  In order for tour operators–who tend to focus on mass tourism–to flourish, authorities need to promote the expansion of charter flights. Even though German operators are increasingly powerful, and therefore able to offer more attractive rates, they cannot break into the French market in any significant way as long as charter flights are "sacrificed" for the sake of regular flights. Other routes between two European destinations are dominated by charter flights, as is the case for flights between the United Kingdom and Spain (82%), Greece (79%) and Turkey (73%). When national tourism authorities promote charter flights by reserving good time slots for them (i.e., travellers' preferred arrival and departure times), the number of flights per week between the destination and the main tourist-generating countries often increases. Thus, the allocation of time slots to charter carriers becomes a significant marketing tool for destinations wishing to boost their foreign tourist quotient.

- *Alliances with tourism-generating countries*
  Typically, a tourism destination cannot be considered in isolation or as a product in its own right. Its market value and appeal depend on a variety of factors that are beyond the control of those responsible for its image. The strategies developed by airlines, large hotel chains, tour operators and leisure-based businesses are established at a global level and are often connected to competing destinations. The authorities in charge of the destination must also take into account contextual aspects such as infrastructures, image (safety, stability and reputation) and its natural, cultural, human and financial resources. Thus, making a destination part of the global strategy of

tourism-based businesses–whether they are local or international–is a very gradual process requiring the kind of major investment that some countries simply cannot raise unaided. Joining forces with large alliances or major players from the various sectors of a tourist-generating country's tourism industry (airlines, hotels, tour operators, etc.) may enable a destination management organization to encourage investment and generate demand in the market segments controlled by these major players.

To develop accommodation infrastructures in their region, destinations are well advised to work with international companies, which are always searching for new markets to develop. Moreover, as previously mentioned, most air carriers are convinced, and have the figures to back them up, that being an alliance member is extremely profitable. However, carriers' expenses are steadily rising, quite apart from the cost of setting up and maintaining an alliance. To increase their revenue and generate economies of scale, carriers who are alliance members must develop an increasingly global network, that is, ensure their hubs are inter-connected on all continents. This interconnectedness engenders an extremely high volume of connecting flights at certain airports. This is true at Lufthansa's hub in Frankfurt, where connections represent approximately 50 per cent of all scheduled flights. Charles de Gaulle, Amsterdam and Zurich also have a high proportion of connecting flights (as high as 40%) (see Chart 21). This focus on increasing the number of connecting flights is advantageous for many destinations, particularly the more remote ones. For example, an Asian destination management organization could draw up an agreement with a foreign carrier such as Alitalia (SkyTeam's newest member) for it to take passengers, perhaps Scandinavian (given sixth freedom rights that permit exploitation of foreign markets), to Asia with a stopover in Rome, Alitalia's hub. The benefits? An increased flow of tourists to the destination and a higher passenger load factor for the carrier.

Returning to the aforementioned example of Hamburg, Germany: after Lufthansa joined Star Alliance, it dropped a number of direct flights from Hamburg to North America and Asia in favour of ones from other hubs. Therefore, it would be a good idea for the Hamburg authorities to attract a carrier from another alliance, such as Delta or Air France of SkyTeam, by offering them peak time slots or advantageous take-off and landing rights. Because SkyTeam is competing with Star Alliance on the German market, the former is definitely motivated to develop a new hub at Hamburg. In taking the spot Lufthansa vacated by joining Star Alliance, SkyTeam could transport passengers from Northern Europe and the Americas directly to Asia. Other European destinations such as Lyon, Marseilles, Barcelona, Naples, Strasbourg, Manchester, Munich, etc. could also benefit by attracting carriers.

- *Local partnerships and the elimination of intra-regional barriers*
  Building local and intra-regional partnerships is an important step towards achieving a critical mass of complete and varied tourism products. Let's take the Middle East, a region with strong growth potential. It could gear its products and destinations to either mass or niche markets. The strategies it implements could involve building associations and partnerships based on each country's particular natural or cultural attractions, so it can offer a more well-developed, sophisticated product. After all, the goal is to present as large a range of products as possible, from the most conventional (for mass tourism) to the highly specialized (for a specific market segment). Moreover, so-called "business" destinations may function as pull products for other destinations with a greater perceived "pleasure or leisure" component. However, facilitating such partnerships requires the elimination of intra-regional barriers, particularly those affecting ground travel (border restrictions, visa requirements, etc.) so tourists can travel freely between countries.

Chart 21
Proportion of Connecting Passengers
at Various European Airports in 1998

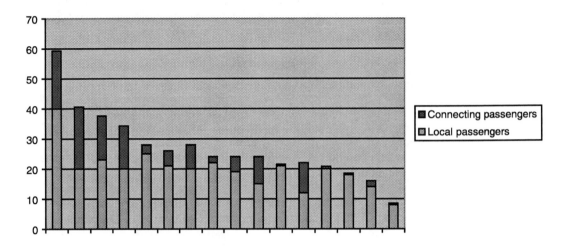

Source: Air Transport Action Group

III.4.3 PARTNERSHIPS BETWEEN GOVERNMENT AND INDUSTRY: AN ESSENTIAL STEP IN BUILDING INFRASTRUCTURE

In order to sustain the increase in demand,[88] the public and private sectors need to join forces and tackle current obstacles together. This collaboration will almost certainly involve building new airports, expanding existing ones and ensuring that the growth of the air traffic control system keeps pace with expansion projects. The runways and overall capacity of numerous international airports, both in the U.S. and Europe (some of the most obvious examples being London, where Heathrow and Gatwick are both exceeding their capacity, Frankfurt, and even Chicago and New York), can no longer meet the increased demand. Consequently, secondary hubs must be established on many continents. In Europe, for example, the growth of airport capacity is a crucial issue for American carriers, given the significant increase in transatlantic air traffic. Even though the Charles de Gaulle Airport in Paris has plenty of room to grow, there is still talk of building a third airport and another one in Spain that could handle approximately 100 million passengers. However, in spite of all this positive momentum, expansion remains a thorny issue, specifically because of environmental impact issues.

Investing in Airports to Meet Demand

Although it has been expanded many times over the years, Zurich Airport, operated by the Zurich Canton, is still unable to meet the steadily growing demand. The "Airport Partners" have drawn up a ten-year infrastructure development plan: a new terminal, a light rail rapid transit line between existing terminals, better access to public transportation, improved cargo facilities, etc. The entire project would require an investment of US$1.15 billion and the overall economic benefit to the area has been estimated at US$3.62 billion.

---

[88] The World Tourism Organization has forecast a 4.1 per cent annual increase in tourism demand (1995-2020) and, according to the International Air Transport Association (IATA), over the next few years there will be a 5.6 per cent average annual increase in international air traffic.

Obviously, any expansion must address the needs for accommodation and basic infrastructure such as access roads, ground transportation, bridges, reliable water and electricity supplies, etc. It is also vital that reception and leisure facilities be set up with the input of the affected communities, who should take part in every step of the planning and development process. In many regions around the world, there is an increasing tendency for the public and private sectors of the host community to work together to set up adequate infrastructures.

DUBAI–The United Arab Emirates

With most of the country's wealth based on oil, the United Arab Emirates decided to diversify its economy through tourism. Led by Dubai, the country developed strategies to open itself up to foreign investment and improve its reception facilities.

Between 1995 and 1999, the average annual growth rate for international tourist arrivals to Dubai was 17.3 per cent, with the country receiving more than 3 million tourists and receipts of US$713 million in 1999.[89] According to Sheikh Mohamed Ben Rached Al-Maktoum, Arab Emirates Minister of Defence and crown prince of Dubai, growth in the tourism sector will increase six-fold over the next ten years and large-scale projects are in the works.[90]

Factors that contributed to the increase in tourist traffic include:

- the presence of large foreign-owned hotel chains: Best Western, Crowne Plaza, Hilton, InterContinental, Howard Johnson, Hyatt, Le Méridien, Marriott, Regent, Renaissance, Ritz-Carlton, Sheraton, Sofitel and many others. From 1995 to 1998 the number of hotels increased by 10.7 per cent, going from 233 to 258, and the number of apartment hotels rose from 3,000 to 3,936;

- the ratification of many open skies agreements, which helped boost the number of airlines serving the region from 53 to 89 between 1993 and 1998: Air Canada, Air France, American Airlines, British Airways, Cathay Pacific, Delta Airlines, KLM, Lufthansa, Qantas, Singapore Airlines, SwissAir, Thai Airlines, etc. At 18 per cent, Dubai Airport's annual growth rate in air traffic is far higher than the world average of 5 per cent.[91] Dubai International Airport spent approximately US$540 million to raise its capacity to 22 million passengers annually, helping make Dubai the tourism industry leader for the United Arab Emirates. The expansion of a third terminal, which would require another $500-600 million, is currently at the planning stage. The airport could double its capacity by 2018, enabling it to handle more than 40 million passengers. Emirates Airlines has established a code-sharing agreement with Thai Airways between Bangkok and Dubai;

- the rapid growth of the cruise sector. In 1993, only one cruise ship put in at Dubai; by 1999 the number had risen to 26;

- expansion of the distribution network. In 1999, there were 800 tour operators in Dubai, compared to only 407 in 1995. The number of international tour operators offering the destination in key markets grew from 258 in 1995-96 to 1,674 in 1998-99;

- promotional efforts by the Department of Tourism & Commerce Marketing (DTCM) and its 15 overseas offices contributed significantly to the increase in tourism;

- development of partnerships. Dubai has positioned itself as the sports capital of the Middle East. Partnerships between the government and the private sector have laid the groundwork for current and upcoming projects in several areas: infrastructure, heritage, hotels, and recreational complexes such as Magic World. Rooted in Arabic culture, this theme park is scheduled to open in autumn 2001.The most ambitious of Dubai's upcoming tourism projects is the construction, over the next several years, of a beach resort on an artificial island shaped like an enormous, 17-branch palm tree. Boasting some 2,000 villas, roughly 40 luxury hotels, shopping centres and a giant water park, the island will add approximately 120 km of coastline to the country's existing beaches.

---

[89] WTO, Tourism Market Trends 2000 Edition–Middle East, p. 79-81 and WTO, Tourism Market Trends 2001 Edition–Middle East.

[90] Luke PHILIPPS, "Une station balnéaire comme un palmier géant," *La Presse*, May 5, 2001, H10.

[91] Susan HACK, "Pyramid Schemes," *Fortune*, April 16, 2001, p. 450.

III.4.4 SUSTAINABLE DEVELOPMENT: A WINNING STRATEGY AND SIGNIFICANT CHALLENGE

In the 1990s, destinations concentrated on increasing their range of products, improving the quality and variety of complementary activities (e.g., pleasure boating, excursions, rafting and hiking) and offering better organized cultural activities. Today, the emphasis is on developing a sustainable tourism industry, one that provides economic benefits without harming the environment or society.

Globalization opens regions up to the free market economy and the growth of mass tourism puts pressure on the environment. Together, they speed up the exploitation of a region's natural, cultural and social resources. In spite of increasing pressure from a variety of economic, social and political groups overly focussed on short-term benefits, public authorities must define a long-term vision. Destinations must succeed in reconciling economy with ecology, development with the environment, and international trade with the protection of its social and cultural identity.[92]

Given the leitmotifs of *BALANCE* and *HARMONY*, destinations need to implement a form of controlled liberalization that is consistent with sustainable development.[93] This implies well-planned development, regulated growth and a clampdown on abusive practices. It means emphasizing added value and distinction: in other words, the quality, not the quantity, of growth. A major issue for tourism growth today is how to limit the number of visitors to fragile yet popular sites (see box). Also, destinations must strive to integrate visitors without being assimilated themselves. Rather than protectionism, these efforts should be seen as respect for cultural identities, the preservation of authenticity and the promotion of diversity.[94]

---

[92] Francesco FRANGIALLI, "Une vision, trois chantiers, une stratégie," Madrid, January 2001.

[93] Ibid.

[94] Ibid.

Visitor Flow Management: A Way to Prevent Overcrowding[95]

The term "carrying capacity" is crucial to the concept of sustainable tourism and refers to the number of people a site can comfortably accommodate while still offering heritage protection, visitor enjoyment, respect for local populations and optimal economic benefits. Determining this number is an indispensable first step to establishing a tourism flow management policy and a tourism manager must create such a policy within the framework of a partnership, not in isolation.

When no thought is given to a natural site's capacity, the site often ends up with an excess of reception facilities and solutions that are implemented haphazardly in an effort to keep pace with growing demand. This creates undifferentiated, "cookie-cutter" landscapes dominated by such eyesores as enormous parking lots, built to accommodate overcrowded trails or lookouts.

Measures to prevent overcrowding:

- stagger visitors in time: introduce early-bird, week-day or off-season specials, to increase attendance during these times;

- stagger visitors in space: set up off-site reception facilities to delay tourist arrivals;

- require greater effort: keep trails rugged, build parking lots further away;

- increase the cost: adjust entrance and parking fees;

- organize the physical area: spread visitors throughout the site, set up barriers and out-of-bounds areas;

- transportation: create no-car zones, provide shuttles;

- build additional structures: interpretation centres, site replicas;

- disseminate information: peak periods to be avoided, peripheral sites in case of congestion and alternate routes;

- marketing methods: pre-confirmed reservations, mandatory guided tours, awareness campaigns aimed at tour guides and operators.

In 1998, the directors of the Ordesa National Park in Spain closed the park to private vehicular traffic and moved the parking lot to the entrance, immediately outside the park's boundaries. A shuttle leaving every 15 to 30 minutes takes visitors into the park and access is limited to 1,800 visitors per day.

---

[95] Anne VOURC'H, "La capacité d'accueil – une notion essentielle dans les sites naturels," *Espaces*, No. 166, December 1999, p. 18-22.

From the outset, sustainable development has been defined as "development that meets the needs of the present without compromising the ability of future generations to meet their own needs."[96] This concept must be implemented on all fronts—economic, social, cultural and environmental. Of course, reconciling economic profit with heritage protection and social development with visitor enjoyment is not an easy task, particularly when culture and nature are considered both as resources to be protected and commodities to be exploited. However, local authorities must take on the task of protecting the rights of populations and regions that have been opened up to tourism: the natural and cultural environments on which tourism is based must be preserved and the guidelines for sustainable development can show the way. They also provide the framework for multinationals to co-operate with and become involved in destination development.

One of the most fundamental and effective means of reducing the negative impacts of mass tourism so often associated with the growth of large multinational groups is education. Tourist-generating countries must find a way to make their travellers ponder the impact of their activities and the influence of tourism on the world,[97] while destinations must convey the purpose and justification of their conservation efforts to both local inhabitants and the visiting public. Another contributing factor to balanced development getting local communities involved in project planning and implementation, regulating development and sharing profits. This enables them to exercise their rights and take part in development rather than have it inflicted upon them.

There are numerous examples of local authorities taking steps to protect the environment. The box below outlines one such example.

The Lascaux Cave at Montignac, Dorgogne, France
Restoration of an Endangered Site[98]

The Magdalenian cave in Lascaux, France, was inhabited by the last great Palaeolithic civilization in Europe and contains some of the most beautiful examples of cave painting in the world. It was discovered on September 12, 1940, and was named a historic site on December 27 of the same year. In 1948, the cave was opened to the public but, over the years, in spite of a variety of protective measures, the constant flow of tourists began to affect the site. Human impact took many forms: the entrance was enlarged, amenities were installed and the floor was lowered. Also, excessive quantities of carbon dioxide generated by the visitors' breath caused the wall and ceiling paintings to fade. There was evidence of biological contamination (large patches of algae, ferns, mosses and mushrooms began to flourish) and thin layers of calcite began to form, threatening to obscure some of the paintings. To stem this deterioration, authorities closed the cave in 1963 and launched a campaign to restore the site to its original state.

Lascaux was saved. Today, only scientists may visit the actual site and access is limited to 5 people per day, 5 days per week. Some 200 metres away, Lascaux II, created by a number of painters and sculptors working from a scanned copy of the original, opened in 1983. This replica offers the public an accurate although partial reproduction of one of the most famous examples of Upper Palaeolithic cave painting.

Another effective means of ensuring sustainable development is by awarding a "seal of approval" to any product or company associated with tourism, as a means of acknowledging its positive efforts. For example, it could be awarded to a hotel company that chooses a style of architecture in keeping with its surroundings or tries to minimize its environmental impact by managing its waste, conserving energy and water, building infrastructures that benefit the community and hiring and training local workers. Other examples of positive effort include an airline company that invests in air pollution research or a tour operator that provides

---

[96] World Commission on Environment and Development's–Brundtland Commission, 1987.

[97] The World Ethics Code established by the WTO represents a first step in this direction.

[98] [http://fr.encyclopedia.yahoo.com/articles/ni/ni_373_p0.html]

maximum visitor enjoyment without endangering resources, provides its clientele with relevant information and establishes partnerships with complementary destination businesses. Local authorities could then promote the seal by telling visitors about the companies' positive behaviour.

Strategies Adopted by the Egyptian Ministry of Tourism[99]

The reforms introduced by the Egyptian Ministry of Tourism to promote sustainable development and liberalize tourism services have directly contributed to the industry's considerable growth in that country. Since 1993, the number of tourists arriving in Egypt has grown by an average of 12 per cent each year, reaching 5.5 million in 2000. Tourist receipts have also increased, by an average of 12.5 per cent annually, for a total of US$4.3 billion. The addition of 30,000 rooms had brought the total hotel capacity to 114,000 rooms by the end of 2000 and, between 1993 and 2000, overnight stays grew by an average of 9.9 per cent annually, for a total of 33 million overnights and an occupancy rate of 73 per cent.

Certain measures implemented in the air travel sector helped open Egypt's borders to tourists:

- improvements to existing airports, specifically those in Hurghada, Cairo, Luxor and Sharm El Sheikh;

- liberalized access to all airports and all tourist destinations for all foreign carriers wishing to offer regular or charter flights, with no reduction in rights at Cairo Airport;

- an increase in regular domestic flights by private Egyptian carriers;

- civil aviation authorities changed their status and became holding companies.

The Ministry of Tourism is encouraging large hotel management companies to do business there, so Egypt can benefit from their international reputations and impressive reservation systems. This strategy is also laying the groundwork for Egypt to set up multinational consortia: a tried and true method already used successfully by the Egyptian tourism industry. Within the context of regional development, the Ministry has implemented a variety of incentives designed to promote tourism development:

- the introduction of a nominal rate for land purchases (US$1 per square metre) and a ten-year payment schedule: a down payment of 20 per cent, followed by a three-year grace period with the balance to be paid over the following seven years; the right to transfer capital and gains;

- a 5 per cent reduction in import duties on all products associated with the project and tax breaks for a period of up to 10 years from the project start date.

In return, the Egyptian government imposes two conditions: the company must comply fully with all environmental regulations and must assume all costs pertaining to infrastructures at the project site.

---

[99] Mamdouh EL BELTAGUI and Mohamed SAKR, *Seminar on globalization and its challenges and opportunities for tourism development in the Middle East and North Africa*, Cairo, Egypt, May 20, 2001.

Strategies Adopted by the Egyptian Ministry of Tourism (cont'd)

All government-run tourism-based establishments are subject to privatization, with the exception of several hotels of significant historic value. The Ministry also supports the following initiatives:

- mergers or strategic alliances among small companies, enabling them to compete more effectively with larger groups;

- training in new technology and new management and marketing strategies;

- improvements to reception and access facilities: public transit systems, customs, etc.;

- public awareness campaigns on environmental issues.

Sustainable Development:
In keeping with the Ministry's guidelines for sustainable development–"Economically feasible; Socially acceptable; Environmentally sound"–companies must meet certain eligibility criteria:

- projects must conform to national development goals;

- project location criteria must reduce regional disparities and exploit untapped resources;

- projects absolutely must involve local communities, maximize employment opportunities and train local populations;

- environmental impact studies must be conducted prior to project approval.

The Ministry has also established limits regarding the number of cruises allowed on the Nile, access to historic sites and the number of hotels and resorts that can be built around the Red Sea and south of the Sinai. Regional zoning laws limiting development, structural and architectural standards, restricted motorized traffic, flora and fauna protection and energy conservation are just some of the Ministry 's environmental protection measures.

It would be impossible for major groups to standardize and integrate the entire tourism industry; smaller players also have a role to play, and there should be room for all types and sizes of business ventures. John Naisbitt, a guru of trend forecast and analysis, has stated: "Global paradox: the bigger the world economy, the more powerful its smallest players. The larger the system, the smaller and more powerful and important the parts." In addition to mass tourism and the standardized products provided by international companies, there must be diversification, specialization and segmentation. As mentioned earlier, the major tourism groups generate an influx of visitors that gives smaller businesses an opportunity to create complementary activities. Whereas conventional tourism products can save tourists time and make them feel more secure, specialization fulfils their needs for individuality, independence, discovery and authenticity. Destinations need to develop products that address these needs, designed for a clientele prepared to step outside the limits of the "all-inclusive" packages offered by tour operators. In keeping with this trend, Costa Rica has developed eco-tourism, France has successfully promoted barge trips along its restored canals and Australia is attracting back-packers who want to discover the country on their own.

III.4.5 DEVELOPING LOCAL INDUSTRY: A PROFITABLE UNDERTAKING

Destinations need to promote the growth of local industry and develop national associations in order to compete more effectively with major groups.

A study conducted by Rodenburg in 1980 showed that small companies performed better than large multinationals when it came to achieving economic goals such as increased profits, trade and investment, job creation, entrepreneurship, and minimal negative social and cultural impacts. According to a study done in Indonesia in 1998, this comparison still holds true today. In fact, the study shows that small and medium-sized businesses fulfil two functions: they stimulate innovation and entrepreneurship in the local economy and they provide jobs. In contrast to its previous policy of automatically conferring large grants to attract foreign investment, towards the end of the 1980s the EU began to target small and medium-sized businesses and local development, on the grounds that they lay the foundation for entrepreneurship and job creation within the community. Events in Wales bear this out: of the 216 projects approved by the Wales Tourist Board between 1990 and 1995, all either attained or surpassed their job creation goals.

III.4.6 INCREASING A DESTINATION'S APPEAL

When a city or region has a wealth of cultural attractions, special events or historic interest, tourism industry players–hotel companies, airlines, the distribution network–will take note and begin developing large-scale markets for that destination. However, there is a great deal of competition among destinations and the increasingly savvy and demanding traveller of today is anxious to get the most from his travel money.

Given these circumstances, a destination must create a strong and unique identity for itself. As long as this identity is based on pull products with sufficient appeal to interest the major players in world tourism, the destination can develop a product of international quality. This brand image becomes the foundation for a well-targeted communications campaign that will distinguish the destination from its competitors and position it in the traveller's mind. The image will also help pave the way for equitable agreements with tour operators that facilitate destination-marketing initiatives; since governments have withdrawn from this area, such initiatives often face financial obstacles.

In the world of e-commerce, developing a brand image is a major financial investment. Obviously, organizations with a well-established image can more easily transfer this identify to the e-commerce environment. For new businesses operating solely on the Internet, acquiring brand recognition is an extremely expensive proposition.

III.4.7 MAKING NEW INFORMATION TECHNOLOGIES PROFITABLE

In spite of rapid growth in information technology and telecommunications, and the meteoric rise of e-commerce, most destination management organizations (DMOs) only began doing business over the Internet in the mid-1990s. Yet the Internet's global network provides companies with the means to exchange information and conduct transactions. For DMOs, the Internet offers amazing potential with respect to the dissemination of information since it allows them to:
- reach large numbers of consumers and transmit information and offer products at a relatively low cost;
- provide complete and more reliable information;
- make client reservations quickly and efficiently;
- reduce the costs associated with producing and distributing printed materials.

However, the technology sector's recent poor performance has done nothing to calm the fears of certain organizations regarding e-commerce. Given the financial markets' infatuation with new technologies, a correction was inevitable. Since January 2000, 555 Internet companies around the world have ceased operations, more than 60 per cent of them in the first 6 months of 2001. In e-commerce, the business-to-consumer (B2C) sector was hardest hit, with 328 companies closing their doors. In spite of the downturn in American e-commerce, companies should not lose sight of the fact that on-line shopping is still growing in popularity and that consumers feel increasingly confident using this medium.

Chart 22
Monthly Variations in On-line Shopping in the U.S.

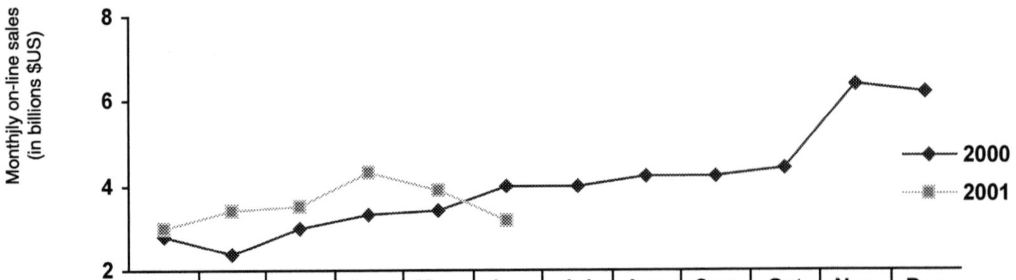

Monthly on-line sales (in billions $US)

	Jan	Feb	Mar	Apr	May	Jun	Jul	Aug	Sep	Oct	Nov	Dec
◆ 2000	2,8	2,4	3,0	3,3	3,4	4,0	4,0	4,2	4,2	4,4	6,4	6,2
▩ 2001	3,0	3,4	3,5	4,3	3,9	3,2						

Source: Forrester Research (2001)

In the midst of this instability, the on-line travel sector is showing some promise with its major players posting surprising earnings. The U.S. industry leader, Travelocity, has declared a profit more than a quarter ahead of schedule and Expedia more than 12 months earlier than expected. The Hotel Reservations Networks agency (HRN) is forecasting profits of more than US$16 million by the end of the present fiscal year. After re-focussing its activities on travel products, Priceline.com should show a first-time profit by the second quarter of 2001.These figures obviously have an impact on the companies' stock-market performance. Following the drop of the technology market in 2000, the stock prices of travel industry leaders began rising again. Between January 1 and June 30, 2001, Priceline.com's share value increased by 590 per cent, Expedia's by 387 per cent, Travelocity's by 153 per cent and Cheap Tickets' by 71 per cent. During the same period, the U.S. technology-weighted composite index, Nasdaq, dropped by slightly more than 12 per cent. At a time when many of the companies rooted in the new economy are being buffeted by the global economic downturn, it is only natural to fear another few months of disappointing growth for the industry. Yet, many analysts are predicting that the stagnant economy will draw bargain-hunters to the Internet in increasing numbers.

Chart 23
Increase (%) in Share Values of Virtual Agencies (January to June 2001)

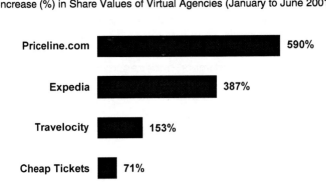

Priceline.com	590%
Expedia	387%
Travelocity	153%
Cheap Tickets	71%

Source: CNET

III.4.8 SPECIALIZATION

In order to sustain tourism development in their region, DMOs need to make greater use of the Internet. Although some destinations have spent millions of dollars setting up extremely high-tech systems, these days a Web site can be created for much less. Faced with strong competition based solely on price, many companies will successfully carve out a niche for themselves in the on-line travel market by specializing. The challenge for DMOs will be to present their destination as a unique product. Non-specialized travel agencies such as Travelocity.com and eBookers.com lack the expertise needed to successfully promote a destination. DMOs provide an opportunity to expand and improve the content on these sites so Internet surfers will visit more regularly. Observers agree that the search for more specialized information will be the justification behind a number of things in the next few years, notably alliances and acquisitions. The strategy of developing a presence on non-specialized agency sites is really a question of accessibility for DMOs, since these sites receive the greatest number of hits. A manager can create the most effective site on the Web, but if nobody knows about it, it is of no use to the organization.

III.4.9 TRANSACTIONAL WEB SITES: AN EXPENSIVE SOLUTION

Once prospective clients have arrived at your site and you have presented a range of potentially interesting products, you must also offer every service available to close the sale. Organizations operating in the on-line market have various transactional options. E-commerce is much more than a technological development; it constitutes a whole new way of doing business. There are many challenges to be overcome before products can be sold over the Web, so it is crucial that the organization develop an effective e-business strategy as part of its overall vision.

Technology makes it possible for destinations to set up Web sites where travellers can purchase travel products. To offer a variety of products through a single site, DMOs cannot afford to ignore the many small and medium-sized businesses, many of whom are not on the Web, that make up the bulk of the travel industry. A desire to remain on an equal footing with all its suppliers may well force a destination to set up a technological environment that can process client reservations in real time. However, with most DMOs being publicly funded, few of them have the financial means to set up such a system, let alone maintain and upgrade it to keep pace with technological innovations. The question is, how can this investment be recouped? Can the expense be justified by the traffic on the site? The myth of Web sites that are "practically free" often distorts a company's impression of the actual cost of doing business over the Internet.

Ultimately, regardless of the method chosen, the main goal of DMOs is still to promote a destination. However, the organization also represents the interests of several suppliers, and one may well question whether its business activities are in conflict with its primary objective. Today, the top travel agencies spend significant amounts creating easy-to-use, effective Web sites. Do the DMOs have the financial resources and technical expertise to compete directly with these major players?

DMOs who do not wish to be directly involved in e-transactions can create links on their official site to the top on-line travel agencies or the reservation systems of their suppliers.

III.4.10 A NEW KIND OF CONSUMER

The tourism industry has to face the facts: the way travellers plan trips has changed with the advent of the information age. As shown in Chart 24 below, the Internet has become a preferred source of information. On-line research is now part of the tourism experience, and the more comfortable consumers become with this technology, the more on-line services they will demand. No longer content to simply research the destinations offered and their asking price, consumers now want to purchase their trips on-line as well.

This new way of shopping has got on-line tourism-based businesses scrambling to offer value-added services. One way to bolster the value of a product or service is to provide consumers with information that helps them make the best decision. Tourism is an information-based industry; its product–travel–is a complex one that requires a great deal of research so information plays a fundamental role. Internet users demand more detailed content, so they can do more than simply research packages and make on-line reservations. New technology enables organizations to present more appealing and up-to-date Web material. The question of price, although generally a factor in on-line purchases, is no longer enough to convince buyers. The development of global markets over the Net gives

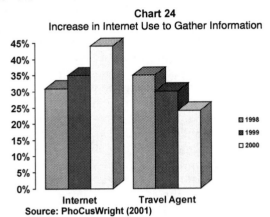

Chart 24
Increase in Internet Use to Gather Information

Source: PhoCusWright (2001)

tourists access to any products, anywhere in the world, so data on travel and tourism must be instantly accessible. Adding value to content is a shift that coincides with the consumer's increasingly active role in travel planning.

III.4.11 THE ROLE OF "INFOMEDIARY"

One of tourism's essential paradoxes is that, 90 per cent of the time, a traveller's decision to visit a destination is motivated by advertising done by the destination management organization. However, it is the other players–hotels, attractions, travel agencies–rather than the DMO who actually reap most of the economic benefits[100]. Acting as intermediaries between suppliers of products and services and consumers, DMOs disseminate information and promote destinations. Although this level of involvement has worked in the past, consumer needs are changing, and with them the conditions under which these organizations operate, forcing them to adopt the new role of "infomediary": either directly or indirectly they are becoming more involved in the purchasing process.

Infomediaries sell neither goods nor services; rather, their role is to facilitate the transaction between consumer and business. It is increasingly difficult for travellers to obtain comprehensive information because of the proliferation of travel-related Web sites. Although experienced Internet users can easily navigate their way through the many sites and links, most people who go on the Net–especially those who are unfamiliar with it–find the sheer quantity of information confusing. The DMO should therefore redefine itself as a "hub," where the traveller can quickly access the necessary information.

III.4.12 CUSTOMER LOYALTY

Destination management organizations deal with the same problem that plagues most e-commerce sites: 60 per cent of on-line shoppers do not have a favourite e-tailer.[101] To boost customer loyalty, DMOs are finding new ways to make the consumer more involved in the decision-making process.

A key component to the success of an infomediary is **trust**. Unless a DMO can guarantee consumers that the personal information they disclose in cyberspace will be completely secure, all its efforts will be in vain.

The Internet is about more than just conducting business on-line. Once an organization has succeeded in getting the visitor's attention, how can it convince him to try its products? Since knowing

---

[100] Michael BORGE, *Involving The DMO's In A Larger Part of The Value Chain*, Enter 2000.
[101] Michael CARLIER, Le voyage en ligne, ESPACECOM, July 2001.

your customer is an absolute prerequisite to succeeding on the Internet, companies these days are drawing up extensive customer-survey strategies. Based on the principle that each consumer is unique, sophisticated computer programs make it possible for DMOs to treat each traveller differently, according to his interests and preferences. By offering tailored products and services, it can establish personal relationships with consumers. According to a study done by IDC, visitors with a personal profile on a Web site visit such sites 2 to 4 times more often than they do traditional sites.

Another Internet characteristic that tends to increase buyer involvement is the concept of community. A virtual community is basically a group of people with one or more common interests. By creating such a community, the DMO enables its clientele to exchange information about the products and services offered and to discuss their experiences as consumers. Such discussion brings travellers closer together and also creates a link between travellers and the organization. This information enables DMOs to better understand their clients' needs and improve their products and services based on what they have learned.

The destinations that will profit most from the Net are those whose sites provide detailed content, guaranteed confidentiality and one-stop shopping for all the customer's travel needs.

III.5 DECISIONAL MODEL FOR DESTINATIONS

This section dealing with choices and strategies for destinations concludes with a decisional model (see below). While it does not provide any answers, it does raise some questions designed to help destinations successfully distinguish themselves from their global competitors.

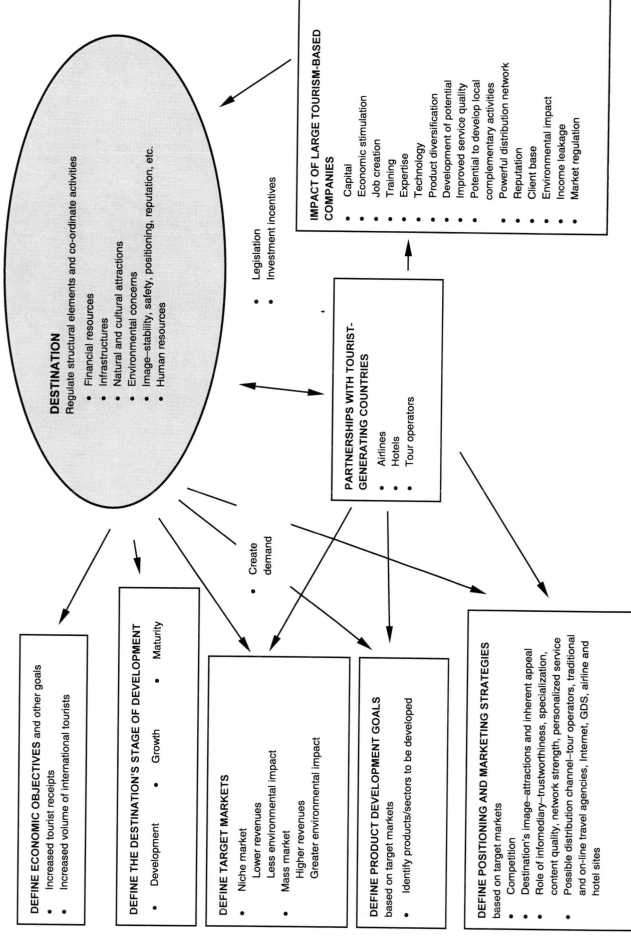

Decisional Model for Destinations

DESTINATION
Regulate structural elements and co-ordinate activities
- Financial resources
- Infrastructures
- Natural and cultural attractions
- Environmental concerns
- Image–stability, safety, positioning, reputation, etc.
- Human resources

- Legislation
- Investment incentives

IMPACT OF LARGE TOURISM-BASED COMPANIES
- Capital
- Economic stimulation
- Job creation
- Training
- Expertise
- Technology
- Product diversification
- Development of potential
- Improved service quality
- Potential to develop local complementary activities
- Powerful distribution network
- Reputation
- Client base
- Environmental impact
- Income leakage
- Market regulation

PARTNERSHIPS WITH TOURIST-GENERATING COUNTRIES
- Airlines
- Hotels
- Tour operators

- Create demand

DEFINE ECONOMIC OBJECTIVES and other goals
- Increased tourist receipts
- Increased volume of international tourists

DEFINE THE DESTINATION'S STAGE OF DEVELOPMENT
- Development
- Growth
- Maturity

DEFINE TARGET MARKETS
- Niche market
  - Lower revenues
  - Less environmental impact
- Mass market
  - Higher revenues
  - Greater environmental impact

DEFINE PRODUCT DEVELOPMENT GOALS
based on target markets
- Identify products/sectors to be developed

DEFINE POSITIONING AND MARKETING STRATEGIES
based on target markets
- Competition
- Destination's image–attractions and inherent appeal
- Role of infomediary–trustworthiness, specialization, content quality, network strength, personalized service
- Possible distribution channel–tour operators, traditional and on-line travel agencies, Internet, GDS, airline and hotel sites

CONCLUSION

The tourism industry is evolving in a constantly-changing business environment. Economic globalization, more accessible markets and the advent of new technologies have created a boom in travelling and have profoundly affected tourism-based businesses. Changes in the hotel and airline industries and distribution network are forcing firms and destinations to alter their practices and are encouraging the emergence of non-traditional entities. As we have seen, to successfully carve out a place for themselves on national and international markets, destinations and small and medium-sized businesses must adapt by devising new management, development and marketing strategies. Regardless of the methods used, they must be innovative, creative and suitably equipped with new technology to distinguish themselves and target specific market niches.

"Tourism and the Trend Towards Consolidation" discusses structural changes that, to be effective, must be part of an overall movement to foster excellence. To this end, the travel industry as a whole must strive to properly satisfy the needs and desires of the most important player in the tourism value chain: the tourist.

PART 4: TOURISM AND CONSOLIDATION: SUPPLEMENTAL INFORMATION

IV.1 THE AIRLINE INDUSTRY

Table 28

Countries Who Have Signed Bilateral Open Skies Agreements with the United States

No.	Year	Month	Country	Remarks
77	2000	1	Slovak Republic	Open skies accord
76	1999	12	Portugal	Open skies accord
75	1999	12	Dominican Republic	Open skies accord
74	1999	11	Tanzania	Open skies accord
73	1999	10	Qatar	Open skies accord
72	1999	8	Argentina	Open skies accord
71	1999	5	Bahrain	Open skies accord
70	1999	4	United Arab Emirates	Open skies accord
69	1999	4	Pakistan	Open skies accord
65	1998	11	Italy	Open skies accord
64	1998	5	Peru	Open skies accord
63	1998	4	Korea	Open skies accord
62	1998	4	France	Major liberalization
61	1998	2	Uzbekistan	Open skies accord
59	1997	12	Netherlands Antilles	Open skies accord
58	1997	12	Romania	Open skies accord
57	1997	10	Chile	Open skies accord
55	1997	7	Aruba	Open skies accord
53	1997	6	Malaysia	Open skies accord
52	1997	5	New Zealand	Open skies accord
51	1997	5	Ukraine	New agreement
50	1997	5	Nicaragua	Open skies accord
49	1997	4	Costa Rica	Open skies accord
48	1997	4	Honduras	Open skies accord
47	1997	4	El Salvador	Open skies accord
46	1997	4	Guatemala	Open skies accord
45	1997	3	Panama	Open skies accord
44	1997	3	Taiwan	Open skies accord
43	1997	2	Brunei	Open skies accord
42	1997	1	Singapore	Open skies accord
41	1996	11	Jordan	Open skies accord
39	1996	8	Pakistan	New agreement
38	1996	3	South Africa	New agreement
34	1996	2	Germany	Open skies accord
33	1996	1	Thailand	New agreement
30	1995	12	Czech Republic	Open skies accord
28	1995	10	Macao	New agreement
26	1995	9	Hong Kong	New agreement
24	1995	6	United Kingdom	Under discussion
23	1995	5	Austria	Open skies accord
22	1995	5	Belgium	Open skies accord
21	1995	5	Denmark	Open skies accord
20	1995	5	Finland	Open skies accord
19	1995	5	Iceland	Open skies accord
18	1995	5	Luxembourg	Open skies accord
17	1995	5	Norway	Open skies accord
15	1995	5	Sweden	Open skies accord
14	1995	5	Switzerland	Open skies accord
13	1995	4	Ukraine	New agreement
12	1995	2	Canada	New agreement

NORTHWEST AIRLINES AT A GLANCE

- Fourth largest carrier in the world
- Revenues: US$9.5 billion
- Destinations: 150
- Fleet: more than 400 planes (Boeing 727, 747 and 757; DC-9,DC-10; and Airbus A319 and A320)
- Employees: over 53,000
- Passengers: 56 million/year

Figure 1
Northwest Airlines and its Subsidiaries

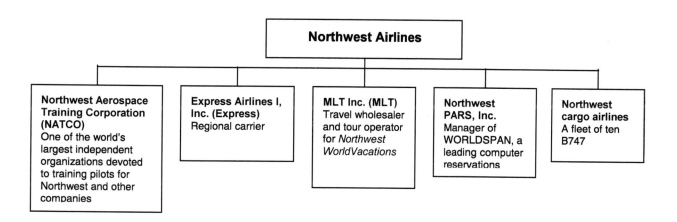

Table 29
Star Alliance at a Glance (June 2001)

	Air Canada (and regional subsidiaries)	Austrian Airlines (including Lauda and Tyrolean)	Air New Zealand (including Ansett Australia)	ANA	bmi British Midland	Varig	United Airlines
Total revenues (billions of $)	6.25	2.0	3.7	8.6	0.92	3.0	19.35
Revenue passenger miles (billions)	37.5	7.2	38.8	33.7	1.9	15.8	124.6
Passengers (millions)	31	8.4	21.8	43.2	6.0	11.0	87
Employees	45,000	8,000	22,966	14,639	6,309	17,740	100,819
Destinations	150	123	190	60	31	120	307
Fleet	376	94	191	144	60	87	604
Main hubs	Toronto, Montreal, Vancouver	Vienna, Innsbruck	Auckland, Los Angeles, Sydney	Tokyo, Osaka	London Heathrow	Rio de Janeiro, São Paulo	Chicago, Denver, San Francisco, Los Angeles, Washington, DC

	Lufthansa	Mexicana Airlines	SAS	Singapore Airlines	Thai Airways International	Total
Total revenues (billions of $)	11.3	1.0	4.66	4.6	3.0	68.38
Revenue passenger miles (billions)	53	7.8	13.3	37.5	25.7	396.8
Passengers (millions)	47	8.25	23.2	12.8	17.7	317.55
Employees	31,305	6,900	27,767	14,600	25,782	322,857
Destinations	349	49	92	119	73	894
Fleet	324	58	190	91	80	2,299
Main hubs	Frankfurt, Munich	Mexico City	Copenhagen, Oslo, Stockholm	Singapore	Bangkok, Chiang Mai, Phuket, Hat Yai	N/A*

*not applicable
Source: Star-alliance.com

Table 30
oneworld at a Glance (June 2001)

	oneworld	Aer Lingus	American Airlines	BRITISH AIRWAYS	Cathay Pacific	Finnair	Iberia	LanChile	Qantas
Destinations	565	31	239	230	44	61	97	44	89
Countries	135	9	52	96	27	30	39	17	21
Passengers (m)	209	6	95	41	10	8	26	4	20
Employees	270,044	5,635	113,806	63,000	13,159	9,214	27,005	9,207	29,217
Fleet	1,852	36	1,007	324	64	57	167	40	152
Operating revenues (m)	--	I£ 832	US$17,730	£ 9,260*	HK$34,520	FIM 9,469	Pts 646,325	US$1,425	A$9,107
Operating expenses (m)	--	I£ 781	US$16,574	£ 8,880*	HK$29,240	FIM 9,172	Pts 636,700	US$1,342	A$8,291
Operating profit (m)	--	I£ 51	US$1,156	£ 380*	HK$5,280	FIM 297	Pts 9,625	US$83	A$602
Frequent flyer program	Yes	TAB (Travel Award Bonus)	AADVANTAGE	Executive Club	Asia Miles	Finnair Plus	Iberia Plus	LanPass	Qantas Frequent Flyer
Year founded	Feb. 1, 1999	1936	Origins go back to 1926	Origins go back to 1919	1946	1923	1927	1929	1920
Ownership	--	95% owned by the Irish Government. 5% owned by employees	Wholly owned subsidiary of AMR Corporation; a publicly traded company on the New York Stock Exchange	Publicly quoted company, with shares traded on the London and New York Stock Exchanges	Public company listed on the Hong Kong and London Stock Exchanges. Major shareholders are Swire Pacific Ltd (45.1%) and CITIC Pacific Ltd (25.4%)	Publicly quoted on Helsinki Stock Exchange and in SEAQ system on the London Stock Exchange. Majority shareholder is the Finnish government with 59%	9% owned by British Airways, 1% by American Airlines, 30% by institutions, 60% floating	Publicly traded company, with 7.8% traded on the New York Stock Exchange, and 9.1% traded on the Santiago Stock Exchange in Chile. Majority shareholders hold the remaining 83.1% of the Company.	Public company listed on the Australian Stock Exchange. British Airways is a major shareholder with 25%
Related carriers	--	--	American Eagle Business Express	BRAL, British Mediterranean, Brymon, CityFlyer Express, Comair, Deutsche BA, GB Airways, Loganair, Maersk Air UK, NJI, Regional Air, Sun-Air, Zambian Air Services	--	--	Binter Mediterraneo, Iberia Regional (Air Nostrum)	Ladeco, LanPerú	Airlink, Eastern Australia Southern Australia Airlines, Sunstate Airlines

Notes: All figures are for main airline and related carriers covered by the oneworld agreement. All financial figures are for the most recent fiscal year. Operating figures the latest published.
*Figures do not include BA non-owned franchise.

American Airlines at a Glance

- Revenues: US$17.73 million
- Destinations: 239
- Employees: 113,806
- Passengers: 95 million/year
- Fleet: 1,007 aircraft, majority made by Boeing, with some Fokker and Airbus

Figure 2
American Airlines: Associates and Partners

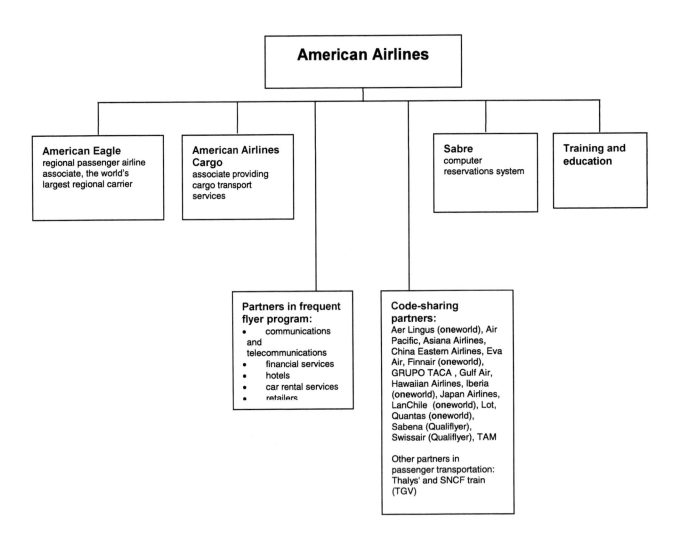

Lufthansa at a Glance

- Revenues: US$11.3 billion
- Destinations: 349
- Employees: 31,305
- Passengers: 47 million/year
- Fleet: 324 aircraft, majority made by Boeing and Airbus — in equal numbers —, some Avro and Canadair Jet

Subsidiaries and associated companies

more than 250 in the following sectors:
- passenger transportation
- logistics
- technology
- catering services
- tourism
- information technology
- ground services

Code-sharing partners

South African Airways, Adria Airways, Air Baltic, Air Dolomiti, Croatia Airlines, Czech Airlines (only on a few routes), Luxair, Qatar Airways, Spanair

Regional partners

Augsburg Airways, Cirrus Airlines, Contact Air, Rheintalflug, Air Littoral and Cimber Air (on selected routes)

Table 31
SkyTeam at a Glance (July 2001)

	SkyTeam	Aeromexico	Air France	DELTA	Korean Air	CSA
Destinations	472 (unduplicated)	50	206	241	69	61
Countries	112 (unduplicated)	7	91	36	26	38
Major hubs	Mexico City Paris-CDG Prague Atlanta Seoul	Mexico Monterrey GUADALAJARA Hermosillo	Paris-CDG Paris-Orly Lyon	Atlanta Salt Lake City Cincinnati Dallas-Ft. Worth New York Kennedy	Seoul Pusan Cheju	Prague
Daily departures	7,091	377	1,715	4,497	368	134
Annual passengers (m)	176.7	8.8	39	106	20.5	2.4
Web site address	www.skyteam.com	www.aeromexico.com	www.airfrance.com	www.delta.com	www.koreanair.com	www.czech-airlines.com
Year founded	2000	1934	1933	1924	1969	1923
Employees	Over 155,000	7,000	54,000 (as of April 1, 2000)	Over 74,000 (as of April 1, 2000)	Over 16,000 (as of April 1, 2000)	4,135
Fleet	1,013	68	220 subsonic 6 Concorde	584	107	28
Operating income		US$70 million (YE Mar. 31, 2000)	€1.176 billion (YE Mar. 31, 2000)	US$1.87 billion (YE June 30, 1999)	US$159 million (YE Dec. 31, 1999)	1.222 billion CZK
Net income		US$60 million (YE Mar. 31, 2000)	€354 million (YE Mar. 31, 2000)	US$1.1 billion (YE June 30, 1999)	US$226 million (YE Dec. 31, 1999)	37 million CZK
Operating revenue		US$1.2 billion (YE Mar. 31, 2000)	€10.3 billion (YE Mar. 31, 2000)	US$14.7 billion (YE June 30, 1999)	US$4.7 billion (YE Dec. 31, 1999)	12.2 billion CZK
Frequent flyer members	35 million	0.9 million	3 million	24 million	7 million	53,151
Frequent flyer program		Club Premier	Fréquence Plus	SkyMiles	Skypass	OK Plus
Ownership		Grupo Cintra (holding company)	Employees: 11% Public: 32% State: 57%	Employees: 11% Public: 89%	Employees: 2% Public: 98%	National Property Fund: 56% Consolidation Bank: 32% Other public: 12%

Source: SkyTeam.com

TABLE 32

Airline Investments in Online Travel Agencies

Air Canada	GetThere.com	equity investment
American	Travelocity.com	through Sabre
America West	GetThere.com Priceline.com	equity investment warrant
British Airways	Rosenbluth Interactive Biztravel.com	equity investment equity investment
Continental	Priceline.com Rosenbluth Interactive Biztravel.com	warrant equity investment equity investment
Delta	Priceline.com	equity investment, warrant
Northwest	GetThere.com Priceline.com	warrant warrant
TWA	Priceline.com	warrant
United	GetThere.com Buy.com	equity investment joint venture

IV.2 THE DISTRIBUTION NETWORK

Figure 3
Preussag Corporate Structure

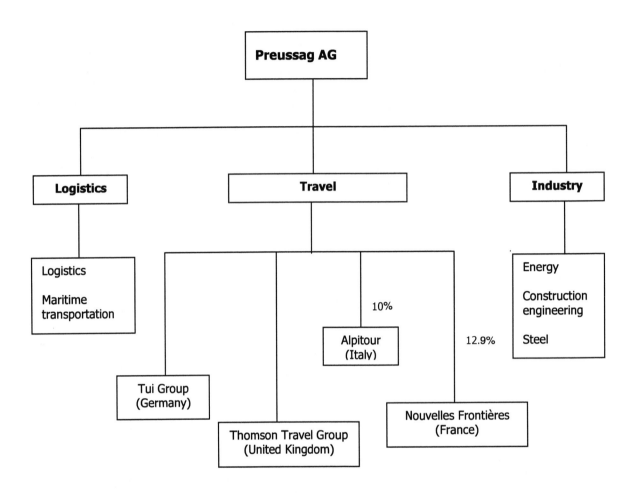

Preussag is:

⇒ a conglomerate of over 500 firms, including TUI Group, Thomson Travel Group and Nouvelles Frontières (12.9%)
⇒ annual sales of approximately US$19.2 billion
⇒ a 50 per cent increase in travel revenues in the year 1999
⇒ 90 planes, 3,600 travel agencies in 13 countries, 75 tour operator brands, both specialized and non-specialized, 21 inbound operators, 250 hotels and approximately 115,000 beds
⇒ over 80,000 employees

Table 33
Primary Brands in Each Group

Group	Tour operators	Travel agencies	Inbound operators	Air carriers	Hotels
TUI GROUP	TUI Schöne Ferien! 1-2-Fly Airtours Wolters Reisen L'tur	TUI Group VTB-VAB Reizen TUI Travel Centers	Ultramar Express Miltours TUI Hellas Travel Partner Bulgaria Tantur Travco	Hapag-Lloyd Flug	Riu, Grecotel, Iberotel, Grupotel, Dorfhotel Robinson Swiss Inn Nordotel Anfi del Mar
Thomson Travel Group	Thomson Holidays Skytours Club Freestyle Just Budget Travel Fritidresor Group Portland Direct	Lunn Poly Budget Travel Regional travel agencies Call centres	-	Britannia Airways	
Nouvelles Frontières	Nouvelles Frontières	Nouvelles Frontières	Nouvelles Frontières	Aerolyon Corsair	Paladien hotels/club

Recent transactions:

December 1998   Acquisition of a controlling share (50.1%) in the Thomas Cook Group, a British network of over 3,000 agencies in approximately 100 countries

February 1999   Take-over of the First chain of travel agencies
Acquisition of a controlling share (51%) in L'tur Tourismus AG

July 1999   Take-over of Touristik Union International GmbH & Co. KG

January 2000   The travel division Hapag Touristik Union becomes TUI Group GmbH

May 2000   Take-over of the Thomson Travel Group, the second largest British tour operator, for US$2.9 billion

November 2000   Acquisition of a 6 per cent interest in Nouvelles Frontières with the option of gradually increasing this share to 34.4 per cent by March 2002

December 2000   Sale of controlling share (50.1%) in Thomas Cook to C & N—to comply with European Union requirements concerning competition

February 2000   Creation of global network for travel professionals—TQ3 Travel Solutions—in partnership with various suppliers: Preussag (through its subsidiary, TUI), Maritz Travel Company (US), Internet Travel Group (Australia), Protravel (France) and Britannic Travel (England)

January 2001   Increases equity investment in Nouvelles Frontières to 12.9 per cent

May 2001   Acquisition of a 10 per cent interest in Alpitour—no. 1 Italian tour operator

Figure 4

Condor & Neckermann Touristik AG–Thomas Cook AG Corporate Structure

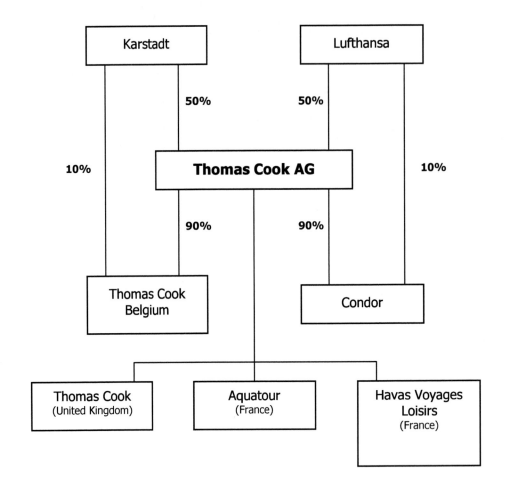

C & N Touristik AG is:

⇒ annual sales of over US$4 billion
⇒ more than 10 million clients
⇒ a fleet of 46 planes (Condor Flugdienst GmbH) and over 8.1 million passengers
⇒ a network of 2,191 agencies in Europe (Neckermann, Holiday Land, Havas Voyages, LHCC, Karstadt / Hertie, Reise Quelle, etc.)
⇒ 55 hotels / clubs (Iberostar, Aldiana and others) and 31,199 beds
⇒ an annual average of over 11,000 employees

Recent transactions:

September 1997   With Lufthansa, 50 per cent investment in Condor & Neckermann (merger of Touristik AG, NUR Touristik GMBH and Condor Flugdienst GmbH)

February 1999   Take-over of Aquatour (tour operator) and its 23 travel agencies in France

October 1999   Merger between Quelle Group and Karstadt AG

April 2000   Acquisition of all assets related to Havas Voyages leisure travel activities in France–394 travel agencies

December 2000   Take-over of Thomas Cook, third largest British travel group–7 tour operators, 1,100 travel agencies world-wide and 800 franchises, and JMC Airlines with its 27 new planes

May 2001   C & N Touristik AG changes its name to Thomas Cook AG and soon all travel activities in the Netherlands and Germany will be distributed under the Thomas Cook brand

July 2001   Purchase of 51 per cent interest in NUR Neckerman in Austria from Swiss group Kuoni, bringing its total shares to 100 per cent

Japan Travel Bureau is:

⇒ annual sales of US$14 billion
⇒ over 750 travel bureaux in 24 countries
⇒ 3 million clients
⇒ 12,400 employees
⇒ the parent company of Sunrise Tours

Figure 5
Carlson Companies Corporate Structure

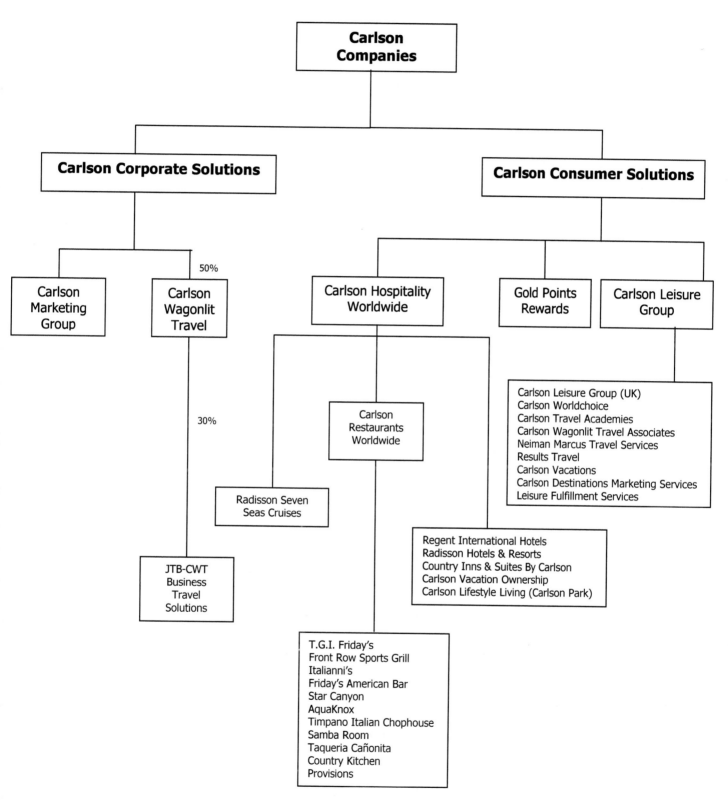

Carlson is:

⇒ one of the largest US private corporations
⇒ annual sales of US$31.4 billion (1999)
⇒ approximately 1,200 travel agencies world-wide
⇒ over 716 hotels and 129,344 rooms
⇒ some 638 restaurants operating under 9 brands in 52 countries
⇒ 5 cruise ships
⇒ 188,000 employees working in 140 countries
⇒ a group of reputable brands such as Radisson and Regent International under Carlson Hospitality Worldwide, Carlson Wagonlit Travel (co-owned with Accor) and Carlson Leisure Group

Recent transactions:

1999   Merger of Carlson's Leisure Travel Business in the United Kingdom with Thomas Cook

2000   Acquisition of Amtra Travel in Bangkok, Thailand
Joint venture with Panorama Leisure Travel in Indonesia
Sale of Thomas Cook to C & N

2001   Creation of JTB-CWT Travel Business Solutions—a partnership between Japan Travel Bureau (70%) and Carlson Wagonlit Travel (30%)

Figure 6

Accor Corporate Structure

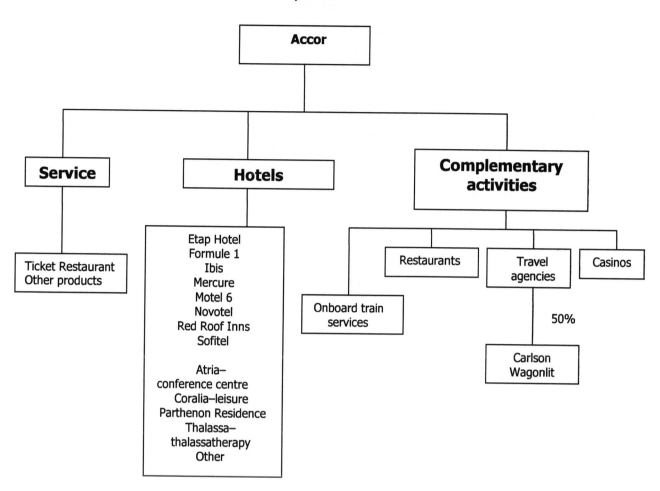

Figure 7

Distribution of Accor Hotel Activities

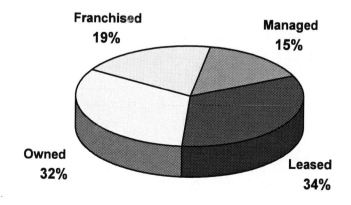

Accor is:

⇒ annual sales of US$ 6.6 billion, with US$6.2 billion from the travel sector
⇒ a world leader in the lodging industry with 3,488 hotels and 389,437 rooms
⇒ number 2 in business travel in terms of traffic, with 50 per cent ownership of Carlson Wagonlit Travel
⇒ manager of 13 casinos
⇒ 145,000 associates in 140 countries
⇒ double-digit growth in revenues for the 7th year in a row

Recent transactions:

January 1999
Acquisition of Good Morning Hotels, a Scandinavian chain
Strategic alliance with Air France creating preferential business ties between the two groups

February 99
Acquisition of Frantour (31 hotels, 86 travel agencies and 7 tour operators)

May 99
Acquisition of Demeure and Libertel

July 99
Take-over of the Red Roof Inns chain in the United States

November 99
Accor sells its 50 per cent ownership in Europcar International to Volkswagen

April 2000
Acquisition of 38.5 per cent interest in Go Voyages, tour operator specialized in no-frills travel

June 2000
Acquisition of 2.5 per cent interest in WorldRes.com Inc. and 19 per cent interest in WorldRes Europe, its European affiliate

July 2000
Acquisition of 20 per cent share in Polish Orbis hotel group

Year 2000
Opens 254 hotels with a total of 34,785 rooms
Wins contract to manage 27 hotels in Australia formerly run by the All Seasons group

Year 2001
Launches new Suitehotel brand on the European market–new 3-star concept aimed at individual business travellers

Figure 8

First Choice Holidays PLC Corporate Structure

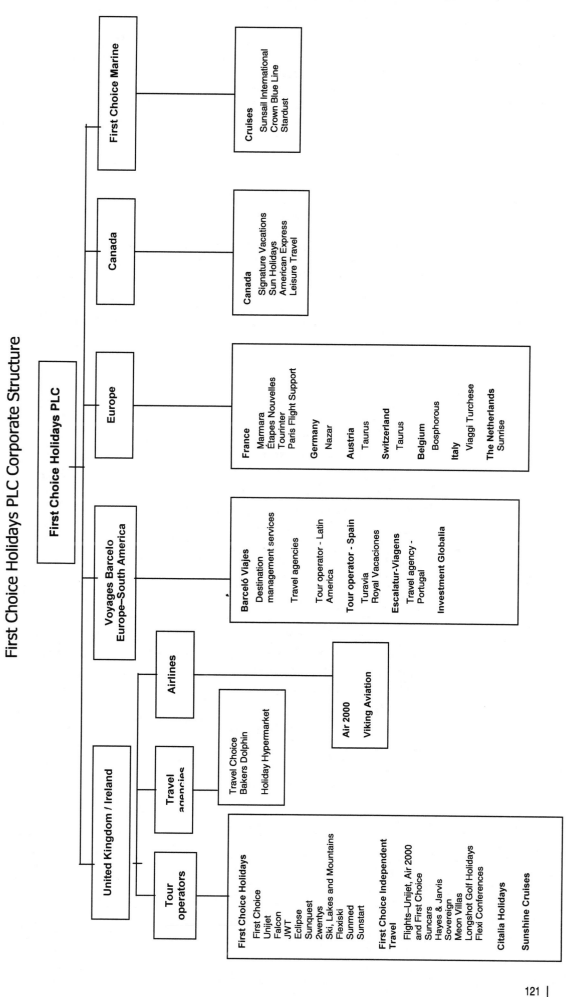

First Choice is:

⇒ annual sales of US$2.7 billion in 2000
⇒ a network of over 650 points of sale
⇒ a fleet of 28 planes
⇒ 6.6 million passengers in 2000

Recent transactions:

1998   Acquisition of tour operators Unijet and Hayes & Jarvis and travel agencies Bakers Dolphin and Intatravel

1999   Acquisition of Meon Travel, a tour operator that includes Meon Villas and Longshot Golf Holidays (US$11.6 million); Sunsail International, cruises and a sports club (US$50.8 million); and FlexiGroup, ski vacations and conferences (US$1.5 million)

2000   Royal Caribbean Cruise Ltd. acquires a 20 per cent interest in First Choice
Acquisition of:
Holiday Hypermarkets–travel agencies throughout the United Kingdom
Ten Tour Group–European tour operator
Barcelo Travel–tour operators, travel agencies and inbound operators in Europe and South America
Taurus Tours AG–European tour operator
Crown Holidays Limited–European tour operator
Stardust Yacht Charters–European and North American tour operator
Sunsail Pty Ltd–Australian tour operator
Sunshine Cruise–cruises in the United Kingdom

2001   Sun Holidays–Canadian travel agencies
American Express retail outlets–Canadian travel agencies
CIT Holidays (Citalia)–UK tour operator
Virgin Sun–UK tour operator
I Viaggi del Turchese S.R.L.–Italian tour operator
Paris Flight Support–French ground services
Escalatur-Viagens E Turismo Lda–Portuguese business travel agencies
Sunrise BV–Dutch tour operator
Tourinter–French tour operator

Kuoni Holding is:

⇒ annual sales of US$2.5 billion
⇒ 7,700 employees world-wide
⇒ present in 20 countries
⇒ the undisputed leader of the Swiss market

Recent transactions:

1998   Acquisition of Euro Lloyd Reisebüro GmbH, German business travel specialist
Association of Kuoni Italie and Italian tour operator Gastaldi Tours to form a
new company, Kuoni Gastaldi Tours
Acquisition of three Danish tour operators who are then merged into Alletiders
Rejser A/S
Acquisition of Voyages Jules Vernes, specialist in direct sales of upscale leisure
holidays in Europe and overseas

1999   Aborted merger attempt between Kuoni Travel Holding Ltd. and First Choice
Holidays PLC
Acquisition of 49 per cent share in the ITV group (Imholz-TUI-Voegele), third
largest Swiss tour operator, owned by Preussag
Acquisition of Intrav, luxury tour operator, based in Saint-Louis, Missouri

2000   Acquisition of 70 per cent share in Inter Holland Travel B. V. (inbound operator)
Acquisition of T Pro, inbound wholesaler based in New York City
Acquisition of 49 per cent share in Swedish tour operator Apollo Resort AB,
based in Stockholm
Equity investment of 12.5 per cent in British TV station, TV Travelshop
Acquisition of Sita Travel, an Indian tour operator specialized in business and
leisure travel and inbound services
Acquisition of specialized tour operator Dane Tours

2001   Kuoni buys remaining shares in Apollo Resort AB, becoming sole owner
Acquisition, via its subsidiary Kuoni Travel India, of inbound operator Tour Club
Sale of its 51 per cent share in N-U-R Neckerman in Austria to Thomas Cook

Figure 9
Airtours Corporate Structure

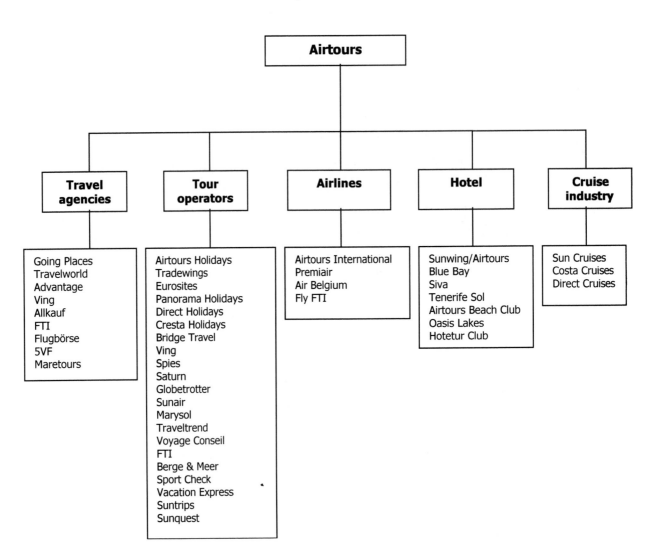

Airtours is:

⇒ annual sales of nearly US$6.5 billion
⇒ a fleet of 52 planes, 4 cruise ships and 132 resort hotels
⇒ over 100 brands
⇒ 70 Web sites
⇒ over 29,000 employees world-wide

Recent transactions:

1999   Acquisition of Travelworld Group, a British wholesaler
Equity investment of 40 per cent in Berge & Meer, German wholesaler of all-inclusive packages
Acquisition of 153 Real Group travel agencies operating in Germany
Acquisition of Marysol and Traveltrend, two Dutch wholesalers
Acquisition of Trivsel/Globetrotter, a Scandinavian wholesaler
Acquisition of 65 per cent share in Blue Bay, a hotel management company active in Mexico and the Caribbean

2000   Acquisition of remaining shares of Frosch Touristik GmbH (FTi)
Acquisition of 50 per cent share in Hotetur Club, a Spanish hotel group that manages 19 hotels in Majorca, the Canary Islands, Cuba and the Dominican Republic

2001   Carnival offers to sell its 25.1 per cent share in Airtours

Figure 10
Transat AT Corporate Structure

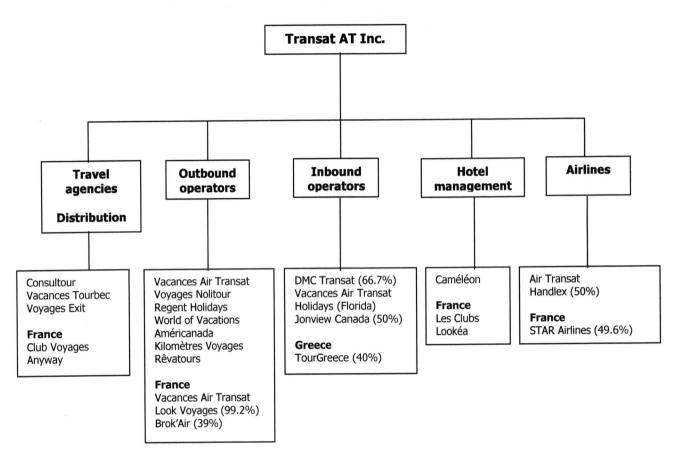

Transat AT is:

⇒ revenues of US$1.26 billion
⇒ a fleet of 22 planes, 6,300 flights to destinations in 27 countries, and a total of 3.5 million Air Transat passengers
⇒ 22 subsidiaries
⇒ approximately 240 points of sale in Canada and France
⇒ two online travel agencies: Exit.ca in Canada and anyway.com in France

TABLE 34
Profile of Global Distribution Systems

	SABRE Inc.	Amadeus Global Travel Distribution	Galileo International	WorldSpan
Year founded	1976 by American Airlines	1987 by Lufthansa, Iberia, Air France and SAS	1993 with the merger of Galileo and Covia Partnership	1990 with the merger of the Delta, Northwest and TWA systems
Headquarters	Dallas, Texas, United States	Madrid, Spain	Rosemont, Illinois, United States	Atlanta, Georgia, United States
Ownership	Public (100%)	Public (40.08%), Air France (23.36%), Iberia Líneas Aéreas (18.28%), Lufthansa (18.28%)	Public (73.2%), United Airlines (17.6%), Swissair (7.7%), Olympic, Air Canada, Aer Lingus Austrian (1.5%)	Delta Air Lines (40%), Northwest Airlines (34%), Trans World Airlines (American Airlines) (26%)
Employees	6,000	3,654	3,300	3,200
Distribution	More than 59,000 travel agencies	54,405 travel agencies in 198 countries (158,651 terminals) and 8,478 airline sales offices (71,331 terminals)	More than 43,000 travel agencies in 107 countries	20,210 travel agencies in 60 countries (47% of these agencies are located in North America)
Revenues–2000	US$2.6 billion, with nearly US$1.6 billion coming from electronic travel distribution	€1.6 billion, a 15.3% increase over 1999	US$1.6 billion (a 7.7% increase)	n/a
Reservations–2000 (volume)	467.1 million, a 6.4% increase over 1999	393.9 million, a 6% increase over 1999	345.1 million (40% from the US market)	n/a
Suppliers	450 airline companies, 53,000 hotels, 54 car rental companies	480 airline companies, 54,641 hotels, 47 car rental companies	511 airline companies, 47,000 hotels, 37 car rental companies	533 airline companies, 47,000 hotels, 45 car rental companies

Source: Chair in Tourism, Université du Québec à Montréal, and annual reports of the global distribution systems

IV.3 THE HOTEL INDUSTRY

Table 35
Hotel-Related Activities

OWNERSHIP / LEASING		
Factors	**Advantages**	**Disadvantages**
• Own the building in which the hotel is located • Lease a property for use as a hotel facility	• In some countries, there are significant tax benefits for real estate investors (i.e., REITs) [102] • Greater flexibility	• Significant investment required • Greater financial and political risk • When buying abroad, there may be access barriers (restrictions with regard to purchases made by foreign companies) • If the owning company has no experience in the hotel industry, it must outsource operating responsibilities
MANAGEMENT		
Factors	**Advantages**	**Disadvantages**
• Manage a hotel A hotel owner can manage the property himself or outsource all management operations to another company • Three types of company: 1. Owner manages his own hotel 2. Hotel chain manages hotels under its brands 3. Independent hotel management company owns no properties and represents no particular brand	• No real-estate investment • Freedom to make management decisions • Owners benefit from management company's expertise and technological transfer	• The management company has to depend on the real estate company that employs it • The hotel management company can also manage the properties of rival brands
FRANCHISER		
Factors	**Advantages**	**Disadvantages**
• Sell a brand and the company formula (standardized procedures for providing products and services) to an independent operator or other company in exchange for a lump sum payment and a share in the franchisee's profits.	• Minimal initial investment • Fastest way to expand • Minimal financial risk since franchisee provides investment capital • Ensures standard product is offered in all hotels under the same brand	• Number of franchisees and geographic distance make it difficult to ensure proper quality assurance • If standards are not maintained, chain's reputation and finances could suffer • If chain goes international, cultural, political and economic differences (etc.) could make it difficult to maintain norms • Possibility of legal wrangling with franchisees
FRANCHISEE		
Factors	**Advantages**	**Disadvantages**
• Purchase a hotel chain's brand and company formula (standardized procedures for providing products and services) from the franchiser for a lump sum payment and a share in the profits.	• Brand recognition • Greater borrowing power (sometimes, financing may be obtained from the franchiser) • Management format • Marketing tools, reservations system already in place, etc. • Savings through group purchases	• Significant investment required • Obligation to abide by franchiser's decisions regarding standards (anything from architectural forms to towel colours) • Possibility of legal wrangling with franchisers • Long-term contract • Significant penalty for breaking the contract

---

[102] Real Estate Investment Trust

CONSORTIUM		
Factors	**Advantages**	**Disadvantages**
• Consortium or affiliation of independent hotels, small properties or chains in order to promote themselves under a single brand • Some target a specific market niche to offer hotel owners marketing services and a recognizable image that comes with a guarantee of quality (i.e., Relais & Châteaux) • Some offer hotel owners a range of marketing services, such as brand affiliation (i.e., Pegasus) • Main services provided by consortia: marketing services and reservations • Initial and annual membership fees	• Freedom to make management and operational decisions • Greater company visibility • Enhanced ability to compete with industry leaders • Short-term, flexible contract • No obligation to conform to standards, as is the case for franchisees • Existing consortia based on themes or categories can improve market penetration prospects	• Some consortia require that prospective members conform to certain standards of quality or image • Members risk losing their own corporate image within that of the consortium

Table 36
Profile of Ten Largest Hotel Industry Giants
(2000)

COMPANY	BRANDS	ACTIVITIES

CENDANT CORP.
Parsippany, NJ, US
 	
1st place
541,313 rooms
6,455 hotels
2000 revenues (travel sector):
US$1.24 billion
 	
Presence in 24 countries
6,455 hotels franchised
	• AmeriHost Inn
	• Days Inn
	• Howard Johnson
	• Knights Inn
	• Ramada
	• Super 8
	• Travelodge
	• Villager Lodge
	• Wingate Inn
		• Real estate
		• Travel (32% of revenues)
		  • Hotel franchiser
		  • Avis car rental franchiser
		  • Timeshare resort
		• Miscellaneous services

BASS HOTELS & RESORTS
London, England
 	
2nd place
490,531 rooms
3,096 hotels
2000 revenues
(hotel sector): US$2.32 billion
 	
Presence in 100 countries
105 hotels owned or leased
344 hotels managed
2,644 hotels franchised
	• Crowne Plaza
	• InterContinental
	• Holiday Inn
	• Holiday Inn Express
	• Staybridge Suites
		• Hotel business (30.6% of revenues)
		  • Franchiser
		  • Manager
		  • Owner/lessee
		• Pubs, restaurants and bars
		• Soft drinks

MARRIOTT INTERNATIONAL
Washington, DC, US
 	
3rd place
390,469 rooms
2,099 hotels
2000 revenues (hotel sector):
US$7.85 billion
 	
Presence in 60 countries
806 hotels managed
1,168 hotels franchised
	• Courtyard
	• ExecuStay
	• Fairfield Inn
	• Marriott Conference Centers
	• Marriott Executive Apartments
	• Marriott Hotels, Resorts & Suites
	• Ramada International
	• Renaissance Hotels & Resorts
	• Residence Inn
	• Ritz-Carlton
	• SpringHill Suites
	• Towne Place Suites
		• Hotel business (78.3% of revenues)
		  • Franchiser
		  • Owner
		  • Manager
		  • Timeshare
		• Services to senior citizens
		• Food services distribution

ACCOR
Evry, France
 	
4th place
389,437 rooms
3,488 hotels
2000 revenues (hotel sector):
US$4.46 billion
 	
Presence in 88 countries
1,129 hotels owned
1,156 hotels leased
531 hotels managed
672 hotels franchised
	• Etap Hotel
	• Formule 1
	• Ibis
	• Mercure
	• Motel 6
	• Novotel
	• Red Roof Inns
	• Sofitel
		• Hotel business (68% of revenues)
		  • Franchiser
		  • Owner
		  • Manager
		  • Lessee
		• Services stock
		• Travel agencies
		• Casinos
		• Restaurants
		• Onboard train service
		• Other

CHOICE HOTELS INTERNATIONAL Silver Spring, MD, US 5th place 350,351 rooms 4,392 hotels 2000 revenues: US$167.5 million **Presence in 41 countries** 4,392 hotels franchised	• Clarion • Comfort Inn • Comfort Suites • Econo Lodge • MainStay Suites • Quality • Rodeway Inn • Sleep Inn	• Hotel business • Franchiser

COMPANY	BRANDS	ACTIVITIES

HILTON HOTELS CORP.
Beverly Hills, CA, US
 	
6th place
317,823 rooms
1,895 hotels
2000 revenues: US$3.45 billion
 	
Presence in 8 countries
139 hotels owned–outright or partially
73 hotels leased
403 hotels managed
1,492 hotels franchised
	• Conrad International
	• Doubletree
	• Embassy Suites
	• Hampton Inn
	• Hampton Inn & Suites
	• Harrison Conference Centers
	• Hilton
	• Hilton Garden Inn
	• Hilton Grand Vacations
	• Homewood Suites
	• Red Lions Hotels and Inns
	• Independent properties / famous hotels like the Waldorf-Astoria (NY)
		• Hotel business
		  • Owner
		  • Manager
		  • Franchiser
		  • Lessee

BEST WESTERN INTERNATIONAL Phoenix, AZ, US 7th place 307,737 rooms 4,065 hotels 2000 revenues: US$157 million **Presence in 80 countries** 4,065 branded hotels	• Best Western	• Voluntary hotel association • Marketing Non-profit organization Every hotel under the Best Western brand is owned and managed by the association member.

STARWOOD HOTELS & RESORTS WORLDWIDE
White Plains, NY, US
 	
8th place
227,042 rooms
738 hotels
2000 revenues: US$4.34 billion
 	
Presence in 80 countries
162 hotels owned/ leased
263 hotels managed
313 hotels franchised
	• Four Points
	• Luxury Collection
	• Sheraton
	• St-Regis
	• Starwood Vacation Ownership
	• W Hotels
	• Westin
		• Hotel business
		  • Franchiser
		  • Owner/Lessee
		  • Manager
		
		Starwood Hotels & Resorts is an American REIT which owns hotel properties.
		Starwood Hotels & Resorts Worldwide manages and operates the establishments owned by Starwood Hotels & Resorts.

CARLSON HOSPITALITY WORLDWIDE Minneapolis, MN, US 9th place 129,234 rooms 716 hotels 2000 revenues: US$4.2 billion **Presence in 63 countries** 682 hotels franchised	• Country Inns & Suites • Radisson Hotels & Resorts • Regent International Hotel • Carlson Vacation Ownership	• Hotel business • Franchiser • Restaurants • Cruises

HYATT HOTEL / HYATT INTERNATIONAL
Chicago, IL, US
 	
10th place
86,711 rooms
201 hotels
2000 revenues: not available
 	
Presence in 38 countries
	• Hyatt Hotels & Resorts
	• Grand Hyatt Hotels
	• Park Hyatt Hotels
	• Hyatt Regency Hotels
		• Hotel business
		  • Manager
		  • Franchiser
		• Golf courses
		• Floating casino

Source: HOTELS' Giant Survey 2000–HOTELS, July 2001 and annual reports of the companies

Table 37
Global Presence of Hotel Groups
(2000)

GLOBAL RANK	COMPANY	NUMBER OF COUNTRIES
2000 1999		**2000** 1999 1998
1 1	Bass Hotels & Resorts	**100** 98 95
2 3	Accor	**81** 81 72
3 2	Best Western International	**80** 84 76
4 4	Starwood Hotels & Resorts	**80** 80 70
5 5	Carlson Hospitality Worldwide	**63** 57 54
6 6	Marriott International	**60** 56 53
7 7	Hilton International	**59** 53 53
8 8	Forte Hotel Group	**55** 51 50
9 10	Choice Hotels International	**41** 36 36
10 9	Club Méditerranée SA	**40** 40 35
11 11	Hyatt Hotels / Hyatt International	**38** 35 34
12 12	Sol Mélià	**30** 27 24
13 14	Cendant Group	**24** 23 --
14 -	Four Seasons Hotels	**21** - --
15 -	TUI Group	**18** - --

Source: HOTELS' Giant Survey 2000–HOTELS, July 2001

Table 38
The Largest Hotel Brands
(2000)

GLOBAL RANK	BRAND	NUMBER OF ROOMS
1	Best Western	307,737
2	Holiday Inn Hotels & Resorts–Bass	290,166
3	Days Inn–Cendant	162,129
4	Marriott Hotels, Resorts and Suites	149,200
5	Sheraton Hotels–Starwood	128,332
6	Ramada Franchise Systems–Cendant	121,431
7	Super 8 Motels–Cendant	119,266
8	Hampton Inn–Hilton Corp.	111,231
9	Radisson Hotels & Resorts–Carlson	101,657
10	Holiday Inn Express–Bass	92,356

Source: HOTELS' Giant Survey 2000–HOTELS, July 2001

Table 39
Companies That Manage the Most Hotels
(2000)

GLOBAL RANK	COMPANY	MANAGED / TOTAL HOTELS
2000 1999		**2000** 1999
1 1	Marriott International Inc.	**806 / 2,099** 759 / 1,880
2 2	Société du Louvre	**540 / 868** 565 / 990
3 3	Accor	**531 / 3,488** 456 / 3,234
4 -	Extended Stay America	**392 / 392** -
5 9	Bass Hotels & Resorts	**344 / 3,096** 175 / 2,886
6 4	Tharaldson Enterprises	**330 / 330** 314 / 314
7 5	Westmont Hospitality Group inc.	**294 / 294** 296 / 296
8 6	Starwood Hotels & Resorts Worldwide	**263 / 738** 204 / 716
9 -	Hilton International	**223 / 223** -
10 -	Prime Hospitality Corp.	**214 / 239** -

Source: HOTELS' Giant Survey 2000–HOTELS, July 2001

Table 40
Companies That Franchise the Most Hotels
(2000)

GLOBAL RANK	COMPANY	FRANCHISED / TOTAL HOTELS
2000 1999		**2000** 1999
1 1	Cendant Corp.	**6,455 / 6,455** 6,258 / 6,315
2 2	Choice Hotels International	**4,392 / 4,392** 4,248 / 4,248
3 3	Bass Hotels & Resorts	**2,644 / 3,096** 2,563 / 2,886
4 4	Hilton Hotels Corp.	**1,492 / 1,895** 1,357 / 1,700
5 5	Marriott International	**1,168 / 2,099** 998 / 1,880
6 6	Carlson Hospitality Worldwide	**682 / 716** 581 / 616
7 7	Accor	**672 / 3,488** 568 / 3,234
8 8	U.S. Franchise Systems	**505 / 505** 374 / 400
9 9	Société du Louvre	**328 / 868** 372 / 990
10 10	Starwood Hotels & Resorts Worldwide	**313 / 738** 299 / 716

Source: HOTELS' Giant Survey 2000–HOTELS, July 2001

Table 41
Ten Largest Third-Party Marketing and
Reservation Providers in the World
(2000)
Ranked by Number of Rooms

GLOBAL RANK	PROVIDER	NUMBER OF ROOMS	NUMBER OF HOTELS
2000		2000	2000
1999		1999	1999
1998		1998	1998
1	UTELL	1,139,708	6,381
1	Brentford, Middlesex, UK	1,802,872	8,700
1		1,500,000	7,700
2	Lexington Services Corp.	515,000	3,975
2	Irving, TX, US	494,000	3,800
2		375,000	3,000
3	Unirez Inc.	262,050	1,747
10	Grapevine, TX, US	60,891	583
-		-	-
4	Supranational Hotels	192,500	1,609
4	London, England	123,563	1,077
4		123,500	827
5	VIP International Corp.	130,475	1,136
3	Calgary, Alberta, Canada	210,320	1,872
3		183,500	1,468
6	IndeCorp Corp.	90,000	418
-	Chicago, IL, US	-	-
-		-	-
7	Leading Hotels of the World	82,000	380
5	New York, NY, US	94,000	340
5		90,200	315
8	Hotusa–Eurostars–Familia Hotels	78,000	977
6	Barcelona, Spain	77,950	976
6		80,000	757
9	Keytel S.A.	74,200	742
7	Barcelona, Spain	76,000	760
7		76,000	700
10	SRS Hotels Steigenberger	71,362	375
8	Frankfurt / Main, Germany	72,000	400
9		60,300	365

Source: HOTELS' Giant Survey 2000–HOTELS, July 2001

Bibliography

ABEL-NORMANDIN, Serge (1999). "Air France et Delta s'associent en vue de fonder une alliance globale," *Tourisme Plus*, July 5, pp. 1-4.

ABEL-NORMANDIN, Serge (2000). "SAir Group consolide le Qualiflyer Group," *Tourisme Plus*, February 14, pp. 4.

ABOCAR, Amran (2000). "Roots Canada veut être le prochain Virgin," *Le Devoir*, June 17-18 , pp. C-7.

ACCOR. *Rapport annuel 2000*, 93 pp.

ACTES DU COLLOQUE (2000). *Le tourisme à l'heure des alliances, des fusions et des acquisitions*, Montréal, November, 109 pp.

ADAMS, Bruce. *Pegasus realigns after acquiring REZsolutions*, [online], May 2000, [www.hmmonline.com/...] (August 23, 2000).

ADER, Jason , Robert A. LAFLEUR and Marc J. FALCONE, *Bear Stearns Equity Research: Internet Travel: Point, Click, Trip, An Introduction To The On-Line Travel Industry*, April 2000, 99 pp.

ADLER, Arthur (2000). "Real Estate Investment Trusts," *Smart Structures in Hotel Investment* –JONES LANG LASALLE Hotels [online], 2000. [http://www.joneslanglasallehotels.com/] (July 2001).

AGENCE FRANCE-PRESSE (2000). "Le patron de British Airways démissionne après une série de déboires," *Le Devoir*, March 13.

AIR TRANSPORT ASSOCIATION, *Airline handbook*, [online], [www.air-transport.org/public/Handbook/...] (March 6, 2000).

AIRLINES INTERNATIONAL (2000). *Driving the Next Consolidated Wave*, July-August, pp.50-51.

AIRTOURS. *Rapport annuel 2000*, 68 pp.

ALFORD, Philip (2000). *E-Business in the Travel Industry–Travel & Tourism Intelligence*, London, 147 pp.

AMADEUS GLOBAL TRAVEL DISTRIBUTION, *Rapport annuel 2000*, 164 pp.

AMERICAN EXPRESS. *Rapport annuel 2000*, 66 pp.

ANDERSEN, Arthur. *Arthur Andersen–New Global Study, Hospitality 2000: The Capital, Examines The Long Term Trends In The Sourcing, Structuring And Use Of Capital In The International Hospitality Industry*, [online], June 6, 2000, [www.hospitalitynet.org/news/...] (August 2, 2000).

ANDERSEN, Arthur. *Hotel Performance in the Middle East and Africa Falters in the First Half of 2001*, [online], August 1, 2001. [www.hotelnewsresource.com/studies/...] (August 2, 2001).

ANDRÉ, Paul and Jean-François L'HER (2000). "Une grille d'analyse des regroupements d'entreprises, *Revue gestion*, Vol. 25, No. 3, Autumn 2000, pp. 137-158.

ANDRÉ, Paul, Walid BEN and Jean-François L'HER (2000). "Regroupements d'entreprises et création de valeur," *Revue gestion*, Vol. 25, No. 3, Autumn 2000, pp. 158-174.

ANTONELLI, Leo. *Does size matter?* [online], March 1999. [www.meetingscanada.com] (August 2000).

ARCHDALE, Gilbert (2000). "NTOs–Managing Change or Adrift in a Changing World," *Eclipse*, 4th Edition.

AVMARK AVIATION ECONOMIST (1987). *Computer Reservation Systems*, May, pp. 21.

AVMARK AVIATION ECONOMIST (1998). *Virtual Mergers, Regulatory Headaches*, Vol. 15, No. 4, pp. 2 & pp. 4-8.

AVMARK AVIATION ECONOMIST (1999). *Differing approaches to alliance strategy*, August, pp. 8-9.

AVMARK AVIATION ECONOMIST (1999b). *US Airline Alliances. Beneficial or Harmful to Consumers?*, Vol. 16, No. 3, pp. 12-17.

AYALA, H. (2000). "Panama's TCR Action Plan: Building Alliances for a Heritage-driven Economy," *The Cornell Hotel And Restaurant Administration Quarterly*, Vol. 41, No. 1, February, pp. 108-119.

BAILEY, Murray. *Travel Agencies Under Pressure: Commissions Shrink as Direct Bookings Grow*, [online], April 10, 2000, [www.arthurandersen.com/] (August 2000).

BARBE, Alain (2000). "Les fournisseurs se moquent de nous," *Bulletin Voyages*, No. 1069, July 31, pp. 10-15.

BARRETT, Amy (2000). "Henry Silverman's Long Road Back: He's fighting to restore Cendant's reputation," *Business Week*, February 28, pp. 126-138.

BASS, *Rapport annuel 2000*, 64 pp.

BEAUREPÈRE, Thierry (2000a). "Voyage au cœur de géants européens," *L'Écho Touristique*, No. 2494, March 3, pp. 22-25.

BEAUREPÈRE, Thierry (2000b). "Le pôle Swissair peut-il contrer Air France ?," *L'Écho Touristique*, No. 2515, September 8, pp. 18-23.

BEAUREPÈRE, Thierry (2001). "Le salut par l'intégration," *L'Écho Touristique*, No. 2547, May 11, pp. 3.

BENAVIDES, David Díaz (2001). "The Sustainability of International Tourism in Developing Countries," *Tourism in the least developed countries*, WTO–United Nations Conference on Trade and Development, 392 pp.

BENHAMOU, François (2000). "Mondialisation de l'hôtellerie : Mythe ou réalité ?," *Espaces*, February, pp.34-40.

BÉRUBÉ, Gérard (2000a). "Les lendemains de la saga Air Canada/Canadian/Onex : Robert Milton a beaucoup appris.". *Le Devoir*, January 20 and 30, pp. C-1 and C-7.

BÉRUBÉ, Gérard (2000b). "La ville à la montagne : L'Expansion de Tremblant s'étirera jusqu'en 2010," *Le Devoir*, July 25, pp. B 1.

BEST WESTERN. *Rapport annuel 2000*, 21 pp.

BEYER, Barbara (1999). "Affecting Competition and Alliances: Canada's One Airline Policy?," *Avmark Aviation Economist*, Vol. 16, No. 8, pp. 6-8.

BILSKY, André (2000). "Un seul monde : Stratagème global pour l'investisseur," *Magazine En Route*, Summer, pp. 48-50.

BOISVERT, Guylaine (1999). "Hôtellerie : tendances de la prochaine décennie," *HRI HÔTELS–RESTAURANTS–INSTITUTIONS*, Vol. 3, No. 1, January 15, pp. 46 & 48-50.

BORGE, Micheal (2000). *Involving The DMO's In A Larger Part of The Value Chain*, Enter 2000.

BOSTON CONSULTING GROUP (2001). "VENTE SUR INTERNET : ACTE II," May, 13 pp.

BOURDAIS, Dominique, Justin LANZKRON and Yannick SIMONART. *European Hotel Valuation Index 2001*, [online], May 2001. [www.hotel-online.com/Neo/...] (May 23, 2001).

BOURGET, Louise and Lucie RENÉ (2000). "Les forces et faiblesses de la franchise : sept franchisés se confient," *Occasions d'affaires*, August-September, pp. 11-18.

BRADY, Diane (2000), "Why Service Stinks," *Business Week*, October 23, pp.118-128.

BRISSON, Benoît and Bernard HAMEL (2000). "Uniglobe Voyages Succès = vision, jeunesse et dynamisme!," *Occasions d'affaires*, August-September, pp. 6-8.

BRISSON, Louis. *Naviguer sur internet*, [online], February 2000, [www.reseau.qc.ca/art2000/20fevrier.htm] (August 2000).

BROUTHERS, Keith D, Joran VAN DEN VEN and Paul VAN HASTENBURG (1998). "If most Mergers Fail, why are they so Popular?," *Long Range Planning–International Journal of Strategic Management*, June 31.

BROWN, P. Anthony. *Hotel REITs–Legislation heralds a new era*, [online], Spring 2000, [ww3.knowledgespace.com/Hosp...] (July 19, 2000).

BUHALIS, Dimitrios (1998). "Strategic use of information technologies in the tourism industry," *Tourism Management*, Vol. 19, No. 5, pp. 409-421.

BUHALIS, Dimitrios (2000). "Destination Management Systems (DMSs): Criteria for Success," *Eclipse*, 4th Edition.

BULLETIN VOYAGES (1999). *La troisième force ? : Air France et Delta forment une alliance globale*, No. 1039, July 5, pp. 2.

BULLETIN VOYAGES (2000a). *Associatour : un nain au pays des géants ?*, No. 1067, July 3, pp. 16-18.

BULLETIN VOYAGES (2000b). *Skyteam : la troisième force est née*, No. 1067, July 3, pp. 32.

BULLETIN VOYAGES (2000c). *ITAG appelle les agents à la révolte*, No. 1069, July 3, pp. 2-4.

BULLETIN VOYAGES (2000d). *Orbitz exigera l'exclusivité sur les meilleurs rabais*, No. 1069, July 31, pp. 24-25.

BUSINESS TRAVELER (2000). *The way ahead*, January, pp. 21.

BUSINESS WEEK (2000). *Airline hawks are ready to strike: British airways-KLM could be just the first cross-border deal*, June 19, pp. 52.

BUTTON, Kenneth and Tae Hoon OUM (1997). "Airline alliances and open skies transport," *Journal of Air Transport Management*, Vol. 3, No. 3, pp. 107.

C & N TOURISTIK A G, *Rapport annuel 1999/2000*, 109 pp.

CANADAY, Henry (2000). "Driving the Next Consolidation Wave," *Airlines International*, Vol. 6, No. 4, pp. 50-51.

CARLIER, Micheal (2001). "Le voyage en ligne," *ESPACECOM*, July.

CARLSON HOSPITALITY WORLDWIDE (2000). "At Market Speed, Carlson Advances," *Hotels*, Vol. 34, No. 5, May, pp. 45.

CARNEY Dan (2000). "Why this new E-biz is raising trustbusters' hackles," *Business Week*, June 19, pp. 51.

CARTON Luc. *6 compagnies aériennes s'associent pour concurrencer Priceline.com,* [online], July 13, 2000, [etourismenewsletter.com/ebusiness.htm] (July 14, 2000).

CARTON, Luc. *Les chausse-trappes du Wireless : Voice-Centric contre Data-Centric,* [online], [www.etourismenewsletter.com/], (October 20, 2000).

CARTON, Luc. *Andbook.com : Accor, Hilton et Forte réunis pour conquérir l'Europe de l'hôtellerie online. L'anti-thèse du projet Orbitz,* [online], 18 April 2001. [etourismenewsletter.com] (August 7, 2001).

CASTELL, Helen and N GUNALAN. *Hotels hold on to rates despite US slowdown,* [online], 25 May, 2001. [www.travelweeklyeast.com/news_article.cfm...] (May 28, 2001).

CAZELAIS, Normand (1999). "Villes du patrimoine mondial : Tourisme historique," *Le Devoir*, December 24, pp. E2.

CENDANT. *Rapport annuel 2000*, 72 pp.

CHABERT, Laurent (2000). "British Airways et KLM discutent d'un rapprochement," *Le Devoir*, June 8, pp. B1-2.

CHOICE HOTELS. *Rapport annuel 2000*, 52 pp.

CLINE, Roger. *Arthur Andersen–Hospitality E-Business in the New Economy,* [online], May 1st, 2000, [ww3.knowledgespace.com/hi/...] (July 19, 2000).

CLOUTIER, Laurier (2000a). "Les fusions et acquisitions échouent dans 83 pour cent des cas," *La Presse*, December 1st, pp. D-11.

CLOUTIER, Laurier (2000b). "Le régional Air Sprint décollera dès September," *La Presse*, June 20, pp. C1 & pp. C-4.

COACH OMNIUM (1999 / 2000). "L'Hôtellerie Économie – Chaînes hôtelières intégrées en Europe," *La Revue*, pp 1-4.

COGSWELL, David (1999a). "A New Wave of Consolidation Is Set To Hit Tour Operators," *Travel Agent*, February 1st.

COGSWELL, David (1999b). "Behind the Tour Operator Buying Frenzy: Which Model Will Work?," *Travel Agent*, July 19.

COHEN, Benjamin. *Les hôtels entrent dans l'ère d'Internet*, CCE International, No. 480 [online], February 2000, [www.sepeg-intl.fr/cce/480/hotellerie.html] (August 3, 2000).

COHENNEC, Yvan (2000). "United Airlines/US Airways : vers une mégafusion," *Air & Cosmos*, No. 1742, June 2, pp. 28-30.

COMMISSION CANADIENNE DU TOURISME (1999). *Enquête sur les agences de voyages et les voyagistes – Rapport de recherche*, 23 pp.

COURTMANCHE, John and Lorraine SILEO. *The PhocusWright Yearbook: Analysis, Assumptions And Assessments For The online Travel Marketplace*, 1999, 115 pp.

COURTMANCHE, John and Lorraine SILEO, *The PhocusWright Yearbook Update: Analysis, Assumptions and Assessments For The online Travel Marketplace*, 6 pp.

CROSS, Larry R. (1998). *L'industrie hôtelière aujourd'hui*, Gueuleton touristique du December 3, 9 pp.

CROTTS, John C., Dimitrios BUHALIS and Roger MARCH (2000a). "Introduction: Global Alliances in Tourism and Hospitality Management," *International Journal of Hospitality & Tourism Administration*, Vol. 1, No. 1.

CROTTS, John C., Dimitrios BUHALIS and Roger MARCH (2000b). *Managing Relationships in the Global Hospitality and Tourism Industry*, New York, Haworth Press.

D'AMOURS, Liette (2001). "Le B2C meurt-il," *La Presse*, May 28, pp. D6.

D'ORGEVAL, Alice (2001). "Le portail aérien européen Opodo prend son envol," *L'Écho Touristique*, No. 2554, June 29.

DALE, Crispin (2000). "The UK tour-operating industry: A competitive analysis," *Journal of Vacation Marketing*, Vol. 6, No. 4, pp. 357-367.

DE SMET, Michel (2000). "Transat A.T. poursuit sa stratégie d'intégration verticale," *Les Affaires – Les 500 plus importantes entreprises au Québec*, pp. 72.

DE LA CRUZ, Tony. *HOTELS' 325*, [online], July 1999, [www.hotelsmag.com] (August 8, 2000).

DE LA CRUZ, Tony. *HOTELS' 325*, [online], July 2000, [www.hotelsmag.com] (August 8, 2000).

DE LA CRUZ, Tony (2000). "FRANCHISING Focus Narrows," *Hotels*, Vol. 34, No. 3, March, pp. 50.

DE LA CRUZ, Tony (2001a). "Forecast 2001: Markets In Flux," *HOTELS*, January, pp. 37-46.

DE LA CRUZ, Tony (2001b). "Kinder, Gentler Franchising," *HOTELS*, March, pp. 51-56.

DENNIS, Nigel (2000). "Scheduling Issues and Network Strategies for International Airline Alliances," *Journal of Air Transport Management*, Vol. 6, No. 2, pp. 75-85.

DESCAZEAUX, Pierre (2000). "Air France, entreprise mondiale grâce à Sky Team," *Espaces*, No. 174, September, pp. 29.

DÉSIRONT, André (2000). "Compagnies aériennes : plus il y a de fous...," *La presse*, June 3, pp. H-8.

DESJARDINS, Stéphane (1999). "Les regroupements, la clé de l'avenir... : Qu'en disent les hôteliers ?," *HRI HÔTELS–RESTAURANTS–INSTITUTIONS*, Vol. 3, No. 6, November 15, pp. 58-60.

DOMKE-DAMONTE, Darla J. (2000). "The Effect of Cross-Industry Cooperation on Performance in the Airline Industry," *International Journal of Hospitality & Tourism Administration*, Vol. 1, No. 1, pp. 139.

DONE Kevin and Deborah HARGREAVES (2000). "BA, KLM in Talks with EU Antitrust Regulator," *Financial Post*, July 1st.

DOORLEY, T. L. (1993). "Teaming up for success," *Business Quarterly*, No. 57, pp. 99-103.

DOUBLET, Jean-Louis (2000). "SkyTeam décolle officiellement," *Le Devoir*, June 23, pp. A-7.

DRAULANS, Ard-Pieter de Man and Henk VOLBERDA. *Alliance capability: Source of competitive advantage*, [online], 1999, [www.kpmg.nl/alliances/] (September 12, 2000).

DUCRUET, H. (2000). "Rewe, nouveau géant du tourisme en Allemagne," *L'Écho Touristique*, No. 2514, September 1st, pp. 7.

DUHAMEL, Alain (2000a). "Air Canada s'installe, les transporteurs régionaux reculent," *Les Affaires*, April 15, pp. 47.

DUHAMEL, Alain (2000b). "Avec la mondialisation, les PME voyagent plus," *Les Affaires*, April 15, pp. 49.

DUHAMEL, Alain (2000c). "Boom des liaisons aériennes transfrontalières, chute dans le nombre des liaisons intérieures," *Les Affaires*, October 7, pp. A-2.

DUHAMEL, Alain (2000d). "D'indispensables rabais pour voyager au moindre coût possible," *Les Affaires*, October 7, pp. A-3.

DUPAUL, Richard (2000). "Allié canadien recherché," *La Presse*, October 4, pp. D-1.

DURIVAGE, Paul (2000). "Les requins du ciel," *La Presse*, May 31.

ECONOMIST NEWSPAPER (2000). *Tour operators–A Place in the sun (Thomson Travel acquired by Preussag)*, May 20.

EL BELTAGUI, Mamdouh and Mohamed SAKR (2001). "Séminaire sur la mondialisation, ses enjeux et ses possibilités pour le développement du tourisme au Moyen-Orient et en Afrique du Nord," Cairo, Egypt, May 20.

ELGONEMY, Anwar R. *Real Estate Investment in 2000*, [online], August 2000. [www.hotel-online.com/Neo/Trends/PKF/...] (December 20, 2000).

ELKIN, Noah. *Travel Consolidated: You Will Be Assimilated*, [online], April 25, 2001. [www.emarketer...] (April 30, 2001).

ELKIN, Noah. *online Travel Market in Latin America Getting Ready for Takeoff*, [online], March 22, 2001. [www.emarketer...] (May 23, 2001).

ELLIS, David G. *Canada's Hospitality Sector; Consolidation, Consolidation, Consolidation*, [online], Winter 1999 / 2000, [www.hotel-online.com/...] (August 16, 2000).

ERNST, David, and others (2001). "A future for e-alliances," *The McKinsey Quarterly*, No. 2, pp. 92-102.

ETUDE COACH OMNIUM (2000). "Chaînes hôtelières volontaires en France : La maturité des réseaux," *L'HÔTELLERIE*, No. 2656, March 9.

FAU, Frédérique (2000). "Globalisation ou proximité, à chaque type d'hébergement sa stratégie," *Espaces*, No. 174, September, pp. 24-27.

FELDMAN, Joan M. (1999). "E-commerce: the Future Is Now," *Air Transport World*, Vol. 36, No. 11, pp. 44-50.

FELDMAN, Joan M. (1998). "Making Alliances Work," *Air Transport World*, Vol. 35, pp. 27-35.

FENSENMAIER, Daniel R., Stefan KLEIN and Dimitrios BUHALIS (2000). *Information and Communication Technologies in Tourism 2000*, Vienne, Springer-Verlag Wien, 518 pp.

FINANCIAL TIMES (2000). *Life is a beach for jostling European tourism companies: Scheherazade Daneshkhu explains why the scramble for spot in the industry is hotting up this summer*, June 14, pp. 23.

FLAIG, Andreas. *Asia Pacific: On the road to recovery*, [online], Summer 2000, [ww3.knowledgespace.com/Hosp...] (July 19, 2000).

FORTUNE (2000). *What's up...*, Special Advertising Section, October 30.

FOUST, Dean (2000). "Low-fliers may be poised to take off," *Business Week*, July 3, pp. 151-152.

FRANGIALLI, Francesco (2001). "Une vision, trois chantiers, une stratégie," Madrid, January.

FRANK, Michel (2000). "Des hôtes et des autres – tourisme et altérité," *Espaces*, No. 171, May, pp. 14-21.

FRENCH, Carey (2000). "E-Ticketing suffers growing pains," *The Globe and Mail*, October 10, pp. T-13.

FRENCH, Trevor (1999). "British Airways and the new airline economy," *Travel & Tourism Intelligence*, No. 6, pp. 13.

FYALL, Alan, Ben OAKLEY and Annette WEISS (2000). "Theoretical Perspectives Applied to Inter-Organisational Collaboration on Britain's Inland Waterways," *International Journal of Hospitality & Tourism Administration*, Vol. 1, No. 1, pp. 89.

GALILEO INTERNATIONAL, *Rapport annuel 2000*, 19 pp.

GIRARD, Michel (2000). " Enfin, de la compétition dans le ciel d'Air Canada !," *La Presse*, October 2, pp. D-1.

GÓMEZ (2001). "The State Of online Travel: Executive Report," 41 pp.

GREEN, Rick (2000). "How the Internet Raises the Bar on Destination Marketing," *Eclipse*, 4th Edition.

GREENE, Gerard and Seamus O'LOUGHLIN (1999). "Hotels in the Middle East: Trends and Opportunities," *Travel & Tourism Analyst*, No. 4, pp. 65-88.

HAANAPPEL, Peter P.C. (1995). "Airline Challenges: Mergers, Take-overs and Franchises," *Annals of Air and Space Law/Annales de Droit Aérien et Spatial*, Vol. XX, No. part I, pp. 179-193.

HACK, Susan (2001). "Pyramid Schemes," *Fortune*, April 16, pp. 450.

HANDSZUH, Henryk (2001). "Séminaire sur la mondialisation, ses enjeux et ses possibilités pour le développement du tourisme au Moyen-Orient et en Afrique du Nord" Cairo, Egypt, May 20.

HANNEGAN, Timothy F. and Francis MULVEY (1995). "International Airline Alliances: An Analysis of Code-sharing's Impact on Airlines and consumers," *Journal of Air Transport Management*, Vol. 2, No. 2, pp. 131-137.

HARBISON, John R. and Peter PEKAR JR (1998). "Institutionalizing alliances skills: Secrets of respectable success," *Best Practice*, Second quarter, pp. 79-94.

HARRIS H. Stephen and KIRBAN, Elise (1998). "Antitrust Implications of International Code-sharing Alliances," *Air and Space Law*, Vol. XXIII, No. 4-5, pp. 166-176.

HÉBERT, Michel (2000), "Le regroupement des transporteurs aériens québécois est en bonne voie," *Le Soleil*, October 19, pp. B8.

HÉGUY, Jean-Baptiste (2000a). "La grande foire des alliances aériennes," *L'Écho touristique*, No. 2003, May 5, pp. 4.

HÉGUY, Jean-Baptiste (2000b). "La rupture de l'alliance Wings crée des turbulences," *L'Écho touristique*, No. 2501, April 21, pp. 16-19.

HÉGUY, Jean-Baptiste (2000c). "Swissair contrôle Air Liberté," *L'Écho touristique*, No. 2503, May 5, pp. 4.

HIGLEY, Jeff. *Franchising doesn't fit all needs*, [online], September 20, 1999, [www.hmmonline.com/...] (February 25, 2000).

HONG, Jung Hwa, Peter JONES and Nihal SIRISENA. *Hotel Development in Southeast Asia and Indo-China*, [online], August 2000, [www.hotel-online.com] (September 12, 2000).

HORWATH (1998). *Enquête sur l'exploitation hôtelière au Québec et au Canada 1998*, 23 pp.

HORWATH INTERNATIONAL. *Hotel Chains Outperform Independents On A Worldwide Basis*, [online], March 5, 2000. [www.horwath.com/...] (May 23, 2001).

HORWATH INTERNATIONAL. *Highlights from the 1999 Worldwide Hotel Industry Study*, [online], 2000. [www.horwath.com/...] (May 23, 2001).

HOTELIER (2000). *"Who owns What?,"* poster, September–October.

HUGHES, Laura, *Waves Across The Atlantic As Airtours Buys TSI*, [online], February 28, 2000. [www.findarticles.com] (October 2000).

INSTITUT DE LA STATISTIQUE DU QUÉBEC (2000). *"Population des MRC et des communautés urbaines, Québec, 1971-2000,"* [online], January 30, 2001. [http://www.stat.gouv.qc.ca/donstat/demograp/regional/207.htm] July 18, 2001.

INTERVISTAS COUNSULTING (2000) *Tourism Impact of Airline Industry Restructuring*, July 5 , 48 pp.

JONES LANG LASALLE HOTELS. *Buyoyant European Hotel Investment Markets*, [online], April 27, 2001. [www.hotelnewsresource.com/studies/...] (June 4, 2001).

JONES LANG LASALLE HOTELS. *Bass the Fastest Mover but Accor Remains Number One*, [online], October 11, 2000. [www.hotelnewsresource.com/studies/...] (June 4, 2001).

JOURNAL DU NET. *Un internaute européen sur six achète en ligne*, [online], July 17, 2001. [www.journaldunet.com/0107/010717nielsen.shtml] (July 22, 2001).

KARSTADT QUELLE, *Rapport annuel 1998*.

KELLEY, Christopher M. and James L. MCQUIVEY (1999). *The Forrester Brief: Canadian online Travel Is Cleared For Takeoff*, December 27, 4 pp.

KIM, K.-H. and M.D. OLSEN (1999). "Determinants of Successful Acquisition Processes in the US Lodging Industry," *International Journal of Hospitality Management*, Vol. 18, No. 3, September, pp. 285.

KIMPEL, Scott (1997). "Antitrust Considerations in International Airline Alliances," *Journal of Air Law and Commerce*, Vol. 63, No. 2, pp. 475-513.

KLEMM, Mary and Bradford PARKINSON (2000). "Managing the Balance of Power: UK Tour Operators and Destinations," *Revue du Tourisme*, pp. 4-13.

KROL, Ariane (2000). "Travelprice.com s'installe à Montréal," *La Presse*, September 7, pp. E4.

KROLL, Karen K. (2000). "The Graying of the Baby Boomers Bodes Well for the Leisure Industry: But will frenetic M&A activity in the sector continue?, *Investment Dealer's Digest*, March 20 .

KUONI GROUP, *Rapport annuel 2000*, 39 pp.

LAINÉ, Linda (2000). "Travelocity et Expedia au top," *L'Écho Touristique*, No. 2511, June 30.

LE MONDE (1999). "Les histoires de fusions finissent mal... en général". *Le Devoir*, 23 and January 24, pp. C-8.

LEGAULT, Julie. *Qu'adviendra-t-il de BonVoyage.com ?*, [online], September 6, 2000, [www.branchez-vous.com] (September 2000).

L'HER, Jean-François and Michel MAGNAN (2000). "Les vagues de fusions et d'acquisitions en Amérique du Nord : modes ou rationalités économiques ?, *Revue gestion*, Vol. 25, No. 3, Autumn 2000, pp. 119-138.

LI, Michael Z.F. (2000). "Distinct Features of Lasting and Non-lasting Airline Alliances," *Journal of Air Transport Management*, Vol. 6, No. 2, pp. 65-73.

LIDDLE, Alan. *Starwood, Marriott, Hyatt shifting $8B budgets to e-purchasing*, [online], 5 June 2000, [firstsearch.oclc.org/FETCH...] (July 19, 2000).

LIVINGSTON, Gillian (2000). "Une compagnie aérienne plein service prendra son envol en partenariat avec Roots," *La Presse*, June 8, pp. E-4.

LUFTHANSA, *Rapport annuel 1999*, 148 pp.

MAILLOT, Jacques (2000), "Nouvelles Frontières, mariage de raison," *L'Express*, October 19, pp.80.

MALHOTRA, Namit. *Canadian Lodging Market: An Overview HVS*, [online], February 2000, [www.hotel-online.com/...] (August 16, 2000).

MARONEY, Tyler (2000). "An Air Battle Comes To The Web," *Fortune*, June 26, pp. 315-318.

MARRON Kevin (2000). "Upstart carriers offer choice and savings," *The Globe and Mail*, October 10, 2000, pp. T-5.

MARSAN, Joan (2001a). "Asia awakens," *HOTELS*, April, pp. 54-60.

MARSAN, Joan (2001b). "Chains To Watch," *HOTELS*, May, pp. 49-54.

MARSAN, Joan (2001c). "European Empires," *HOTELS*, June, pp. 48-56.

MARSAN, Joan (2001d). "Growing In Spite Of The Odds," *HOTELS*, June, pp. 56-59.

MARSAN, Joan and Sally WOLCHUK (2001a). "Hotels' 325," *HOTELS*, July, pp. 46-47.

MARSAN, Joan and Sally WOLCHUK (2001b). "Corporate 300," *HOTELS*, July, pp. 49-70.

MARSAN, Joan and Sally WOLCHUK (2001c). "Consortia 25," *HOTELS*, July, pp. 72-76.

MATHEWS, Vinitia E. (2000). "Competition in the international hotel industry," *International Journal of Contemporary Hospitality Management*, Vol. 12, No. 2, pp. 114-118.

MCARTHUR, Keith (1999). "RootsAir links with world airlines," *The Globe and Mail*, June 19, pp. 1-12.

MCGEE, J. William (2000). "Vacation.com and TAN Accelerate Consortium Consolidated Trend," *Travel Agent*, April 26.

MCINERNEY, Joseph A. *The State of the Asia Pacific Hospitality Industry*, [online], June 11, 2001. [www.hospitalitynet.org /news/...] (June 15, 2001).

MCNEECE, James R. (2000). "DuPont — Comparison of Major Airline Alliances," *Avmark Aviation Economist*, Vol. 17, No. 6, pp. 15-18.

MCWHIRTER, Alex (2000). "Allied victory?," *Business Traveler*, January, pp. 28-29.

MEDINA-MUNOZ, Diego and Juan Manuel GARCIA-FALCÓN (2000). "Successfull relationships between hotels and agencies," *Annals of Tourism Research*, Vol. 27, No. 3, pp. 737-762.

MICROSOFT CORPORATION, *Rapport annuel 1999*, 33 pp.

MILCENT, Blandine (2000). "Grandes manœuvres dans le tourisme allemand," *L'Express*, May 25.

MILLER, Griffin (2000). "Consortia React, Reinvent To Compete," *HOTELS*, November, pp. 63-68.

MINISTRY OF CULTURE & TOURISM KOREA (1998), *OECD-Korea Conference: A New Era in Information Technology: Its Implications For Tourism Policies*, November 10-11, 238 pp.

MOON, David and Christian E. HEMPELL. *Hospitality eDistribution in the new economy: Redefining the value chain for consumers*, [online], 2000, [ww3.knowledgespace.com/Hosp...] (July 19, 2000).

MOONSHINE TRAVEL MARKETING (2000a). "Destination Image," *Eclipse*, 1st Edition.

MOONSHINE TRAVEL MARKETING (2000b). "Tourism Information for Travellers," *Eclipse*, 2nd Edition.

MOSTELLER Jeff (1999). "The Current and Future Climate of Airline Consolidation: the Possible Impact of an Alliance of Two Large Airlines and an Examination of the Proposed American Airlines-British Airways Alliance," *Journal of Air Law and Commerce*, Vol. 64, No. 2, pp. 575-603.

MOWAT, Bob. *Marketing, Technology & Financial Rewards: The Jewels Of GEM's Success*, [online], August, 1999, [www.travelpress.com] (August 2000).

MOWAT, Bob. *Vacation.com Acquires GEM Canada, Poised To Launch National Branding Strategy*, [online], September 6, 1999, [www.travelpress.com] (August 2000).

MULRONEY, Catherine (2000). "Gunfight at the on-line corral," *The Globe and Mayl*, October 10, 2000, pp. T1-2.

MURPHY, Anne and Gérard KOK. *Leap into the future: Managing differences*, [online], April 2000, [www.kpmg.nl/alliances/] (September 12, 2000).

NGUYEN, Bernard (2000a). "Les avions de moins en moins à l'heure," *Les Affaires*, April 15, pp. 51.

NGUYEN, Bernard (2000b). "Le transport aérien à bas prix est en expanxion," *Les Affaires*, April 15, pp. 50.

NIELSEN/NETRATINGS. "Nielsen/NetRatings Global Internet Trends," September 2000.

NOËL, Kathy (2000). " Régionnair connaît à son tour des difficultés," *Les Affaires*, October 7, pp. A-8.

NON, Sergio G. *online travel, games stocks lead techs*, [online], July 2, 2001. [news.cent.com/news/...] (July 16, 2001).

NORMAND, François (1999). "Les jeux ne sont pas faits : Certains transporteurs pourraient changer leur fusil d'épaule, selon le vice-président d'Air France," *Le Devoir*, December 16.

NOZAR, Robert A. (2000). "Private capital might dominate hotel future: Atlanta conference speakers see more profits, added consolidation in lodging industry's future," *Hotel & Motel Management*, April 17, 2 pp.

NUNES, Natalia and Stephen FARAGO and Johanna TRAVIS. *The Economic Impact of International Airline Alliances*, [online], May 1997, [http://www.pc.gov.au/research/other/aircraft/index.html] (April 11, 2000).

O'CONNOR, Peter (1999). *Electronic Information Distribution in Tourism and Hospitality*, CABI Publishing.

OCDE. *International Strategic Alliances: their role in industrial globalisation*, [online], July 2000. [www.oecd.org/dsti/sti/prod/sti_wp.htm] (August 17, 2000).

OCDE. *Cross-border Mergers and Acquisitions: Their Role in Industrial Globalisation*, [online], July 2000. [www.oecd.org/dsti/sti/prod/sti_wp.htm] (17 August 2000).

O'TOOLE Kevin and Tom GILL (2000). "Buying power: The global alliances are only just starting to use their combined buying power," *Airline Business*, January, pp. 44-45.

OUM, Tae and Jong-Hun PARK and Anming ZANG (2000). *Globalization and Strategic Alliances: The Case of the Airline Industry*, Pergamon, 252 pp.

OUM, Tae and Jong-Hun PARK (1997). "Airline alliances: current status, policy issues, and future directions, *Journal of Air Transport Management*, Vol. 3, No. 3, pp. 133-144.

PAGE, Isabelle (2000). "Air France revendique un premier rôle dans la refonte du ciel européen," *Le Devoir*, June 14.

PALMERI, Christopher (2000). "Heavy housekeeping at Hilton," *Business Week*, July 10 , pp. 87-88.

PEGASUS SYSTEMS, *Rapport annuel 2000*, 67 pp.

PERREAULT, Mathieu (2000). "La compétition choisit ses niches," *La Presse*, September 3, pp. A-9.

PEYMANI, Bijan. *Tour Operator Takes Aim*, [online], June 8, 1999, [www.arthurandersen.com/] (August 2000).

PEYMANI, Bijan. *Tour operator takeovers in Europe: Merger mania near end?*, [online], July 13, 2000, [www.arthurandersen.com/] (August 2000).

PHILIPPS, Luke (2001). "Une station balnéaire comme un palmier géant," *La Presse*, May 5, H10.

PHOCUSWRIGHT REPORT (1999). THE PARTNERSHIP PHENOMENA: PUTTING TOGETHER DEALS THAT WORK, Vol. 1, No. 2, January.

PHOCUSWRIGHT REPORT (2000). *Airlines And The Internet: Nonstop Growth And Competition*, Vol. 2, No. 4, June.

PHOCUSWRIGHT REPORT(2000), *The PhocusWright Report: The online Travel Investor Report, Travel Dot.Com And Dot.Com-ers Face The Street,* April 2000, pp. 1-88.

PINARD, Guy (2001). "L'Égypte recherche des investisseurs," *La Presse*, April 14, pp. H10.

PITCHER, George (2000). "Patient players triumph in travel industry takeover; Travel operators are consolidating methodicaly, as demonstrated by Thomson's decision to turn down C&N Touristik's offer in favor of Preussag's," *Marketing Week*, May 18.

PKF. *European Hotels Celebrate Millennium With Record Breaking Performance*, [online], July 20, 2001. [www.hospitalitynet.org/news/...] (July 20, 2001).

POON, Auliana (1993). *Tourism, Technology and Competitive Strategies*, CAB International.

PRESSE CANADIENNE (2000a). "Air Canada créerait trois filiales, selon ses pilotes," *La Presse*, June 13, pp. C-7.

PRESSE CANADIENNE (2000b). "Air Canada et Canadian intègrent leurs systèmes de réservation," *La Presse*, October 11, pp. D-16.

PRESSE CANADIENNE (2000c). "Québec subventionnera un nouveau transporteur," *La Presse*, October 19, pp. D-19.

PREUSSAG, *Rapport annuel 2000*, 135 pp.

PRICELINE.COM, RAPPORT ANNUEL 2000, 47 pp.

PRICEWATERHOUSECOOPERS LLP (1999). GLOBAL INDUSTRY TRENDS, GLOBAL LODGING CONSOLIDATION ACTIVITY, March 13, 6 pp.

RAMSAY, Laura (2000). "Thriving airline industry connects the North," *The Globe and Mail*, October 10, 2000, pp. T-11.

REED, Stanley (2000). "Airline Hawks are ready to strike," *Business Week*, June 19, pp. 52.

REVUE ESPACES (2000), *E-tourisme*, No. 170, April, pp. 13-33.

REVUE TOURISME PLUS (2000), *Navigant acquiert GTS Global Travel Solutions*, Vol. 20, No. 35, October 16, pp. 1.

RHOADES, DAWNA L. AND HEATHER LUSH (1997). "A typology of strategic alliances in the airline industry: Propositions for stability and duration," *Journal of Air transport Management*, Vol. 3, No. 3, pp. 109-114.

RICE, Kate. *Commentary: Orbitz, the site, the stragegy*, [online], June 7, 2001. [www.webtravelnews.com/...] (June 14, 2001).

RIVIÈRE, Bruno (1998). "Pourquoi ces Alliances Stratégiques Mondiales ?," *Aéroports Magazine*, No. 293, pp. 11-21.

ROBERT, Michel and Bernard RACINE (2000). *Stratégie Internet pure et simple*, Les Éditions TRANSCONTINENTAL inc.

ROBITAILLE, Louis-Bernard (2000) "Refus Global," *Magazine En Route*, September, pp. 57-62.

ROULEAU, Danielle (1999). "The Boutique Bandwagon," *Hotelier*, September–October, pp. 71-72 & 75-76.

RUSHMORE, Stephen. *Top Markets, Predictions & Opportunities*, [online], January 2001. [www.hotel-online.com/Neo/...] (January 18, 2001).

RUSHMORE, Stephen (2001). "Dont't Worry About The Recession," *HOTELS*, May, pp. 36.

SABRE HOLDINGS CORPORATION, *Rapport annuel 2000*, 64 pp.

SAN FILIPPO, Michele (1999). "United They Stand," *Travel Agent*, August 23.

SHELDON, Pauline J. (1993). "Destination Information Systems," *Annals of Tourism Research*, Vol. 20, pp. 633-649.

SHELDON, Pauline J. (1997). *Tourism Information Technology*, Oxon, CABI Publishing, 224 pp.

SHELDON, Pauline J., Karl W. WÖBER and Daniel R. FENSENMAIER (2001). *Information and Communication Technologies in Tourism 2001*, Vienne, Springer-Verlag Wien, 386 pp.

SHILLINGLAW, James (1999a). "A Merger of Technology and Bulk Aims to Shake the Agency World," *Travel Agent*, June 28.

SHILLINGLAW, James (1999b). "Agencies Put Vacation.com Mega-Merger Under a Microscope," *Travel Agent*, July 5.

SHILLINGLAW, James (2000a). "Marrying Clicks With Mortar," *Travel Agent*, January 3 .

SHILLINGLAW, James (2000b). "Carlson Gets "Results" Focused," *Travel Agent*, May 22 .

SIMONS, Michael S. (2000). "Global Airline Alliances — Reaching Out to New Galaxies in a Changing Competitive Market — the Star Alliance & Oneworld," *Journal of Air Law and Commerce*, Vol. 36, No. 10, pp. 44-47.

SOLON, Daniel (1999). "Differing Approaches to Alliance Strategy: American Airlines-British Airways and KLM-Alitalia," *Avmark Aviation Economist*, Vol. 15, No. 6, pp.8-9.

STARWOOD HOTELS & RESORTS WORLDWIDE. *Rapport annuel 2000*, 12 pp.

SWIG, Rick. *Ready, Willing, and Unable?*, [online], August 2000, [www.hotel-online.com/...] (August 22, 2000).

TATU, Natacha (2000). "Nouvelles Frontières : les copains passent la main," *Le Nouvel Observateur*, No. 1870, September 7-13.

TELFER, David J. (2000). "Tastes of Niagara: Building Strategic Alliances Between Tourism and Agriculture," *International Journal of Hospitality & Tourism Administration*, Vol. 1, No. 1, pp. 71.

THE ECONOMIST (2000a). *Tour Operators–A place in the sun*, May, pp. 75-76.

THE ECONOMIST (2000b). *Room for reservations*, July 1st, pp. 64.

THE ECONOMIST (2000c). *How mergers go wrong*, June 22, pp. 19 & 67-68.

THE ECONOMIST (2000d). *Canada's not-so-open sky*, September 2, pp. 59.

THE ECONOMIST (2000e). *Emerging-market indicators*, October 7, pp. 124.

THE ECONOMIST (2001). *Is there life in e-commerce?*, February 3, pp. 19-20.

THE TRELLIS GROUP INC. (2001). "Le commerce électronique dans les services de voyages au détail au Canada," Industrie Canada et Commission canadienne du tourisme, 19 pp.

THOMPSON FINANCIAL SECURITIES DATA. "The World is Not Enough... to Merge Worldwide Announced M&A Volume Soars to Record $3.4 Trillion in '99" [online], 2000, [www.tfsd.com/news_room/archive/] (October 23 2000).

TINARD, Yves (1994). *Le tourisme : économie et management*, Ediscience.

TINARD, Yves (1997). "Les grandes tendances du tourisme mondial : l'émergence de l'Asie de l'Est ?," *Espaces*, March-April, pp.36-44.

TINARD, Yves (1999). "L'aménagement du territoire face à la déréglementation aérienne," *Espaces*, September, pp. 32-41.

TOUPIN, Gilles (2000). "Canadien régional : devant le Sénat, les TUAC crient à la mesure insensée," *La Presse*, June 13, pp. C-7.

TRANSAT A.T. INC. *Rapport annuel 2000*, 68 pp.

TRANSPORT Canada. *Rapport annuel 1998*.

TRANSPORT Canada. *Cadre pour la restructuration de l'industrie du transport aérien au Canada*, [online], August 1999, [www..tc.gc.ca/...] (April 4, 2000).

TRAVEL AGENT (2000). *Bid for Britain's Thomson: C&N's $2.08 bil proposal for Thomson Travel has been rejected; C&N runs travel shops in UK, charters on Germany's Condor*, Vol. 299, No. 4, April 10.

TRAVEL TRADE GAZETTE UK & IRELAND (2000a). *C&N's sights still on UK operators*, May 22 , pp. 7.

TRAVEL TRADE GAZETTE UK & IRELAND (2000b). *C&N eyes Cook's as takeovers intensify*, June 12 , pp. 1.

TRAVEL TRADE GAZETTE UK & IRELAND (2000c). *Kuoni joins C&N in duel for Cook's*, June 19 , pp. 1.

TRAVEL & TOURISM INTELLIGENCE (1997). "Global Trends in Airline Alliances," *Travel & Tourism Analyst* , No. 4, pp. 81-101.

TRAVEL & TOURISM INTELLIGENCE (1998a). "Travel Distribution: Who Owns Whom in the European Travel Industry," *Travel & Tourism Analyst*, No. 3, pp. 41-59.

TRAVEL & TOURISM INTELLIGENCE (1998b). *The International Hotel Industry: Corporate Strategies and Global Opportunities, by Murray Bailey,* RESEARCH REPORT, 2nd Edition, Londres, 609 pp.

TRAVEL & TOURISM INTELLIGENCE (1999a). "The Travel Trade: Travel Agents in Canada," *Travel & Tourism Analyst,* No. 1, pp. 71-86.

TRAVEL & TOURISM INTELLIGENCE (1999b). "Accommodation: Capital investment in the US hotel industry to 2005," *Travel & Tourism Analyst ,* No. 5, pp. 69-87.

TRAVEL & TOURISM INTELLIGENCE (1999c). "British Airways and the new airline economics," No. 6, pp. 3-16.

TRAVEL & TOURISM INTELLIGENCE (2000). "The impact of branding on the UK hotel industry," *Travel & Tourism Analyst ,* No. 2, pp. 65-82.

TRAVEL AND TOURIST ANALYST (2000), *Travel Distribution: Outbound Travel Agencies in Asia,* No. 4, pp. 37-49.

TRAVEL AND TOURIST ANALYST (2000), *E-Business Models in the Travel Industry,* No. 3, pp. 67-89.

TRÉVIDIC, Bruno (1999). "Les compagnies régionales à l'heure des grandes alliances internationales," *Aéroports Magazine,* No. 394, pp. 38-41.

TURENNE, Martine (2000). "La montagne aux dollars," *Actualité,* Vol. 25, No. 8, May 15, pp. 56.

ULRICH, Daniel (2000). "Les transporteurs jouent la carte du service," *Espaces,* No. 174, September, pp. 28-29.

UNITED STATES DEPARTMENT OF TRANSPORTATION. *Global deregulation takes off: first report,* [online], December 1999, [www.ostpxweb.dot.gov/ aviation/intav/alncrpt3.pdf] (August 4, 2000).

UNITED STATES GENERAL ACCOUNTING OFFICE. *Domestic Aviation: Effects of Changes in How Airline Tickets are sold,* [online], 1999, [www.gao.gov] (August 4, 2000).

VALLIÈRES, Martin (2000). "L'immobilier peut contrer la volatilité," *La Presse,* December 4, pp. D1.

VOURC'H, Anne (1999). "La capacité d'accueil – une notion essentielle dans les sites naturels," *Espaces,* No. 166, December, pp. 18-22.

WAGUESPACK, Blaise P. *An exploratory examination of a typology of alliances in the global airline industry,* [online], 1998, [www.sbaer.uca.edu/ docs/proceedingsII/98sma179.txt] (April 19, 2000).

WALLER, Fletch (2001). "Chain Marketing Muscle? It Isn't Necessarily So," *HOTELS,* January, pp. 20.

WALSH, Dominic. *Hotel groups seal online European joint venture,* [online], May 10, 2000, [www.the-times.co.uk...] (July 28, 2000).

WANHILL, Stephen (2000). "Small and medium tourism enterprises," *Annals of Tourism Research,* Vol. 27, No. 1, pp. 132-147.

WATKINS, Ed (2000). "The Internet as Distribution Weapon," *Lodging Hospitality,* Vol. 56, No. 3, March 1st, pp. 30+.

WATKINS, M. *Une politique de niche*, [online], 14 October 1999, [www.horeca.tm.fr/...] (February 25, 2000).

WHITFORD, Marty. *Top 100: Merger-and-acquisition activity dominates lodging landscape*, [online], September 2, 1998, [www.hmmonline.com/...] (February 25, 2000).

WHITFORD, Marty. *Proliferation of chains and independents offers hotels a two-way street to success*, [online], May 3, 1999, [www.hmmonline.com/...] (February 25, 2000).

WILSON, Tim (2000). "Hotels Centralize," *Internet Week*, April 24, pp. 35.

WOLFF, Carlo (2000). "Keeping up with Digital Joneses," *Lodging Hospitality*, Vol. 56, No. 8, June, pp. 31.

WORLD TOURISM ORGANIZATION (1998a). *Yearbook of Tourism Statistics*, Vol. I, 50th Edition.

WORLD TOURISM ORGANIZATION (1998b). *Yearbook of Tourism Statistics*, Vol. II, 50th Edition.

WORLD TOURISM ORGANIZATION (1999a). *La commercialisation en ligne des destinations touristiques : Stratégies pour l'ère de l'information*, Madrid.

WORLD TOURISM ORGANIZATION (1999b). *Tourism Market Trends 1999 Edition: Middle East*.

WORLD TOURISM ORGANIZATION (1999c). *Tourism Market Trends 1999 Edition: East Asia & the Pacific*.

WORLD TOURISM ORGANIZATION (1999d). *Yearbook of Tourism Statistics*, Vol. I, 51th Edition.

WORLD TOURISM ORGANIZATION (1999e). *Tourism 2020 Vision: Executive Summary*.

WORLD TOURISM ORGANIZATION (1999f). *Marchés émetteurs de tourisme : Vue d'ensemble et situation par pays*.

WORLD TOURISM ORGANIZATION (1999g). *Marketing Tourism Destinations online: Strategies For The Information Age*, September.

WORLD TOURISM ORGANIZATION (2000a). *Yearbook of Tourism Statistics 1994-1998*, Vol. 1 and 2, 52nd Edition.

WORLD TOURISM ORGANIZATION (2000b). *Tourism Market Trends 2000 Edition: Africa*.

WORLD TOURISM ORGANIZATION (2000c). *Tourism Market Trends 2000 Edition: Americas*.

WORLD TOURISM ORGANIZATION (2000d). *Tourism Market Trends 2000 Edition: East Asia & Pacific*.

WORLD TOURISM ORGANIZATION (2000e). *Tourism Market Trends 2000 Edition: Europe*.

WORLD TOURISM ORGANIZATION (2000f). *Tourism Market Trends 2000 Edition: Middle East*.

WORLD TOURISM ORGANIZATION (2000g). *Tourism Market Trends 2000 Edition: South Asia*.

WORLD TOURISM ORGANIZATION (2000h). *Tourism 2020 Vision: Africa*, Vol. 1.

WORLD TOURISM ORGANIZATION (2000i). *Tourism 2020 Vision: Americas*, Vol. 2.

WORLD TOURISM ORGANIZATION (2000j). *Tourism 2020 Vision: East Asia & Pacific*, Vol. 3.

WORLD TOURISM ORGANIZATION (2000k). *Tourism 2020 Vision: Europe*, Vol. 4.

WORLD TOURISM ORGANIZATION (2000l). *Tourism 2020 Vision: Middle East*, Vol. 5.

WORLD TOURISM ORGANIZATION (2000m). *Tourism 2020 Vision: South Asia*, Vol. 6.

WORLD TOURISM ORGANIZATION (2000n). *Faits Saillants 2000*.

WORLD TOURISM ORGANIZATION (2001a). *Yearbook of Tourism Statistics 1995-1999*, Vol. 1 and 2, 53th Edition.

WORLD TOURISM ORGANIZATION (2001b). *Tourism Market Trends 2001 Edition: Middle East*.

WORLD TOURISM ORGANIZATION (2001c). *Tourism Market Trends 2001 Edition: The World*, provisonal edition.

WORLD TOURISM ORGANIZATION (2001d). *Compendium of Tourism Statistics 2001 Edition*.

WORLD TOURISM ORGANIZATION (2001e). *Tourism In The Least Developed Countries: Third United Nations Conference on the Least Developed Countries*.

YESAWICH, Pepperdine & Brown and Yankelovich Partners (2000a). *The YP&B Yankelovich Partners 2000 National business travel monitor*, Orlando, April 28.

YESAWICH, Pepperdine & Brown and Yankelovich Partners (2000b). *The YP&B Yankelovich Partners 2000 National leisure travel monitor*, Orlando, April 7.

YOUNG, Joanne W. (1999). "Airlines Alliances — Is Competition at the Crossroads?," *Air and Space Law*, Vol. XXIV, No. 6, pp. 287-293.

YU Larry. *The International Hospitality Business: Management and Operations*, The Haworth Hospitality Press Inc., New York, 1999, 404 pp.

ZELLNER, Wendy (2001). "Where the net delivers: Travel," *Business Week*, June 11, pp. 142-144.

COMPANY WEB SITES *

ACCOR. [www.accor.com].
AIR CANADA. [www.aircanada.ca].
AMERICAN AIRLINES. [www.aa.com].
AMERICAN EXPRESS. [www.americanexpress.com].
BASS HOTELS & RESORTS. [www.bass.com].
BEST WESTERN INTERNATIONAL. [www.bestwestern.com].
BONVOYAGE.COM. [www.bonvoyage.com].
CANADIAN PACIFIC HOTELS & RESORTS. [www.cp.ca].
CARLSON HOSPITALITY WORLDWIDE. [www.carlson.com].
CARLSONWAGONLIT. [www.carlsonwagonlit.com].
CENDANT CORP. [www.cendant.com].
CHAÎNE HÔTELIÈRE HÔTE. [www.chainehote.com].
CHIP HOSPITALITY. [www.chipreit.com].
CHOICE HOTELS INTERNATIONAL. [www.choicehotels.com].
DATALEX. [www.datalex.com].
DELTA AILRLINES. [www.delta-air.com].
FINANCIAL TIMES. [www.ft.com].
FIND ARTICLES.COM. [www.findarticles.com].
FOUR SEASONS HOTELS & RESORTS. [www.fourseasons.com].
GRACIENT SOLUTIONS. [www.gochannel.com].
HANDELSBLATT. [www.handelsblatt.com].
HAVAS VOYAGES. [www.havasvoyages.fr].
HILTON HOTEL CORP. [www.hilton.com].
HÔTELLERIE CHAMPÊTRE. [www.hotelleriechampetre.com].
HOTWIRE. [www.hotwire.com].
HYATT INTERNATIONAL. [www.hyatt.com].
IATA. [www.iata.org].
IBM. [www.ibm.com].
INTER-RÉS@. [www.interresa.ca].
ITA SOFTWARE. [www.itasoftware.com].
KARSTADTQUELLE. [www.karstadtquelle.com].
LEADING HOTELS OF THE WORLD. [www.lhw.com].
LEXINGTON SERVICES CORP. [www.lexres.com].
LUFTHANSA. [www.lufthansa.com].
MARRIOTT INTERNATIONAL. [www.marriott.com].
NORTHWEST AIRLINES. [www.nwa.com].
OACI. [www.icao.org].
ONEWORLD ALLIANCE. [www.oneworld.com].
ORACLE. [www.e-travel.com].
ORBITZ. [www.orbitz.com].
PEGASUS SOLUTIONS, INC. [www.pegsinc.com].
QUALIFLYER. [www.qualiflyergroup.com].
RELAIS & CHÂTEAUX. [www.relaischateaux.fr].
ROYAL HOST HOTELS & RESORTS. [www.royalhost.com].
SAIRGROUP. [www.sairgroup.com].
SKYTEAM. [www.skyteam.com].
STAR ALLIANCE. [www.star-alliance.com].
STARWOOD HOTELS & RESORTS WORLDWIDE. [www.starwood.com].
SWISSAIR. [www.swissair.com].
THOMSON TRAVEL GROUP. [www.thomsontravelgroup.com].
UNION EUROPÉENNE. [www.eurunion.org].
UNITED AIRLINES. [www.ual.com].
U.S. DEPARTMENT OF TRANSPORTATION [www.dot.gov].
VACATION.COM. [www.vacation.com].
VIP INTERNATIONAL CORP. [www.vipintcorp.com].
WESTLB PANMURE. [www.westlbpanmure.com].
ZOHO. [www.zoho.com].
* Sites consulted between May and July 2001.

WEB SITES CONSULTED

[cyberatlas.internet.com/big_picture/...]
Europe's E-Commerce Profits Up for Grabs (July 25, 2001).
Where in the World is the Best E-Commerce (May 15, 2001).

[eMarketer.com]
Global B2C: Slow and Steady Wins the Race (July 27, 2001).

[www.allianceanalyst.com]
Dispelling the myths of alliances: The new realities of successful alliance management (July 18, 2000).

[www.atwonline.com]
Austrian foresees $25 million benefit from Star, April 3, 2000 (April 3, 2000).

[www.biz.yahoo.com/prnews]
Southwest Airlines on Pace to Exceed $1 Billion in Internet Revenue for 2000, February 28, 2000) (February 28, 2000).

[www.digitrends.net]
Top 15 Sites for Customer Loyalty, Ebiz News (July 25, 2000).

[www.europe.eu.int...]
Harmonisation des règles et des procédures dans l'aviation civile (May 4, 2000).
Application des règles de la concurrence (May 4, 2000).

[www.euunion.org...]
European commission states condition for approving lufthansa/SAS/United Airlines alliance, June 8, 1998 (April 19, 2000).

[www.expressindia.com]
Airline alliances in musical chair game, June 24, 1999 (April 19, 2000).

[www.findarticles.com]
Fitzgerald Urges Justice Department Review of Airline Merger, June 14, 2000 (July 27, 2000).
United's Goodwin Tells Congress: Airline merger a win-win for Consumers, June 13, 2000 (July 27, 2000).
AirTran Airways' CEO Addresses Senate Commerce committee on State of Competition in the Airline Industry, June 21, 2000 (July 27, 2000).
Bigger Gets Bigger, May 29, 2000 (July 27, 2000).
Virtual Mergers: With traditional mergers difficult to pull off, airlines are finding creative ways to consolidate, January 31, 2000 (July 27, 2000).
Virgin Atlantic and EasyJet critical of British Airways/KLM merger, June 8, 2000 (July 27, 2000).
KLM seeks 30 per cent share in merger with British Airways, June 9, 2000 (July 27, 2000).

[www.freep.com/news/airtravel/...]
Airline alliances uneasy for fliers, May 24, 1999 (April 19, 2000).

[www.ft.com]
Preussag reports 11 per cent rise in nine-month profits, August 29, 2000 (September 1st, 2000).

[www.geoscopie.com]
Transports, facteurs de mondialisation (February 25, 2000).

[www.handelsblatt.com]
Preussag to expand tourism business beyond Europe, August 28, 2000 (September 1st, 2000).

[www.hotel-online.com/...]
Canadian Hotel Investment Report: Colliers International Hotel Realty 2000, Ideas & Trends, February 1st, 2000 (August 31, 2000).
Marriott International and Hyatt Corporation to Launch E-Based Procurement Network for Hospitality Industry, Special Report, May 2, 2000 (August 21, 2000).
Alliance Between Four of the World's Largest Hotel Companies (Starwood, Accor, Hilton & Forte) Will Create Joint Internet Portal for Selling Rooms online, Special Report, June 19, 2000 (August 21, 2000).
Accor, Bass, GranadaCompass, Hilton International and Whitbread Creating a Web-based Exchange, August 3, 2000 (August 31, 2000).
Canadian Hotel Transaction Overview: Colliers International Hotel Realty, Special Report, August 3, 2000 (August 31, 2000).
Preferred Hotels & Resorts Worldwide Announces a Plan to Create a New Business Organization to Allow Independents to Compete Sucessfully Against Hotel Goliaths, News, August 14, 2000 (August 15, 2000).
Marketing Alliance Formed Between 54 Relais & Châteaux Hotels and 43 Leading Hotels of the Wolrd Hotels, Special Report, August 15, 2000 (August 17, 2000).
Cendant Corporation to acquire AmeriHost Inn and AmeriHost Inn and Suites Brand Names and Franchising Rights, Special Report, August 18, 2000 (August 21, 2000).
Sol Meliá to Acquire the Madrid-based TRYP Hotel Chain, Special Report, August 20, 2000 (August 22, 2000).
New Zoho Suppliers Add Over 50,000 Products To Growing online Hospitality Marketplace, Ideas & Trends, August 30, 2000 (August 31, 2000).
With Potential Economic Slowdown a Possibility, the REIT Modernization Act Should Soften Impact on Hotel REITs, December 28, 2000 (January 4, 2001).

[www.house.gov/judiciary/...)
Statement of Delta Airlines inc. before the house judiciary committee regarding the state of competition in the airline industry, May 19, 1998 (April 19, 2000).

[www.hsmai.org/...)
HSMAI releases list of hospitality industry trendsetters to watch in the new millennium, April1st, 2000 (July 19, 2000).

[www.mesnouvelles.com/affaires/...]
Air Canada regroupera ses transporteurs régionaux, January 20, 2000 (May 5, 2000).

[www.newswire.ca/releases/...]
Royal Host first hotel REIT to fully internalize management, September 17, 1998 (August 21, 2000).

[www.ntaonline.com]
National Tour association's Market Development Council, Industry Report–Consolidation (September 11, 2000).

[www.quid.fr/WEB/TOURISME/...]
Hôtellerie en France : Statistiques (August 23, 2000).

[www.travelpress.com]
Canadian carriers (May 5, 2000).

[www.webtravelnews.com]
Orbitz consumer advocate responds to ITSA (July 13, 2000).
Giant retailer Wal-Mart drops online travel site (September 1st, 2000).
Orbitz names travel partners sets timetable (September 8, 2000).
Four major airlines plan Web travel portal, November 9, 1999 (May 18, 2000).
11 European airlines launch Web travel portal, May 12, 2000 (May 18, 2000).
Orbitz and Hotwire help airlines lose money, (July 21, 2000).
Airline-owned T2 travel portal answers charges, June 9, 2000 (June 12, 2000).
23 airlines join big four on travel Web site, January 13, 2000 (June 12, 2000).
United Airlines E-tickets now surpass paper tickets, June 21, 1999 (May 18, 2000).
Asian-Pacific airline portal in the works, July 11, 2000 (July 13, 2000).